THE LEONARD FEENEY
OMNIBUS

THE
LEONARD FEENEY
OMNIBUS

A Collection of Prose and Verse
Old and New

SHEED & WARD
New York • *1944*

810.8
F

To Francis X. Talbot, S.J.

ACKNOWLEDGMENTS

THE AUTHOR is grateful for special permission to use in this collection poems from individual books still available from these publishers: to The America Press for selections from *In Towns and Little Towns* (copyright, 1927); to The Macmillan Company for selections from *Riddle and Reverie* (copyright, 1933), *Boundaries* (copyright, 1933), for *Song for a Listener* (copyright, 1936), and for selections written by this author from *The Ark and The Alphabet* (copyright, 1939). The author is also grateful to the editors of the following periodicals for permission to use material originally published in: *America, Thought, The Boston College Stylus, The Boston Pilot, The Catholic Digest, The Missionary* and *The Month*.

PREFACE

THIS BOOK contains the things I like best of all I have written up till 1943. It does not contain the things I hope to write from now on. And so, though it is called an "omnibus," it is not to be taken as an "obituary."

My publishers have been very kind in letting me make my own choices. A number of things have been omitted, over protest of my friends. But a poet—if such I be—must ultimately be his own critic, his own chooser. It is one of the few freedoms left a man in this merciless age.

I am not, as one critic has kindly suggested, "a poet of many personalities." I am a poet of one personality who has had many moods. I realize I could have made a much greater reputation for myself if I had written everything in one groove. But in this matter I took a cue from God the Father—who is the poet, *the maker*, in God—and who could have made a much greater reputation for Himself if He had made the lion and omitted the mosquito.

Other than this, I offer no apologies.

L. F.

August 6th, 1943.

Contents

NOTES

SURVIVAL TILL SEVENTEEN

POEMS

POEMS—*Continued*

VERSE

VERSE—*Continued*

THE LEONARD FEENEY
OMNIBUS

Sketches

———◆———

FISH ON FRIDAY

TO THOUSANDS of our fellow Americans we Catholics are known merely as the people who eat fish on Friday. It amuses us (up to a point) to be thought of in this way, as some queer sort of "Sixth Day Adventists" waiting with out-stretched frying-pans for the weekly arrival of the fishmonger, or rushing periodically to market and hollering for halibut or clamoring for clams in order to fulfill a strange religious superstition.

It is a pity so little is known about us. We now number twenty millions in this country, and sooner or later we are bound to be reckoned with as a Christian body in terms of something more substantial than our Friday fare. For it never fails to happen that people who know only a little about us get that little wrong. As a matter of fact we do NOT eat fish on Friday. That is to say, not unless we like fish and want to eat it of our own accord. I am one of those many moderately good Catholics in whom the persuasive power of Canon Law has not developed a taste for fish either on Friday or any other day, and stands no chance of doing so. It is true I do not eat meat on Friday, but the distinction between abstaining from meat and partaking of fish is not too difficult to comprehend, and ought to offer food for thought.

Oddly enough, the learned explanations of why we eat fish on Friday are more stupid than the stupid ones. The ordinary friendly Protestant who sits beside us in restaurants and notices our hebdomadal horror of meat, puts us down as "just a little

bit queer on that point," somewhat in the manner of the ortho-
dox Jews, who are "a little bit queer" on the subject of ham all
the year round.

We like this simple explanation of our Friday observance best
of all those which do not explain it. A misunderstanding is
never unpleasant provided it is straightforward and uninvolved.
What drives us to desperation is a treatise on the subject of
"Catholics and Friday Fish" by a savant, a theological psychol-
ogist, or a student of "comparative religion."

We are amazed to learn from Professor Puffles that the prac-
tice of eating fish was introduced into the Christian ritual be-
cause the Apostles were fishermen; or to be informed by more
erudite authorities that, whereas pictures of little fishes were
enscrolled on the walls of the Catacombs, the early Christians
became gradually devoted to fish worship, which aroused in
them intermittently a religious symptom known as "an icthy-
ophagus esophagus."

What annoys us in the theories of these polysyllablists is not
what they say, but what they imply. They imply, of course,
that the Christian tradition is merely a superior form of myth,
and if archeologists and other diggers had time to go into the
matter, it could probably be shown that the Roman Pontiff is
a development of the god Neptune, and that the Holy Virgins
of the Litanies were originally a school of mermaids.

The true explanation of the ICTHUS inscribed as a devotional
rebus in the Catacombs, has no more to do with our practice of
eating fish than the presence of an embroidered pelican on the
back of a Benediction vestment has to do with our failure to
eat pelicans, whether embroidered or otherwise. If our religious
development followed the psychological rules which professors
of religion imagine, we would most certainly be consuming
lambs and devouring doves on Friday, instead of avoiding them
in favor of fish, because, of all the animal symbols employed by
Christians in their sacred liturgy, unquestionably the common-
est and most pronounced have been the lamb and the dove.

In my younger days, when our adversaries were the good old (and thoroughly honorable) Protestant Evangelicals, who had sense enough to see that what we were doing on Friday was not eating fish but abstaining from meat, there was often quoted against us the text from Saint Matthew: "Not that which goeth into the mouth defileth a man"; and I remember the great flurry which occurred in the "Question Box Departments" of Catholic magazines in trying to answer this difficulty.

What a pity the Catholic apologete of those days had not tact enough to be less apologetic! Instead of trying to belabor the exegesis of a Scriptural text—to nobody's satisfaction, not even our own—he could have pointed out the enormous compliment we were paying to meat by considering its absence from our table to be a hardship. One does not offer God by way of penance what one thinks is bad but what one thinks is good. And nobody really understands how good meat is until he tries going without it one day a week. And why has it not been noticed that whenever a big feast of the Church—let us say Christmas—falls on Friday, we become joyously carnivorous out of schedule, openly abandon our loyalty to fish and transfer it to roast turkey? Indeed, the truth of the matter is, if we dared tell non-Catholics the number of reasons which will legitimately permit us to eat meat on Friday, they would be scandalized. And I have always considered this a most amusing situation, namely, the constant danger we are in of giving scandal to those outside our Faith, should we neglect to do what they would think it absurd for us to do, even if we did it.

There is, in view of these considerations, a resolution we ought to make. And it is this: not to waste our time and the time of unbelievers in discussing our religion with them any longer in terms of its non-essentials. There is no use trying to explain Friday fish, devotional prayers, incense, holy water, candles, relics, medals and such incidentals to anyone who has not studied the Catholic Faith "from the ground up." We only beget confusion of mind in those who question us, and arouse inordinately our own risibilities.

I remember once being asked by a very ponderous Protestant Divine: "When you read Matins in your Breviary, do you believe everything that is written in the lessons of the Second Nocturne concerning the lives of the Saints?"

"Well," I replied, "that all depends on what you mean by the word 'believe.' I do not BELIEVE them as part of the Christian Revelation. Nevertheless I credit them with some authority, let us say as the best record of a saint's life available when an account of it was being prepared for recitation in the Divine Office."

"You know," he added, paying not the slightest attention to the explanation I had given, "the French pay compliment to a skillful liar by saying, 'He can lie like a Second Nocturne.'"

I laughed out loud. But my reverend adversary, strange to say, did not laugh at all. He looked very serious.

Now why did I laugh, and why did he not laugh, at a joke which was entirely on me? For the simple reason that I have, in common with those of my Faith, a sense of humor radically different from that of an outsider. There are—let there be no mistake about it—Catholic quips and drolleries which no one but a Catholic can tell, and no one but a Catholic can see the point of. I hate to analyze a joke, but let me do so for once, in order to illustrate what I mean.

Every Catholic knows that our Church sometimes speaks directly in the name of God. To each phrase of God's revelation we attach a sacredness that would not warrant our making a joke about it. If anyone (even a Frenchman) should say about a liar, "He can lie like the Apostles' Creed," I should not only resent the remark, I should not only think it not in the least funny, but I should promptly wither my opponent with one of the retorts I keep at hand for just such a situation.

But the lessons of the Second Nocturne do not always come to us directly from God. Many of them were written not by inspired writers, but by some holy old monks whose purposes were not historical but panegyrical, who were trying to compose not chronicles but eulogies. Now there is between a good panegyrist and a good prevaricator an apparent similarity, in that both over-tell their story, the former to delight, the latter to deceive. That is why a comparison of the two is so funny. But the universal law of all humor achieved by comparison demands that underneath an apparent similarity there be a real difference. And if one doesn't see the real difference, one doesn't see the joke.

Furthermore, every authentic Christian joke is at once humorous and pathetic. One smiles not in ridicule but in tenderness at the poor old scribe who wrote lessons for the Second Nocturne in order to commemorate a saint whom he loved, and who tried so hard to tell the truth, he told it too well. For charity is the most childlike of all the virtues, and it thinks sometimes, in its innocence, it can do service for every other virtue besides itself, even for the virtue of veracity.

This idea as it exists in the minds of simple Christian folk was brought home to me strikingly on a certain lovely morning in Galway, when I went for a walk, and asked an Irish peasant to tell me how far it was to—let us call the place, for I forget it—Corofin.

"Good morning! How far is it to Corofin?"

He was sitting on a wall. He raised his hat and gave me a bow.

"About a half mile down the road, Father. And God speed you!"

"Thank you."

I walked a half mile. I walked another half mile, examining sign-posts as I went. And another half mile. And another. And not until I had duplicated this distance twelve times did I arrive at Corofin, for it was six full miles away.

When I returned in the late afternoon, I met the same Irishman sitting on the wall. I went up to him indignantly.

"What did you mean by telling me Corofin was only a half mile away?" I shouted. "It was six miles away! You knew that when I spoke to you! Why didn't you tell me the truth?"

"Well, you poor man," he answered quietly and with great seriousness, "I didn't want to knock the heart out of you, and you looking so tired in the early morning. I gave you a half mile to Corofin. That got you started. Somebody else gave you another half mile. That drove you on a bit further. In Ireland we do be always wanting to soften the journey of a stranger by giving him little dribbles of encouragement. Sure, there'd be nobody going any place here on a hot day, if people knew how far they had to go to get there."

"Now listen," I said, refusing to smile, "I don't think that's really funny. It may be Irish, but it isn't honest. I just came from England. In England one doesn't get fooled that way. An Englishman takes great care in giving any information that is asked of him, and he takes great pride in giving it truthfully."

"Do you know the trouble with the English, Father?" he replied vehemently, as he pounded the wall with his fist. "Do you know the trouble with the English? They wouldn't think enough of you to tell you a lie!"

I am not defending the naïveté of this Galway playboy, nor holding it up as either a convincing or authentic example of Christian perfection. To be an ideal Catholic, it is not enough to be a Celt. One needs also to be a saint. But surely there can be detected in him a thorough sense of self-forgetfulness not found in any save the children of the Faith, whose failing it is to love a person more than a thing and a man more than a measurement. Undisciplined Christian generosity of this sort has its drawbacks, I admit, but I prefer it greatly to the cold exactitudes of post-Reformation skeptics, whose social courtesies are governed solely by an undistracted interest in their own good breeding. True, they are pleasant people to meet on a short walk, especially when one is in need more of information than of affection, but in the long run give me "a half mile down the road to Corofin" any day, and I'll walk the rest of the way myself.

It can be seen from this homely example, that one source of Catholic humor is human nature itself in the act of being transformed (with all its absurdities, stupidities, scruples and superstitions) into something serene and noble. For a religion as universal as ours embraces all classes, and patiently tolerates among its members even the most ridiculous types, provided they be men of good-will.

But this is to take Catholic humor in its passive sense. This is not what makes a Catholic laugh. It is what makes him laughable. I am anxious to discover, in some fashion or other, what is the inner secret of our joy, and what it is that makes us laugh by ourselves, and within ourselves, even when we are alone.

I am sure the reason lies in our knowing, through the light of Faith, paradoxes too magnificent to be contradictions. And this is the secret not only of our mirth, but of our sorrow as well. There is an empty amusement and an empty sadness that come from a mere knowledge of life's contradictions. But these are the portion of the skeptic and the stoic, who seldom laugh and seldom weep. But the Christian may look into a world of mystery in which all contradictions are reconciled, even though paradoxes remain. And the fruit of his wisdom is his gayety and his tears; for laughter and tears are the safety valves of sanity, and by these beautiful outlets the strain within our nature is relieved.

I may illustrate this animadversion by another little story.

There is a convent not far from where I live, to which I have gone on occasions to give a retreat. At this convent one meets a very nice old lay sister, who has charge of the priest's dining-room, and whom I may call Sister Mary.

Sister Mary spends half the day indoors and half the day outdoors, for her duties are twofold: to feed the chaplain and to feed the chickens. Now this in itself is a paradoxical situation, and I am sure accounts for the merry twinkle in Sister Mary's eyes, who, knowing nothing of either Evolution or Relativity, has faith enough to see, apart from apparent similarities, the enormous difference between a chaplain and a chicken. Indeed, I have often thought it would be delightful if Sister Mary should some day get her functions confused, and should walk out to the hen-coop with a cup of coffee, and come clucking into the chaplain's refectory throwing handfuls of corn.

"Sister Mary," I said to her one day, as I sat beaming over a splendid dinner which she had just brought in on a tray, "if you were going to order a nice meal for yourself, what dishes would you choose? What would you like best to eat?"

She rubbed her hands on her apron and stood for a while speculating, and then said, finally and decisively: "I think I'd love a nice thick beefsteak!" Whereupon she began to laugh, and laughed and laughed and laughed, until tears streamed from her eyes.

I must confess I was not prepared for such a mirthful explosion, and it puzzled me. I knew, of course, the traditional Christian custom (which nuns observe most scrupulously) of laughing whenever anything pleasant is either spoken of or thought of. But this was sheer hysterics, and seemed unwarranted by anything either Sister Mary or I had said which was so dreadfully funny.

It was only after I returned to my room and had time to meditate on the matter, that I arrived at a solution of my perplexity. I am sure the reason for Sister Mary's hilarity, even to the point of turning herself into a fountain, was her use of the word "love" in the sentence, "I think I'd love a nice thick beefsteak."

One begins to see how funny this concept is when one remembers the love employments of Sister Mary's heart during the rest of the day. My question, I daresay, had distracted her from some holy thought. She is not often asked about the amours of her appetite. But being asked, she must admit that the same heart which loves God and His angels and archangels in her moments of contemplation, has lowlier and less ethereal preferences when she studies a bill of fare. Now it is a shatteringly laughable experience to transfer one's attachment suddenly from something sublime and eternal to something desperately temporal and comestible, to be loving at one moment a living angel and at another a dead cow. But, because a Seraph is just as real to Sister Mary as a sirloin, she saw the absurdity of their conflict in her heart's affections, and went into a paroxysm.

It is interesting to notice that in non-Catholic circles, and in Catholic circles which have been influenced by non-Catholic culture, (and many of us have adopted, more than we are willing to admit, the moods of the pagans and the manners of the heretics in whose midst we live) there is no genuine humor of this kind. An honest Christian joke, in which the very roots of one's being are shaken with laughter, has been supplanted, in this country at least, by what is known as a wise-crack. A wise-crack is a bogus form of humor in which a ridiculous sense of the sublime is combined with a sublime sense of the ridiculous. Its physical reaction is not a laugh but a snigger. Being rarely capable of more than two variations, the one uncharitable, the other unchaste, it is noticeably the most tiresome form of humor ever invented. It will eventually destroy one's power to laugh altogether, as well as raise havoc with one's nervous system. There is no reckoning how much mental harm is being done to the amusement audiences of America by reading and listening to professional wise-crackers, to whom their own fun-making is a drudgery, and who, after a short spasm of popularity, inevitably succumb to melancholia, alcoholia and other poisons.

But where am I who, a few pages back, started to write on fish? I am where every Catholic finds himself who undertakes to write on anything. I am writing on everything. For if one is a Catholic, one cannot think without being cosmical, or without being comical either, because the Faith links all realities together and fills the world with surprises.

Nevertheless, in deference to one of the favorite penitential practices of my co-religionists, I feel bound to say something directly favorable about my subject before I conclude. So I shall say this: On that day of the week when meat is forbidden me, I like to go to a Catholic kitchen and listen to little fishes being fried in their skins. Because I think one of the very nicest of all noises is the sound of hot silver sizzling in a pan. But the palatability of these little creatures, when they arrive on my dinner plate, depends upon whatever success I have in obliterating their natural flavor with strong doses of fish-sauce. Which reminds me, that I have never yet seen a bottle of fish-sauce which did not claim to have won a medal at the World's Fair.

GOOD CHRISTIANS

UNTIL THE summer of 1931, the Y.W.C.A. meant nothing more to me than the feminine gender of Y.M.C.A., formed by turning the M upside down. And of the Y.M.C.A. I knew little beyond the fact that it had swimming pools in most of the large American cities. It was interesting, therefore, one August, on the Continent, in a crowded railway carriage (which on European trains are compartmental, and so make for easy conversation and acquaintanceship) to meet two Young Women Christian Associates returning to the United States after a five years' missionary sojourn in Japan.

We did not speak at once; English and American tourists never do, the former because they are soured with the superior airs of Anglicanism, the latter because we are tainted with the

odd manners of Methodists. We went through the usual pre-
liminary ritual of pretending to be uninterested in one another,
of unnecessary clearings of one's throat, unnecessary windings
of one's watch, unnecessary mistings and dryings of one's spec-
tacles, and all the foolish frigidity of behavior that came to
be regarded as "good form" when the Reformers ruined the
natural comradeship of Christianity.

It was a very nice Polish gentleman, a Catholic, traveling in
our compartment with his wife and family, who shamed us
into conversation. After vainly trying to make friends with us
by cordial little blinkings of his eyes, tiltings of his nose, churn-
ings of his mouth, and shruggings of his shoulders, his warm
Catholic heart, eager to give and receive affection, drove him,
as a last desperate effort, to open his lunch basket and offer us
each, for pity's sake, a cheese sandwich.

It was cruel to refuse him, but we Americans did, the ladies
for their own reasons, and I because my usual railway head-
ache was with me, and was doing quite well, thank you, with-
out any further caloric assistance. However, we tried to make
it up to him with much gracious bowing and smiling, and I
good sport, and I wasn't refusing because I feared the Poles
tried to tell him in gesticulated Polish that he was an awfully
bearing gifts, but only because I couldn't manage a cheese and
a headache on the same journey.

After this episode the Y.W.C.A. and the R. C. Church felt
we could exchange a word or two without violating the con-
ventional canons of Christian conduct. Hitherto we had had
nothing in common (except a language, a flag, an Unknown
Soldier, a human nature, and an original father and mother).
Now, by God's mercy, we had acquired something definitely
in common, something that would warrant our turning Hem
and Haw into Hello. Even Emily Post would forgive us now
for speaking without being introduced. We had established a
point of social contact. We had refused a cheese sandwich con-
jointly. (And, incidentally, they were the largest cheese sand-

wiches in point of cheese I have ever witnessed. There was an absolute geometrical minimum of bread to them, just enough to give one a sanitary grip on the cheese. And the nice Polish gentleman, after taking a gigantic bite out of his, showed us, by a round smile and a luscious bulge on his cheek, that we didn't know what we were missing.)

It was not to be expected, although we chatted for three hours, that the Y.W.C.A. ladies should give me their names. And in a way I am rather glad they did not do so, as it will allow me to write about them with less embarrassment and more elbow-room. So whether they were Carrie and Cora, or Daphne and Dora, or Fifi and Flora, or some other selections from a feminine litany not usually associated with *ora pro nobis*, for purposes of this tale let X = Y.W.C.A.; let 2X = two ex-missionaries returning from Japan; and let 3X = three exiles in Europe, who became friends in a Continental railway compartment, all over a cheese sandwich.

If there is any bitterness in these lines so far, and there seems to be, it is directed against a heresy, and not against these Young Women Christian Associates personally. Personally they won my regard and admiration much more than they will ever know. Indeed, this paper is intended to be a eulogy of their splendid goodness, a eulogy I feel will be all the more sincere because they will never read it or even dream of its existence. And when I salute them as "Good Christians" I do so in no spirit of irony. I do so with reverence and respect and a little tinge of sadness.

I have never been privileged to meet young women more refined and gentle in their deportment or more shining in their natural goodness. They were dressed with taste and simplicity. They wore plain felt hats that seemed to have come from the same bargain counter, and their flowered dresses, almost identical in design, were modest, thrifty and charming. Their complexions were innocent of all artifice. They were bedecked with the jewelry of the poor. Their voices were low and lady-like. One of them spoke with the bewitching drawl of Georgia, the other with the sprightly accent of Illinois. They seemed wonderfully healthy in an unathletic way. It was not the health of a gymnasium (that forced, inferior sort of health that destroys one's nicer sensibilities and turns one's brain into a biceps); it was the health of wind and sunshine, of boating and bathing and roaming in the fields, the health of a good appetite, a good conscience, and a good night's sleep.

Their books and their baggage all bespoke the temper of their character. Their books especially interested me. They were good books, clean books—travel, biography, ethnology, educational essays, interesting and wholesome reading for interesting and wholesome minds. Their talk about the countryside, the people, the customs, culture, art, cathedrals of Europe, was all intelligent and sympathetic, and full of nice observation and generous impulse. They spoke of their work in Japan with a likeable restraint. They were loath to be called "missionaries" because the word seemed to smack of the heroic. They preferred to call their enterprise "welfare work," or "Y work," undertaken, they said, partly in a spirit of zeal and partly in a spirit of adventure. There were times when I suspected them of possessing, at least in a few brief flashes, the sublime virtue of humility.

They were most delicate and resourceful in avoiding any issue with me on the subject of religion. Not that I tried even remotely to force any, but it requires a great deal of tact to talk in loose, watered terms about "Christianity" and "the Christianizing of the Pagan," etc., with a man who displays his religion in his clothes. But they managed it skillfully, and I evinced a real sympathy for them when they complained of the bad influences effected by American movies, American magazines, and even American tourists, in destroying in the minds of the native infidels the ideals of Christian modesty and Christian social behavior which the Y workers were trying to instil. I assured them also that I was very proud of the fact that Christian ladies of their type were giving the better features of our civilization at least some representation in the Orient. This small show of tolerance on my part thawed our small talk and melted it nearly to the point of authentic friendship. They seemed suddenly to breathe more freely and to cherish the fact that I had not been despising them in secret. And anxious to be generous to me in return, one of them unbent so far as to remark, almost with warmth, almost with pride, almost without any trace of condescension: "You know I have a friend who is a Catholic nun. She is a Madame of the Sacred Heart."

I expect always to remember the little cold chill that ran down my spine at the mention of this name on her lips. In all my life I had never before heard a Protestant speak of "The Sacred Heart." In the present instance it was an incidental and official use of the term, to be sure, but it was none the less unusual and astounding. It was as though I had seen Mr. Hoover bless himself; as though I had heard Lindbergh recite the Hail Mary; as though I had listened to the Salvation Army singing the Tantum Ergo.

With this shock for a start, I had only to close my eyes and allow all sorts of strange things to happen in my imagination. I began to picture how goodness could be transmuted into saintliness in the lives of these two young ladies who sat across the aisle, if only they could discern in their Messiah any traces of the real Sacred Heart.

If only their pleasant philosopher, their excellent citizen, their skillful mouther of sweet slogans, their other Abraham Lincoln, would flare for one moment into the Incarnate Word of God, alone and incomparable, who came to earth not to plague His people with platitudes but to stiffen them with a challenge and amaze them with a revelation, there might be some feeling in their souls for a Kingdom not of this world, there might be some message to bring from Jesus to the Japanese.

If only Christ should seem to talk to them with dogmas and

not with drivel, if He should stop saying, "I am your Big Brother, your Big Pal, your Big Friend, your Goody-goody What-you-may-call-me" and lapse into some great and God-like announcement like "Unless a man eat My Body and drink My Blood he cannot have life in him," if He would speak more like Jehovah and less like Santa Claus, they, who had very nearly reached the limit of spiritual excellence allowed them in their faded pattern of Christianity, might, on a supernatural basis, slip into that lovely company of virgins for which by character, temperament and generosity they were so eminently fitted. They might reach out for God like a moth for a star. They might be seized with the Divine madness of trying to be perfect as their Heavenly Father is perfect.

Those flowered dresses would lengthen and darken. Girdles would bloom at their sides. Two white wimples would creep up and encircle their faces. And long black veils would journey across their hair and drop in folds over their shoulders. They would walk soft-footed and to the tinkle of rosary beads. And on each breast a little silver crucifix would swing. Their awkwardness would be supplanted by the lovely manners of the cloister, and their nervous self-assurances would yield to a mighty certitude and an inward peace.

I dared not open my eyes. The picture was too lovely to spoil. And so, when we came to their station and they were up and ready to depart, I pretended to be sleeping. It was a censurable insincerity, I know, even though I was not due to leave the train until another station. But anyhow, I am so very sure that my Good Christians will go safely to Heaven when they die (for God loves us for our efforts and forgives us our ignorances) that, if I shall have managed to get there myself, there will not have been any need for having said good-bye.

SKHEENARINKA

SKHEENARINKA is not a Russian actress, a Hawaiian swimmer, or a Japanese billiard player. It is a very small schoolhouse in Ireland, in the County Tipperary, on the road that goes west from Clonmel, near a village I cannot remember, at the foot of a mountain I cannot spell.

Skheenarinka leaves a pleasurable tinkle in your mouth when you say it, but more than that, it is full of surprise and delight in its meaning. It means in Irish "the little dancing bush." Being by profession a schoolmaster, and by folly a rhymer, how could I resist the schoolhouse of the little dancing bush? I did not resist it. I walked boldly up to it, and tapped at the window. Master Connolly's scholars swiveled their small heads like a squadron of sparrows frightened at a noise, and the master himself came shuffling to the door to unlatch me a welcome.

One of the greatest charms of the Irish character is the easy formality of making friends with it. There is never any need of "How do you do?" or "Have I met you before?" or "Have we been properly introduced?" And one is never required to resort to subterfuges like "Could you tell me the time of day?" or "Is this the road to Currabinney Junction?" One has only to select one's Irishman, walk up to him casually (not nervously or jerkily, for he is bee-like in his behavior: his sting for the wary, his honey for the candid) and say something like this: "I am trying to remember a tune called 'The Peeler and the Goat'; could you whistle it for me, please?" With perfect imperturbability, as though the incident were prearranged, he will wet his whistle and blow you the tune. Then, for good measure, he will tell you a story about a peeler, or, even better, a story about a goat. In ten minutes you will be intimate enough with him to borrow his pipe. If it is near mealtime you will dine in his cottage. If it is nightfall you sleep in his extra bed.

At the risk of running ahead of my story, let me spend

myself in praise of Master Connolly's quality as I eventually came to discover it. And whereas I know, at present writing, five Irish schoolmasters, he may stand as typical of their immense goodness. (And if you, Michael of Burncourt, and you, Fionna of Dublin, should ever read this, be aware, with a blush, that you are bracketed with the great Connolly in my admiration and affection.)

The old master of Skheenarinka is a tall man with adjustable spectacles, reddish-brown hair patched with silver, and a countenance of amazing sweetness and sincerity. For all his sixty years, his eyes are fresh and young, and his face is full and wrinkleless. His mouth (and this is the surest outward test of culture) is easy and flexible in its movements. He breathes his syllables quietly and with relish, and while his lips are molding them into sound, the red maneuverings of a trim mustache lend emphasis and variety to their meaning. His voice is eminently pedagogical, the voice of a story-teller. His arms are long, and they slide out of his shirt-sleeves for unbelievable distances when he gesticulates. But his feet are small and suitable for dancing. His esthetic nature betrays itself in a bright waistcoat with assorted buttons. He wears a gay tie. And he manages, with only moderate success, an extra lick in his hair. In his day he was a sportsman, rode a good saddle, shot a good shot, and fished a good fish. But at sixty, at eventide, he keeps to his garden and his orchard. Indoors, he plays a masterly game of cribbage, and can squeeze a tolerable melody out of an old concertina, something plaintive, aboriginal, Druidic, that makes you want to cry.

Master Connolly's share of erudition is not large (for books are expensive, and Ireland is even poorer than you think it is) but his native intelligence is astounding. When the topic of conversation moves into the sure field of his own capacities (and they are many) he speaks with clearness, brilliance, and authority. His mind is an elegant instrument, faultless in its logic, practiced in its idiom, and beautiful in its metaphor.

Frequent excursions into the realm of the supernatural have given it a warmth and a charity not of this world. He looks upon his calling as a challeng^ and a trust. Nightly on his knees he importunes God to make him a good master, true to his tradition, valiant in his faith, and honest in his utterances.

Such then, all inadequately, is the genius of this lovable philomath of Tipperary, who, for a few shillings a week, in a shack in an open field, shadowed by an ancient tree, by the side of a dancing bush, at the foot of an unspellable mountain, sits patiently with his thirty ragged schoolboys, and tempts their little minds to struggle and fly. Barelegged and rumple-haired they come over boreen and meadow at the crack of the morning bell, with their three books and a slate, trotting through potato patches and climbing over walls. Their naked feet, calloused and cut by pebbles, are clean and wet from dewy anointings in the spongy acres of bog. Their eyes, blue, hazel, green, orange and chestnut, are restless with sparkle and squinty with sunshine. All knees and elbows, cluttering and squirming like a herd of he-kittens, they wait for the master in the school-yard. They are nature's children, unspoiled by artifice, untouched by modernity. Bred in the hallowed bodies of pure womenfolk; laid in their baptismal bonnets and chris-tening dresses on Our Lady's altar, and offered to her for pro-tection; nurseryed in a storyland of wonder and poverty and prayer; clean-lunged and lithe from roaming in the fields; friendly with the fairies and intimate with young Jesus; by these few little ones, the last and the loneliest, Ireland renews herself again, and takes hold on one more generation of men.

But let me tap again at the window and watch the old master of Skheenarinka coming out to greet me at the door.

"Good morning, master," said I.

"Good morning to your Reverence," said he.

"We are strangers," said I.

"We might easily be friends," said he.

"I come from a land," said I, "where they name schoolhouses

after dead philanthropists and live politicians. Will you let me come in?"

The master smiled, sniffed me a bit, seemed to find me genuine, reached out his hand and said "Welcome!" After little or no formality he threw open the classroom door and ushered me to the visitor's seat. Thirty pairs of eyes looked at me with mingled reverence and alarm. The master introduced me in Irish, saying something evidently very courteous, for they all nodded to me respectfully, and something very funny, at which they all laughed. I stood up a trifle abashed and, trying to recall old tricks, made my début before the younglings of Ireland. One false step, and I knew they were lost to me forever. One sure stroke, and they would be mine irrevocably. "I came in, boys," I said, watching them cautiously, "to stump you in your Catechism."

A roar of laughter, like a clap of musical thunder, broke forth in those four narrow walls. It was more than the laughter of nervousness set at ease; it was the laughter of exquisite contempt. It was vibrant with a hundred disdainful replies. "Stump us in our Catechism! We! The Irish! We who were fed Christian Doctrine with our first sups of milk! Stump *us!* The crack batsmen of the Roman Catechetical Church! Who have faced undauntedly the mouths of a dozen Canons, Bishops and Monsignori! The progeny of Patrick! The scions of a race that never knew a doubt and never held a heresy! Come on, with the best there is in you!"

I began with the usual things: the Blessed Trinity, the Incarnation, Our Lady, the Sacraments, Prayer. But it was like tossing elephants into the air for champion marksmen to shoot at. I then threw a few questions with a spin on them. They were returned with the spin reversed. I led them out into deep water and they followed fearlessly. And only when, in my absurdity, I began talking like the Council of Trent, did I get hesitating answers. And even then, they never said anything definitely wrong. They were merely puzzled that anyone could conceive such silly difficulties in regard to facts so patent and childlike as the truths of the Catholic Faith.

It was Bartley, the village butcher's boy, who broke up the encounter and enabled me to retire from my quiz gracefully. Bartley is only four and a half years old. He is allowed to come to school as a privilege, because his mother is dead, and his father cannot find time to manage him in the butcher's shop. He sits in the back of the classroom and draws pictures under Master Connolly's direction. He is a pet, and he knows it. He seems even to understand that he has not reached the use of reason, and so can enjoy liberties that are denied to full-fledged intellectuals. Bartley evidently grew tired of my heretical effrontery in trying to dislodge the Rock of Peter with pin pricks, so he waddled disgustedly down the aisle, and taking hold of Master Connolly's fingers and snuggling his little face in the master's hand, he cried out fervently: "I believe in God! I believe in God!"

"Do you, my little love?" said Master Connolly with infinite tenderness. "Well now, here's a big jump for you up to the sky!" And little Bartley went sailing up to the ceiling in the teacher's strong arms. And winking at me, the master remarked:

"He's a shrewd gossoon, Father; he knows that besides being meritorious in Heaven, these cute professions of Faith are good for an apple at recess time."

The master then took the class in hand, and we had specimens in reading and sums and geography. Some of it was done in Irish, with running translations for my benefit by the master. There was a story about a daisy, read in unison by the class, with inflections and cadences that were fascinating. There was some swift and brilliant work in mental arithmetic. And, in my especial honor, there was a treatise on the soil, the climate, and the inhabitants of the United States of America. Then came early dismissal which I was allowed to declare officially. And last of all the prayer for the closing of class. I shall never forget that prayer. It was the prayer of vision. The Irish do not merely talk to God. They coax Him. They cajole Him. They breathe on Him, like children pressed close to their Father's bosom and cradled in His arms.

It was on the road to the master's cottage (where one would have been dragged by the coat-tails if one had refused to go) that the great Connolly opened his heart to me; and during a delightful hour in the garden, and over a monster dinner prepared by his lovely wife and sweetened by her presiding presence at the tea-pot; and in the master's study, after our conversation had been whetted by a glass (maybe it was two glasses!) of noble wine; and during the whole of an autumn afternoon, until the sun had gone down behind the hill, and my day's schedule had been totally abandoned. And when at night I raced down the road to the station house, I was barely in time to catch the last train for Dublin.

Skheenarinka is now a permanent word in my vocabulary. It has the flavor of a good swear word, and serves me in that capacity when the devil tempts me to profanity. It is also my word of magic. Skheenarinka! . . . Run along to school, you Tipperary toddlers! A little fairy is clinking her castanets! A little bush is dancing in the wind!

A MADONNA OF THE KITCHEN

MRS. BOGGIANO, née Katie Zdrojefska, was born at Moulmoon on the Slwotz River in Latvia. My maps do not locate the river or the town, but this is not surprising. Her parents were Poles and had slipped up into the Latvic (then Lettonic) peninsula before Katie was born, and they carried, as is the custom, old and familiar names to strange places. "Slwotz" may be a corruption of "Slutsk" which is a real river near the Pinsk Marshes in West Poland, where Katie's people came from. I have little skill at geography and less at genealogy, so this short statement of the lady's antecedents will have to suffice. The point to remember is that she is a Christian peasant, born and bred in a mysteriously small nation of Northern Europe; and that she left it and came to America.

Mrs. Boggiano arrived in this country at the age of twelve, the spring before the Great War. Her sister, Ralolla Zdrojefska, had emigrated ten years previously and had already married Zingamesh Psduhishwish. (I am weak on invertebrate names, but this approximates it, and besides it sounds like a wave on the Baltic Sea, and may give this story a little local color in case I get courage to use it again.) Katie lived with her sister for a few years, and then hired out as second laundry-girl to the Elkinses, a well-favored family of these parts, who live in a mansion with sixteen servants and are very unhappy.

Romances are always interesting, so I shall sketch Katie's briefly. She was very beautiful, and is so to this day. I have a theory that expressions and not features are beautiful, and that lovely thoughts make a lovely face; but if you hold an opposite opinion, I might mention that her eyes are Baltic blue (a blue with a difference), her hair is silky and honey-colored, and I feel sure a lady novelist expert at facial descriptions would produce a long paragraph in praise of her neck and nose; there would be a page on her profile and a chapter on her chin.

The eldest Elkins daughter was a student of art, and often called Katie from the laundry, draped her in some outlandish fashion, and made her pose for a picture. One summer afternoon she was put on display before a crowd of esthetic visitors who had motored out to a house party. She was ordered to appear in the garden and wait beside the fountain, wearing her striped skirt, her checkered waist, her red shawl, and her mother's gold loops in her ears.

Poor Katie, utterly bewildered, twisted her fingers nervously during this ordeal and like a frightened bird tried many times to run away. The guests gathered about and discussed her as they would a vase or a rug. It was all very clever and very cruel. The gentlemen of the party called her "interesting" (a delicately ill-mannered expression, indicating no sense of verbal discrimination, and applicable equally to an archangel or an alligator); while the ladies agreed she was a "type"—which is a word employed by ugly débutantes in order to designate and belittle the good-looking daughters of the poor.

And then it happened. One afternoon in summer, when Katie and the first laundry-girl, who was also Polish, were hanging the last of a heavy washing on the dry-lines in the trellised enclosure south of the big mansion, a little pink-eyed rabbit darted under the hedge. Katie, forgetting her dignity as second laundry-girl, and remembering only that she had just turned sixteen, chased the rabbit. As it started to cross the road, there happened to be strolling home from work one Tommaso Boggiano, a railroad blacksmith, tired, sooty, and lonely. The dark eyes of Italy met the light blue eyes of Latvia. Tommaso caught the rabbit. And the Elkinses were out a second laundry-girl.

Mrs. Boggiano at the age of twenty-six has been married ten years and is the mother of six children. It is amazing how Providence sees to it that the simple of heart reproduce their kind in great abundance. Nature is constantly at work sloughing off its skeptics and sophisticates by sterility or self-destruction, and is continually replenishing the world with those who have a sense of reverence and a sense of humor. It is good that this is so. It is good that the meek possess the land.

Most young girls find marriage a problem, and are not always happy after they are wedded. The reason is that during the feverish days of courtship they fail to remember that incompatability of temperament is the normal condition between the sexes, and there can be no love without discipline and no fidelity without self-sacrifice. Mrs. Boggiano solved this problem by marrying a man ten years her senior, different to her

in all his sensibilities, indeed, whose very language she did not
understand. It would be true to say that she never fell in love
with him. Rather, she had always been loving something like
him, something innocent, deficient and unfulfilled, that needed
the richness of her nature to establish it and make it contented.
It was in her quest of a little pink-eyed rabbit that she ran into
a dark-eyed man.

Boggiano is a leathery little fellow with close-cropped hair,
large ears, a parabolic nose, and excellent teeth. His face in
repose is decidedly homely, and is seldom well-washed, but,
due to the influence of a ready and mischievous smile (much
more than to soap and water) it achieves a certain brightness
of texture and harmony of design, and could at moments be
called handsome. In his working clothes he looks not only
presentable, but even distinguished. Dressed up he becomes a
complete bumpkin. He has a ravenous appetite, has a flair for
poultry, and is good at gardening. He is especially skillful at
chores, chopping wood, raking leaves and fixing fences, and
always at his work he whistles and sings beautifully. He is not
so much Katie's companion as her complement—for the Italians
are gay and the Poles sad. And by his dramatics, tricks and
practical jokes he safeguards her sanity and her sense of the
ridiculous. She calls him in Polish (though I do not know the
word for it) her "private comedian."

He looks so funny when he crawls into a boiled shirt on
Holy Name Sunday and she helps him to fasten in the gold
buttons. He looks so funny with lather on his mustache when
he shaves. He looks so funny when, with clownish gallantry,
he catches her by the hand and entreats her to waltz with him
in the pantry. Katie wouldn't exchange him for any other
husband in the world. He is too enjoyable and, above all, too
uninvolved. He gets angry, but never moody. He sometimes
uses profanity, but even in his greatest temper would not harm
a kitten. He worships her little ones, takes them up tenderly
when they cry, and sings them to sleep with operatic airs.

Day by day he stares contemplatively at this lovely, blue-eyed creature from the North, whom he wooed with a few words of broken English—all of it ungrammatical and most of it slang—and who, for some sweet, secret reason she has never disclosed, was willing to become his possession, wash his clothes, cook his meals, and bear his children.

I sometimes think mothers get more pity than they require. There is much talk lately about how difficult it is to bear a child, and too little talk about how nice it is to have one. Someone should put a stop to the considerable screaming being done by unmarried lecturers in the throes of giving birth to imaginary children on public platforms. Motherhood is never honored by excessive talk about the heroics of pregnancy. If babies were not worth the pains and confinements they cause, there would not have been a billion of them born in the last hundred years. It is true they have come mostly from black, yellow and brown women, and our western civilization is dwindling. But it is nice to know that the heroine of this story, imported to our shores in pig-tails at the age of twelve, has been responsible for the complexions of six little snow-white Americans. In this way our country is kept populated with a few Caucasians, and the Constitution goes on.

Katie Zdrojefska has never heard the reasons advanced for the restriction of families, and would probably not comprehend them if they were explained to her. She knows it is hard enough to be poor and have children. She would think it unbearable to be poor and have none. Fidelity to nature's laws has left her will unhampered by hesitancies, inhibitions and phobias. Her body has become the instrument of a pure spirit able to melt every inch of it and make it maternal. Her fruitfulness has never been outraged by drug-store deviltries, and so there are no cross-purposes in her nerves needing to be untangled by a psychiatrist. Hither and thither she moves at her nursery tasks, bothered but not bored, tired but never in a tantrum, her children's chiefest plaything, continually tugged at by the apron strings. It is her way of learning that life is very good and God is very wonderful—God, who breathed on the little make-believe daughter she used to fondle in far-off Latvia, and turned it in this land of exile into a living doll: her namesake, now seven years old; now able after a brief coaching to arrange the kitchen table for supper, beautified with her mother's eyes, shadowed with her light brown hair, vibrant with the identical shift of her shoulders, the turn of her head, as she utters a patient and imitative sigh when the cups run short, or the sugar bowl is discovered hiding behind the bread tin.

It must be obvious that this unlettered Polish woman is a splendidly civilized person and a most valuable member of society. She is a minimum of annoyance to her neighbors and a minimum of expense to the state. No high-salaried social scientist is required to adjust her to the simple problem of living. And if intelligence is—as it is—half a moral virtue, there need be no hesitancy in calling her highly intelligent. Her mind touches the realities of life by swift intuitions and certitudes. Unlike her psychic sisters of the INTELLIGENTSIA, she does her thinking for herself. It is not done for by nervous philosophers, diseased dramatists, sullen poets, and melancholy writers of fiction, whose purposes are anti-social and whose friendships are unwholesome. Her tradition is that of the Christian peasant, the soundest of all metaphysicians, and, under the influence of Divine grace, the profoundest of all mystics. . . .

It is Springtime. The birds are twittering in the trees outside my window. My room becomes stuffy. Indoors becomes intolerable. So I decide to cajole a much-prized walking companion into a jaunt on the highway.

We march merrily along, and I am cheered by the sweet afternoon air and the brightness of the fields and the sky.

A quarter of a mile down the road we pass the cottage where

the Boggianos live. Three of the little ones: Tommy, Catherine, and Anna Maria, are playing in the yard. They run to the fence to hail us as we pass.

The smoke curls at the chimney top. The little pigs grunt in the sty. The mother-hen scratches for her brood under the hay wagon. Soon, Mrs. Boggiano appears in the doorway. She wears a faded house dress, old shoes, and no stockings. Her hair is parted straight in the middle and bound with an elastic band behind her head. Her forehead is covered with perspiration and with steam from the stew pot, boiling on the stove. Her arms are bare to the elbow, and there is a bad grease burn on her right forearm. She looks a bit fatigued (Boggiano says the new baby is only one month away), but there is ever in her clear blue eyes aloofness, serenity, purity and calm. She beams with delight when she sees us talking to the children, and curtseys in the manner of a princess. And half in Polish, half in English, she greets us with a prayer: "May Jesus bless you, Reverend Fathers; and may the Blessed Mother be your protection at all times."

"Hello, Mrs. Boggiano!" we answer in the cold, clumsy manner of Americans . . . but down in our hearts we are saying: "And may Jesus love you and bless you too. And may Our Lady keep you forever in the blue shadow of her mantle, Katie Zdrojefska, from Moulmoon, on the Slwotz River, in Latvia!"

EVANGELINE

WE WERE waiting in the reception parlor, waiting to go in to dinner. It happened in England, and it wasn't far from London. Our hostess, who was busy with many things, had not had time to introduce us all round. There were some guests arriving late, there were name cards to be set at the proper plates, flowers to be straightened in vases, and a final challenge to be issued to the cook. There were probably innumerable other details needing attention. I have never been a hostess. I can only weakly imagine what nervous delights and delicious flurries reward that noble function and make it worth while.

I think it only proper that guests should suffer a little in return for the sweets of hospitality. I think it behooves us to stand around as awkwardly as possible while we are waiting to be introduced. I always try to look especially uncomfortable. I even try to look disgruntled. I endeavor to give the impression of wishing I had not come at all. I make a strong effort to suffuse my face with a horror of food, a horror of pleasantry, and a horror of company. It is even a good idea to become rigid, plastic, to stop breathing if possible—though this last is rather difficult.

And when the room has degenerated into a morgue or a mausoleum where everyone is statuesque, inanimate, and hateful, then let our hostess walk in and touch us into life with her own personality. Let her put us at our ease, because we needed terribly to be put at ease. Let her charge us with affection and friendliness. For the real triumph of a hostess comes, not after the dinner, for which, since she did not cook it, she can take credit only with reservations; but before the dinner, when she assumes her delightful prerogative of establishing her guests in their various identities, by walking into her waiting parlor and taking slime of the earth and breathing into it the soul of a dowager, a doctor, a coquette, or a clergyman; and sends them all chattering and alive into the dining-room.

We were standing about, waiting to go in to dinner, and everyone, as far as I could see, was observing the ritual of good guesthood I have described above. We were all Punch-and-Judy figures, wooden and soulless, waiting for someone to jiggle our strings. Now and then, a pasteboard gentleman would twist on his hinges; now and then, a sawdust lady would stir in her rags; but this was to be expected, as even marionettes are subject to the laws of mechanics and gravity. There was occasionally a cough or a sniffle or a sneeze or a yawn, that sounded dreadfully human and inappropriate. But for the most part, it was as dull as a doll shop deserted by clerk and customer, and littered with uncompanionable crockery.

At a moment of great stillness, the voice of our hostess could be heard telephoning in the hall. We all listened, as little eggs in a nest might listen to their bluebird. It was a voice full of song, full of promise, a prenatal music heard by unhatched fledglings. Soon it would come chirping into the reception parlor and peck at our shells, and we would emerge and cheep merrily, and become happy and fluttersome, and open our mouths for dinner.

Feeling, for reasons best known to myself, exceptionally irritable and uneasy, I undertook to glance at myself in a mirror near which I happened to be standing. I wanted to see if I looked as waxlike and expressionless as I was trying to look. It was a quick glance, but it startled me, for there were two of me in the glass. I saw myself double. Two black suits, two rabats, two turned-about collars, two sacerdotal somebodies of the same build and height. Horrors! Was it possible that in trying to suppress my personality, I had actually reduplicated it!

I switched my gaze into the mirror again and saw, to my indescribable relief, that there was another priest in the room. My other reflection was a young cleric who stood in an opposite corner leaning against the mantelpiece. I turned my head and scrutinized him in the flesh. He looked very much like me. But he was not me. And for that I thanked God profusely.

This incident led me, unsportingly if you will, to violate the rules of the game and come to life ahead of time. I decided not to wait for the arrival of the lady of the house. I blossomed into vitality at once. I became myself prematurely. But I think I ought to be excused for doing so.

There happens to be in this world of strange social conventions, one friendship that transcends all conventions and knows no rules. It is the brotherhood of Catholic priests. There is not, I swear it, under the stars, an intimacy more reckless or more profound than the bond between one Catholic levite and another. It needs no coaxing, no prelude, no ritual. It is subject to no formality. We meet and possess one another instantly. There is not the shadow of a barrier between us, neither age, nor antecedents, nor nationality, nor climate, nor color of skin. Ours is a blunt, rough-hewn affection. It almost forgets to be polite. I can dine at his table without invitation; sit in his study and read his books before I have ever met him; borrow his money or his clothes with no bail; his home is my home; his fireside, my fireside; his altar, my altar. I can give him my confidences promptly and without reserve. I can neither edify nor scandalize him. We can quarrel without offense, praise each other without flattery, or sit silently and say nothing, and be mutually circumvented.

How and why all this can happen is our own precious secret. It is the secret of men who climb a lonely drawbridge, mount a narrow stair, and sleep in a lofty citadel that floats a white flag. Singly we go, independent and unpossessed, establishing no generation, each a conclusion of his race and name; yet always companioning one another with a strange sympathy, too tender to be called fellowship, too sturdy to be called love, but which God will find a name for when He searches our hearts in Eternity.

I walked over to the mantelpiece where my priestly colleague was resting his elbow. I was very casual. Comrades are always casual. I spoke to him quietly, almost indifferently. "I didn't know there were two of us." That was all I said. And I took his hand . . . but somehow or other it didn't shake properly. There was something either too stiff or too loose about it, I don't know which.

"How do you do?" he said very suavely. (We never say

"How do you do?" and we never say it "suavely.") "You're an American, aren't you?"

"Yes."

"Are you stationed in London?"

"No. Just visiting."

"I'm just visiting, too."

"Where do you come from?" I asked.

"Well, you see, my wife and I—"

BANG! A sheet of ice fell between us and shattered at our feet.

You fooled me, little High Churchman, Low Churchman, Broad Churchman, or whatever you are. I don't dislike you. I like you very much. You have clean, honest eyes, and though my principles depend on a creed, my friendships do not. And I like clean, honest eyes. But we are not friends yet. This is a dinner party. And who are you and I, sir, to speak before we have been properly introduced? . . .

Whereupon our hostess came in, radiant and charming, with a Fiat Lux in her eye. And she introduced us. He was Mr. Plummer, and I was Father Who's-this. And we were terribly delighted with each other as we walked in to dinner.

Was it fate, or a *faux pas*, or my Guardian Angel trying to be funny, that put me at dinner next to Mr. Plummer's wife? Whoever it was, or whatever it was, I thank them. For Mr. Plummer's wife was the most unspeakably (one moment, please, while I change the sheet in my typewriter)—

I am given to superlatives. I overstate things. My friends have rebuked me for it. I have tried to correct it. But I haven't. I can't. I say "most" when I mean "much." Without the words "tremendous," "wonderful," "amazing," and "astounding," my vocabulary would collapse. I couldn't talk. I couldn't think. Megalomania is like a bad devil. It can be driven out only by prayer and fasting. And I have neglected to fast sufficiently.

Let me be restrained, therefore, at least on this occasion. Let me not say that Mrs. Plummer was the most beautiful woman

I have ever seen in my life. She was in her early twenties. It is probable that she was twenty-two, possible that she was twenty-three, but unthinkable that she was twenty-four. She looked ever so young to be married. She looked almost too young to be in love. Her Christian name (which Mr. Plummer let slip in the course of the dinner) was Evangeline.

It was very clear that Mr. Plummer had had something to say as to how she dressed and wore her hair. After all, the pastor's wife should set a good example to the congregation, and the length of her skirts, the width of her eyebrows, and the shine on her fingernails might well determine the standard of the parish gossip. I do not know what the parish gossips said or thought about her, for parish gossips can manage to streak ink on a sunbeam, but Mr. Plummer's wife satisfied perfectly my anticipations of an angel. I could not tell you what I ate while sitting beside her. I have a vague remembrance of seeing an oyster on a fork on its way to my mouth. But I have no notion of what became of it.

Mrs. Plummer made no effort to shine at the dinner. Yet no one listened to or looked at anybody else. And in her simplicity she seemed entirely unconscious of the fact that she was the glory of our feast. Two or three débutantes, whose gowns were very garish and hung perilously from their shoulders on spider threads, sat like manikins and watched her score her easy triumphs without a single display of cleverness or a single sentence spoken for effect. Several inveterate table talkers like myself, who switch all conversations into the neighborhood of their own anecdotes, utterly subsided lest their ears should miss the rapture of Mrs. Plummer's voice saying nothing more considerable than "Please pass the celery!"

Across the table from me sat Mr. Plummer beaming with satisfaction. He was enormously pleased with his little consort and the specimen of charm and decorum she was achieving in the name of the clerical profession. And it is embarrassing for me to say so, but Mr. Plummer spent half the time looking at his wife, and the other half looking at me. There was pity in his eye. The wave-length of pity is very delicate, but there is no mistaking it. It is easy to look daggers and miss your mark, but the shafts of pity are suited to the eye's most unerring performance. Even Mrs. Plummer detected it, and endeavored to shield me in her sweet charity.

"It must be fine, just the same, to be a priest," she said, and the strangeness and suddenness of the statement startled me into inarticularity.

"I remember," she went on (oh, why did she go on?), "when we were in Italy last summer. My husband went walking in a little side street in Padua. And a group of children met him and thought he was a priest, and danced about him, and kissed his hand, and called him *Padre mio*, and thought he didn't belong to anybody but them!"

Mr. Plummer wilted and I dropped my head. And then it dawned on Mrs. Plummer what she had said. And I call upon a righteous Reformation, a loving Luther, a happy Henry, and a kind Calvin to witness that when they gave Evangelines to Evangelicals and took away from them the children in a side street in Padua, they made it possible for a woman to give a man the saddest, most hopeless and most poignant and most repentant look I have ever seen a woman give a man in my life. And if this be an overdose of superlatives, it is not an overdose of truth.

ASTHORE

I AM, if I may be allowed to stress one of my qualities, a good companion for an old person. My early life, up to my eleventh year, was spent in constant association with an aged grandfather. In those years of our childhood (his second and my first), my grandfather and I took a sympathetic interest in each other's joys and miseries. He preferred me to any of his old cronies, and I him to any of my playmates. We were kindred spirits and loved each other dearly.

It was my business, when his memory became unreliable, to solve my grandfather's bewilderments concerning the time of day, the hour of dinner, and the whereabouts of his spectacles. I had not only exclusive access to his thoughts, but also extraordinary privileges about his person. I was allowed to tie his boot laces, dust his hat, wind his watch, and light his pipe. And my youthful ear had a monopoly on his stories.

His stories were invariably about Ireland, and rigidly Irish in flavor; but there was universal stuff in them: ghosts, fairies, christenings, wakes, weddings, famines, battles. The battles were my favorites, fought, it seems, from the beginning of the world, against an army of ruffians called "low Briddish." The "low Briddish" kept coming across the sea in order to persecute our people, the "high Bernians." We were a peaceful and gentle race. They were unkind and cruel. They killed our orators. They poisoned our potatoes. Many a summer's afternoon my grandfather and I sat on the front doorstep with our chins in our hands, shaking our heads and hating the "low Briddish," wishing them bad luck, and calling them the names they deserved.

From my grandfather I acquired many of my personal characteristics: the habit, for instance, of licking back my hair with my hand when I am annoyed, or of putting my thumbs behind my suspenders when I am amused. From him, too, I derived my sole musical talent, the art of humming Irish tunes. My grandfather took pains to teach me these ancestral arias with great thoroughness; and though I never tried to put words to them (nor did he), I learned to manage them in melody behind a closed mouth with unmistakable authenticity and sweetness. Even to this day native-born Irishmen will testify that I am a splendid Celtic hummer, with an extraordinary nasal range, and a most interesting repertory of hums.

Every child in the course of his development makes at least one precocious remark. Some children, provided they be unusually bright or abnormally stupid, make many. But no child fails to make at least one. I made one, I am quite sure *only* one, but I think it was a very good one.

My grandfather and I were sitting—need I say?—on the front doorstep one drowsy afternoon in July. It was getting late. The sun was ready to go down. Our voices were weary and our emotions tired. Finn McCool, a large-jowled Irish chieftain, had just executed some fine stunts for us in the movies of our imaginations. At intervals we had cleared our soft palates and strummed a little music, keeping it in time with a metronome accompaniment of heel and toe. My grandfather had made a few meditative remarks on his favorite holy topic, the Blessed Mother of God, at the mention of whose name he invariably raised his hat, even though it occurred twice in a sentence. I, being hatless, was in the habit of paying my devoir to any spoken syllables indicating Our Lady's reality by making her a reverential flick of my hair. But, as I said, at last we grew tired, tired of talk and romantics. And we lapsed into one of those long silences we often had together when the conversation lagged.

My grandfather sighed. It was a long, deep sigh, indicating not the fatigue of a day but the fatigue of a whole life. He was growing very feeble at the time, only six months before his death. He sighed again, and looked at me for ten intense minutes that were full of flashes issuing from the core of his soul to the kernel of mine. "I am all through!" he said without speaking. "You must carry on. You must keep alive the thoughts, and the dreams, the stories we once shared together."

I sighed back at my grandfather to show him that I understood his message, and was assuming my burden with pride and regret. And in some dim way I promised him with my eyes that if ever I had a grandson, I would see to it that our stories were kept alive and that our tradition did not die. I did not know at that time that it was God's holy design to make me the last of my line.

When this sacred trust had been executed and I had in silence received it, my grandfather shriveled, and for some moments after seemed to lose his individuality. His hands grew cold, his face expressionless, and his head dropped dismally on his breast. For a little while he stopped being anybody's grandfather, even mine, and became just an old hulk of a body with a spirit floating somewhere inside it, a soul unrelated to material dimensions and movements, without a function or any human purpose. I pulled his head down, and putting my mouth close to his ear, whispered, "Is it lonely in there, grandfather?" . . . I hope I am allowed to consider this a remarkable question, very precocious, and, indeed, deeply mystical.

My grandfather saw to a nicety the point of my strange query. He wiped his bad eye with the back of his hand—he had one bad eye which, for the last ten years of his life, was constantly inflamed, and which my mother had to bathe three times a day with boric acid and warm water—and answered, "It is, *asthore!*"

There is, in Irish, no expression of endearment so delicate in its nuance, or so extravagant in its meaning, as the term *asthore*. It is very probably the loveliest word in that language. It is elusive in its emotional significance and impossible to translate straightforwardly into English, much like the word *doux* in French. I once heard Hilaire Belloc struggling to render in good Anglo-Saxon the expression *le doux air d'Anjou.* "The *sweet* air of Anjou" he said would never do. Nor would "the *gentle* air of Anjou." But possibly Chesterton's phrase, "the *quiet kindness* of the Angevin air" would indicate the spirit of the word. "Asthore" is even more difficult.

The best way to convey the meaning of "asthore" is to state the relationship which must exist in persons between whom its employment is warranted. "Asthore" supposes in general what

I may call "an affectionate, protective superiority" on the part of the one using it toward the one to whom it is used. A young person never calls another young person "asthore"; nor would a child use it to an elder, nor elder people among themselves. There are three situations in which the word achieves its power and its point, which usages I may designate as (1) The Lover-Beloved, (2) The Parent-Child, and (3) The Grand-parent-Grandchild.

(1) The L-B use of "asthore" is always dead serious. It is, in this case, never a mere pet word, nor one to be employed in any light flirtation. For instance, an Irish lad would never think of saying to a pretty girl at a cross-roads dance, "You have nice eyes, asthore," or "What are you doing next Tuesday evening, asthore?" This would be an utter profanation of the word. It would be in impossible bad taste, much as though a young American "fresh guy" should say to an indefinite blonde waitress in a café, "Hello, bright eyes! I can see right on the spot that God meant you from all eternity to be my comfort, my joy, and my delight. Would you mind telling me your name and letting me take you to the movies?"

No. When a young man calls his sweetheart "asthore," it is required (a) that she be not merely his sweetheart, but his "sweet soul"; and (b) that they be realizing for the moment some phase of the spiritual quality of love, its sacrificial character, its burden, its rapture, and its mystery. "And will you love me when I am a weeshy, scrawny, wither-may-jingle old woman?" says she. If she has asked it smilingly, he will answer: "Yes, acushla [or mavourneen or machree]," meaning, "Yes, my darling, or my honey, or my sweet one." But if she asked this question *with tears in her eyes*, his answer is "I will, asthore!" That's the way the word goes among lovers.

(2) The Parent-Child use of "asthore" is playful. It is the term of affection by which fathers and mothers (or their equivalents: aunts or uncles or very close neighbors) indicate to youngsters what adorable annoyances they are, what agreeable

nuisances. When a father calls his little son "asthore," he means: "I love you because you are my little son. I love you because you are at once such a joy to me, and such a bother. I wouldn't swap you for ten million pounds. And I wouldn't give tuppence for ten more like you!" This is the second meaning of "asthore."

(3) The Grandparent-Grandchild use of "asthore" is the most sacred of all. It is a word of ritual, the love cry of a tribe, the call of the blood overleaping a generation. It is the means by which an aged human heart asks its own posterity, not for affection but for existence, not for companionship but for continuation. It makes vocable an act, not of love alone, but of love and faith fused into one virtue, which we call "hope," and which we rightly set highest of all the operations of the human spirit in its present condition of probation and exile. If King David had written his psalms in Irish, he would have called his Royal Grandchild "asthore."

The night my grandfather died, just before the death rattle began in his throat, he raised a blessed candle and waved goodbye to all his neighbors and kindred, to the whole world and all its countries and peoples. And then, with the last bit of strength left in him, he whispered, "Good-bye, asthore," to me. Shortly afterward, the undertaker arrived, to dress his lifeless body in its coffin clothes, surround it with candles, and give it a parlor respectability. I have never had a grandfather since that time. . . .

Freudians, psychoanalysts, and chemical philosophers, who are anxious to dissect and desecrate all forms of honorable human affection, will be interested in this personal confession. It may give rise to a whole new department in the field of behavioristic studies hitherto left untouched: "the little-boy-old-man neurosis"; or maybe, "the atavistic perversion"; or more likely, "the Abraham complex." And if their textbooks can prove that the implications of any psychic irregularity are sufficiently degenerate and gloomy to arouse popular interest,

science will hand over a fresh inspiration to literature. A new
form of melancholy will develop among our novelists. Amer-
ica's leading dramatist will put me in a play.

THE JOURNEY

EVANS INGRAM TOWNE (that is not his exact name, but it is
very nearly the flavor of it) sat next to me in the train. He was
traveling all alone from Albany to Boston. Evans Ingram
Towne, eleven years old, his travel money folded in his hand-
kerchief, his ticket in his blouse pocket, and a nervous little
grin on his face that seemed to say to his fellow-passengers,
"Don't you people think I'm a pretty brave little boy to be
traveling all alone from Albany to Boston?" was as pleased
with himself as could be, because he was making such a long
journey without his father or his mother or his aunt or his
uncle or anybody with him.

True, his aunt had put him on the train at Albany, and his
father was going to take him off the train at Boston. But think
of all the railroad-sleepers he was riding over all by himself,
and the miles and miles of steel track rolling under him, and
the millions and millions of trees and people and cows and
clotheslines and telegraph poles and villages and advertisements
and barns and woodpiles he was looking at without anybody to
help him!

"I'm eleven years old, and I'm traveling all alone from
Albany to Boston. What church do you preach in? Would
you like a ham sandwich? I've got two story books. Would
you like to read one of them? . . ."

I was a little bewildered at this barrage of questions from the
small somebody in the seat next to me. I had intended speaking
to him after I finished another "story book," which I read
under pain of mortal sin every day (and I hate to interrupt a

psalm in the middle, because you have to begin it over afterwards). But even prayer must yield to politeness. And after all, what is the liturgy for but to teach us good manners?

I closed my Breviary and looked at him. Wishing to make a good impression, I said I had preached in any number of churches, clearing my throat as I said so, to indicate a slight exaggeration. I said I approved of ham sandwiches at all times. I would be awfully glad to read one of his story books. And I felt sure that a non-stop railroad journey from Albany to Boston, undertaken SOLO at the age of eleven, was undoubtedly a world's record and ought to get in the papers.

After our story book apiece, we had a ham sandwich apiece, which we ordered with great ceremony from the porter, along with two bottles of milk, to make sure we were getting all the vitamins that were coming to us.

Evans Ingram Towne was a gallant little man, intent on observing all formalities. "I'm to pay for the lunch," he said, "because I was the one who suggested it."

I assured him that when two people were traveling together, it was always the privilege of the older person to pay for the lunch, no matter who suggested it.

"No," he said very earnestly, "mother says that when you invite anybody to lunch, you should do the paying."

I then suggested that we match coins to see who would pay for the lunch, just to be good sports. We did so, and he won, much to his delight. So then I suggested we should match coins again to see who would NOT pay for the lunch. He won again. So we compromised by letting me pay for the lunch and letting him tip the porter.

Having dined together, and having jointly contributed to a mutual amusement fund: four match tricks, two thumb tricks, ten conundrums, and the completion of one one-hundredth of a cross-word puzzle, we felt firmly established in friendship and came to a point where we could indulge in a few little confidences.

His first mother was dead, and now he had a second mother. He felt fairly sure that his second mother liked him well enough, and she did often give him a "hurry-up kiss," but she was different from his first mother in this, that she never did any real worrying about him. "She seems to think I never need any worrying about and that I am always all right, and sometimes I'm not all right, especially when I'm sick or have tonsilitis, when I really ought to be worried about." He scratched his little head as he said this, and gave me a most wistful look, as if to indicate that he wasn't complaining, but just telling me the facts.

Now the secret of the charming intimacy that exists between all Catholic children and all Catholic priests, lies precisely in the fact that our children know they can come to us at any time and be worried about without any red tape or delay. Lest I seem to be forcing the point, I can speak entirely from my experience as a child. When I was eleven years old, I knew I had only to meet a priest, any priest whatsoever, and if circumstances permitted, there was sure to follow a little dialogue of worry questions and responses, in which I loved my part because I knew it so well, because it was so terribly important, and so terribly easy to play.

"Are you a good boy?"

"Yes, Father."

"Are you getting big and strong?"

"Yes, Father."

"Do you say your prayers?"

"Yes, Father."

"Night and morning?"

"Yes, Father."

"And do you ask God to protect you and bless you?"

"Yes, Father."

"Why did God make you?"

"God made me to know Him and love Him and serve Him in this world, and to be happy with Him forever in the next."

It may be objected that this last line is found on page 3 of the Penny Catechism, and I had learned it like a parrot. I can only answer that Hamlet's soliloquy is found on page 103 (if you have my edition) of Shakespeare, and I once learned that like a parrot, too. It is not necessary to have composed a line of great drama in order to relish its meaning or to sense its magnificence on one's lips. And it is no small distinction at the age of eleven to have the whole Catholic hierarchy always at one's beck and call, anxious to be amazed at one's youthful histrionics, dumbfounded at one's wisdom, eager to magnify in terms of the Penny Catechism one's sacredness and importance in a world where otherwise one seems so little, so helpless and so insignificant.

But this was as between me as a child and my priests, or me as a priest and my children. How could I undertake to worry about Evans Ingram Towne, when the reasons for my worry were not, as they needed to be, taken for granted? Nevertheless, I determined to try.

"What is the best day in the year?" I asked him by way of sparring for an opening.

"Christmas Day?" It was half question and half answer.

"That's right!" I replied. "And why is Christmas Day the best day in the year?"

"Because that's the day Christ was born." (I forgot to mention that Evans Ingram Towne goes to the Unitarian Church on Sundays, and his pastor's name is something like Rev. Mr. Judson Bumbleberry.)

I was amazed at such a dogmatic utterance from such a source. "And who was Christ?" I continued.

"He was God," he answered promptly and with perfect assurance.

"You are right, dear," I said, not a little surprised; "that's just who He was. And God became man. He came down to earth and became a little boy like you. Wasn't that a lovely thing

for God to do? And Our Lady is Our Lord's Blessed Mother.
Did you ever hear of God's Blessed Mother?"

"Well, I've heard them speak of that once or twice at home,
but I don't think they have that much in our town. I think
that's confined mostly to the larger cities, isn't it?"

I decided not to waste any time trying to decide statistically
just what cities "that" was confined to, but determined to go
as far as I felt Rev. Mr. Jumbleberry would allow me, in telling
this priceless little wayfarer something of that traditional
theology which gives Christian children of my acquaintance
such comfort and delight. And if I could induce him to make
in his own way some simple act of perfect love, the Holy
Spirit might be willing to transmute it at once into Baptism of
Desire. But I had to work quickly, because I was leaving the
train at Worcester, and the porter was already dust-ragging my
bag.

"You see, it's this way," and I decided on a number of swift
short sentences, "God made you. . . . He loves you. . . .
You're His little boy. . . . Nobody owns you as much as He
does. . . . Even when your first mother died, you went on liv-
ing . . . because you really don't belong to anybody but God.
. . . He worries about you all the time. . . . He never lets
you out of His thoughts. . . . He counts the number of steps
you take when you walk and the number of breaths you
breathe in your sleep. . . . Everyone who is good and kind to
you He blesses and rewards. . . . Everyone who is mean and
unkind to you He punishes. . . . When you do wrong and are
sorry He forgives you and forgets it. . . . When you do good
He never forgets it. . . . You weren't really made for this
world. . . . I wasn't. . . . Nobody ever is. . . . That's why
we're all a little bit restless all the time and a little bit lonely.
. . . We're all waiting for our real life which begins in Heaven
after we die. . . . Heaven is where we will see God and know
how beautiful and lovely He is. . . . And then we will be

happy. . . . We will be happy forever and ever. . . . We can't see God now . . . but we will see Him some day. . . . He sees us, though . . . and He loves us. . . . He wouldn't have made us if He didn't love us . . . and He wants us to love Him . . . and He will help us to love Him if we try. . . . You love Him . . . don't you?"

"Yes." This was fine, but I wanted to make sure of it. And the trainman was shouting "Woooooooster!" and I had but a few seconds more to remain.

"Well, do you love God more than you love anybody else?"

"Yes, I do."

"Well, say you do."

"I do."

"With all your heart?"

"Yes."

"Just for His own sake, because He's so good? And you're sorry if you ever offended Him?"

"Yes, I am."

"Well, say, 'Almighty God, I love You with all my heart.' "

"Almighty God, I love You with all my heart."

"Better than I do anybody."

"Better than I do anybody."

I shook his small hand.

"Good-bye."

"Good-bye."

"And always remember," I added hurriedly as I prepared to rush for the door, "that God loves you so much He came down to earth to be a little boy like you. And that's why Christmas Day is the best day in the year, because it's the day God was born into the world for love of little boys. Will you remember now why it's the best day in the year?" I was ready to make my sprint and dive for the Worcester platform.

"Yes, I'll remember," he said with a knit of his brow. "But of course I don't think it can compare with the Fourth of July. . . ."

I leaped off the train as it started to move out of the station. My head was buzzing and my heart was sick. I gave my bag to a red-cap porter and then took it away from him again. I sat down on a bench on the railroad platform. Distances, distances were running through my mind. I was measuring them off, counting the hours, counting the miles. From Albany to Boston. From Albany to London. From Albany to Paris. From Albany to Paradise! That's a long journey. For a little boy. To be taking all alone. At eleven years of age. Whose first mother is dead. Whose second mother doesn't seem to worry. And whose lovely Blessed Mother is confined mostly to the larger cities.

JOE PALLAVICINO

JOE PALLAVICINO is my barber and I am his customer.

On Sunday mornings he loves to come to Solemn Mass and behold me standing at the high altar, clad in the gorgeous vestments of a celebrant. I shine amid a blaze of lights. I am bowed at by respectful attendants in their flowing maniples and braided gowns. I am showered with incense by graceful altar-boys. I raise my hands majestically and speak aloud the beautiful phrases of the Latin prayers. I burst into song and am answered from the distance by a triumphant organ and a full-throated choir. I walk to and fro in an aura of mystery, surrounded by golds and marbles, linens and flowers. I gesticulate to the accompaniment of chimes. One thousand pairs of eyes approve and interpret my every movement. I raise this multitude to its feet when I go to read the Gospel. I drop it on its knees with the pæans of the Sanctus. I send it into a hush at the sacred moments of the Consecration. I am the protagonist in the greatest drama that happens under the stars. I am Joe

Pallavicino's hero of heroes. He has never met anyone in the world so wonderful as me.

On Monday morning it is quite different. I walk into Pallavicino's barber-shop with all my glory gone from me. I am the most nondescript-looking person imaginable. I am dressed in somber black. I wear an unkempt hat, unpolished shoes, and shiny trousers. I shed my coat and collar and sit down like any other mortal and am meekly wrapped in a barber's sheet. I possess, strange to say, a very ordinary head of hair, which Joe Pallavicino can actually take hold of and clip with a scissors and rake with a comb.

But Joe Pallavicino refuses to forget me as he saw me on Sunday. My image in its moment of grandeur has been burned into his memory. And it will not vanish on Monday when I sit down to be sheared, and am ignominiously exposed in my shirt-sleeves and suspenders. He still treats me with the greatest reverence, tempered with a deliberate nonchalance that is calculated to cover up any embarrassment I might suffer from being touched and handled. He is most particularly anxious to protect me from the worldly chatter of customers in neighboring chairs. Whenever any coarse voice is heard in which he detects the possibilities of a profanity or an indelicacy, he clicks loudly with his scissors, grunts with his diaphragm, and shuffles with his feet.

Soapy Face in the next chair has a coarse voice, and Joe Pallavicino is afraid of it. Soapy Face has come in after I have been draped and disguised as an ordinary customer, and is unaware of the distinguished personage in whose presence he is being shaved. Joe Pallavicino makes a SNIP, SNIP, SNIP with his fingers in an effort to attract Soapy Face's attention. Soapy Face pays no attention, but launches into a monologue about prize-fights, midnight cabarets, and nigger pool. SNIP, SNIP, SNIP goes Joe Palavicino again, determined to catch Soapy Face's eye and give him an admonition. This ruse is fatal. Soapy Face finally turns his head, stiffens his half-lathered jaw and mutters with great annoyance, "What the hell is the matter with you?"

Joe Pallavicino wilts. He is disgraced. His face blazes with anger as if at a sacrilege, and then melts into an expression of supreme supplication. The whole performance is, of course, clearly visible to me in the mirror. Joe Pallavicino indicates me to Soapy Face with frantic pointings of his finger. "A priest! A priest!" he whispers with exaggerated and inaudible lip-movements. And then as a final gesture of despair, drops his instruments, and makes on his forehead and breast a violent sign of the cross.

Soapy Face replies with a gesture of bewilderment, sulks a little, stretches his legs, closes his eyes, and subsides in the fumes from a hot towel.

I became Joe Pallavicino's hero by being his priest. But I became his intimate friend by becoming his disciple. If you want a man to like you a lot, ask him questions. Make him an authority. Let him tell you something you never knew before. Giving information is the most rapturous of all social pleasures.

There are plenty of things Joe Pallavicino knows that I do not know. So each time I appear in his shop, I ask him questions about matters in which he is expert and I am not. I ask him about barber-chairs, for instance, those mysterious contrivances which can twist a customer into any shape, and deliver him to the operator, perched at any angle. I ask him about the tastes and temperaments of his patrons. He takes the greatest delight in instructing me, in supplementing my conjectures, and in correcting my ignorances.

But the charm of his conversation is enhanced by the occur-rence in it, every now and then, of certain little curio-locutions, the formula for which I have never been able to discover. I have attempted several times for my own amusement to reproduce slips-of-the-tongue like Joe Pallavicino, but none which I have devised are as good as the "originals." Here are some examples:

"Joe, do you ever use any of that hair tonic on your own hair?"

"No, Father, I don't. I don't use anything on my own hair except cold water. Except once in a while I might use some hair tonic. Once in a while I might. But not very often. If I go to a party I might. Or if I go to a show I might. Or if I go to a dance I might. Or, for instance, if I go to a wedding I might."

I think the delayed use of "for instance" is rather delightful.

"Are your parents living, Joe?"

"Yes, Father. My parents are both living, thank God. They're both living. They live with me. I support them. You see, they're old, so I take care of them. And I try to be as nice to them as I can. I think a fellow ought to be nice to his parents, don't you, Father? So I try to be nice to my parents. I think when a fellow grows up, if he isn't nice to his parents, he's no good. I think he's a piker, in other words."

"In other words" is precious, is it not?

"Do any ladies come into this shop, Joe?"

"Very few, Father. Very few. Once in a while a lady comes in to get her hair cut, but not very often. This is a man's barber-shop. As a matter of fact I don't like to work on ladies. I don't like to cut their hair. I don't think it ought to be cut. I think a lady ought to let her hair grow long. I think it's more beautiful that way, much more beautiful. Of course, it's none of my business, as I said before, but that's the way I look at it."

"As I said before" is altogether too charming.

Across the street from Joe's barber shop is a row of fruit stalls. These fruit vendors are his steady clients.

"Joe," I said, "do those fruit merchants earn a good living? Do they make much money?"

"No, Father. They don't make much money. They have to work pretty hard, you know. And they really don't make very much money. They have to sell a lot of fruit to make any profit. And they don't make very much. If they sell a whole crate of oranges they only make about a half a dollar. And it takes them a long time to sell a whole crate of oranges. And besides they always find some bad oranges in the crate that they can't sell. Sometimes in a crate of oranges they find as many as five or six bad ones. And SOMETIMES," he put down his instruments and continued with emphasis, "and SOMETIMES as many as SEVEN OR EIGHT!"

I thought he was going to say: "And SOMETIMES as many as TWENTY OR THIRTY!" Didn't you?

CHARLIE MALONEY

IT WAS in the smoking car of a fast express going from Boston to New York. The first thing I do, when I get on a train, is recite my Breviary. Then I go at once to the smoking car. And there always seems to be somebody there who has been waiting for me to come.

"How d'ye do, Father? You're a Catholic priest, aren't you? . . . I thought so. . . . Oh, I dunno. . . . I can tell you priests by just lookin' at you. . . . Oh, I dunno. . . . I just size you up for a minute or two and then I say, 'There's a priest!' or else, 'There ain't one!' . . . Oh, I dunno. . . . It's like lookin' at an automobile. I say, 'There's a Packard, or a Buick, or a Rolls-Royce!' It's the same way when I see a priest. . . . These Episcopalian ministers with their Roman collars don't fool me. . . .

"My name is Charlie Maloney, Father. I come from Schenec-
tady, New York. I'm a traveling salesman. I'm on the road sell-
ing gelatine. I work for the Cosmopolitan Gelatine Company.
. . . There's one of my cards, see? 'Cosmopolitan Gelatine
Company; Representative: Charles J. Maloney!' . . . That's
yours truly. . . .

"Of course we're not exactly cosmopolitan. . . . As a mat-
ter of fact we're only in two states, New York and Massachu-
setts. But Cosmopolitan sounds big. Makes it sound like a big
league company, see? . . . And that goes big with the cus-
tomers. Sounds like International Harvester, or Standard Oil,
or League of Nations; see what I mean? . . . Big stuff! See
what I mean? . . .

"What do they use GELATINE for? . . . Who? . . . You
mean the public? . . . What do they use GELATINE for? . . .
Say, what are you tryin' to do, Father—kid me? . . . What
do they use GELATINE for? . . . Wow! That's a good one.
Why, did you know one eighteenth of the food you eat is
made of gelatine? . . . You didn't know that? . . . Of course
it is! . . . Certainly! . . . Pies, cakes, jellies, soups, desserts,
ice cream. Didn't you know there was any gelatine in ice
cream? . . . Why of course! Didn't you know that the gela-
tine industry is the ninety-seventh largest industry in the
United States?. . . Why certainly! Gelatine is a basic product
like wheat and corn and sugar. . . . You didn't know, did you,
that if the country stopped producin' gelatine New York'd go
bankrupt tomorrow? . . . Well, it would! Why, just think of
all the bakeries closin' and all the ice cream parlors! Why,
there'd be a famine! . . . What do they use GELATINE for?
Gee, that's a good one! . . . Of course I'm not blamin' you,
Father. That's not your business. Gelatine after all isn't your
business. Your business is 'Dominus Vobiscum, et cetera,' isn't
it? . . . But naturally it sounds kind of funny to ME bein' in
the business MYSELF to hear anybody ask ME, 'What do they
use GELATINE for? . . .'

"Sure I'm married. I got four kids. . . . Just a minute and I'll show you a picture of my family! . . . There you are! There's the whole gang! . . . That's my wife, Ella! . . . That's my oldest daughter, Eleanor! . . . Then there's Margaret and Alice! . . . And finally the baby, Charles, Jr., named after his old man! . . .

"My wife's a wonderful woman! . . . A wonderful woman and a wonderful Catholic! . . . Yes, sir, she's right there with the goods when it comes to religion! She belongs to the Married Ladies' Sodality and the League of the Sacred Heart and about everything else that we have at the church up home. . . . And talk about prayers! I never saw anybody say so many prayers as she does. She keeps prayin' all the time. And of course she keeps prayin' like the deuce for me so that I won't go off the handle when I'm on the road. . . . A couple of weeks ago we had a Mission in our parish, and one night the priest gave a sermon on the General Judgment, an' my wife comes home after the sermon and she says to me: 'Charlie, on the Last Day which are you goin' to be, one of the sheep or one of the goats? . . . ' An' I said: 'Well, which one am I supposed to be? Which one gets saved?' . . . She couldn't remember which one gets saved, only she thought it wasn't the goats. . . . Which one DOES get saved, Father? . . . The sheep? . . . Oh, I see! The sheep go up and the goats down, is that right? . . . I must remember that! . . .

"My wife worries about the funniest things. One of the things she's worryin' about now is because her name Ella ain't a saint's name. . . . She said the priest who gave the Mission at our church said that all the Catholic girls ought to have saints' names. And she can't find no Saint Ella anywhere in her prayer-book . . . And I said, 'Well, what's the use of worryin' now? I can't take you down and get you baptized all over again, can I?' And she says, 'No. But I wish I had a saint's name just the same. . . . ' And I says, 'Well, what do you want me to do, start callin' you Mary Magdalene? . . . ' An' she says, 'No,

I don't want you to do that.' . . . 'And besides,' I says, 'you got other names besides Ella. Look at all the other names you got: Ella, Margaret, Mary, Veronica Maloney? Every one of them's a saint's name except Ella!' . . . And she says, 'Well, anyhow, I'm glad we named our little girl Eleanor instead of Ella. Because Eleanor is a real saint's name. . . .'

"And by the way, Father, I don't like to talk about my daughter Eleanor, but between you and me she's a wonder. She's really a wonder. . . . She's nine years old and the Sister down at her school told me she's the very brightest girl in her class, especially in Geography and Catechism. . . . 'Mr. Maloney,' the Sister Superior said to me, 'Mr. Maloney! Your daughter is the very brightest girl in her class, especially in two things, Geography and Catechism! . . .' Father, you ought to hear that kid recite her Geography! . . . It's simply uncanny! . . . You can ask her where any place on the map is and she'll tell you. North Dakota, South Dakota! Any place! . . . Bays, rivers, mountains, capes, she's got them all right on the tips of her fingers! . . . Just imagine that, an' only nine years old, eh? . . . And Catechism! Boy! . . . You ought to hear her recite her Catechism! It's simply uncanny! It's marvelous! The answers she knows in her Catechism, it's simply marvelous! . . . When I come home at night she says to me, 'Daddy, would you like to hear my Catechism lesson?' And I say, 'Why certainly! Give me the book! . . .' So I open the book and ask her the questions. . . . Of course I put up a bluff that I know some of the answers without the book, but between you an' me, Father, I don't think I'd be so very hot without the book in my hand. . . . The other night I was askin' her questions in Catechism, an' I says, 'Of which should we take more care, our soul or our body?' 'Our soul,' she says. Right off! Just like that! Not a moment's hesitation! . . . Why did you know, Father, she actually knows the names of all the Apostles? . . . Think of that, at nine years of age! . . . Yes, sir! I said to her the other night, I says, 'Eleanor, name the Apostles! Name the Apostles,' I says. And right off she starts namin' them. . . . 'Peter, Andrew, and so forth and so forth! . . .' 'James, Joseph, and so forth, and so forth! . . .' She didn't miss one Apostle out of the whole darn bunch, true as I'm tellin' you! . . .

"Wait a minute! I want you to look at the pictures of my other three kids. . . . There's Margaret! She's seven. She's next to Eleanor. Margaret's a little bit delicate, I'm sorry to say. She's got weak eyes, for one thing, and she has to wear glasses. But, boy! Does she love her father and mother! . . . She thinks I'm the greatest thing that ever lived. She thinks I'm a big shot in every way; you know what I mean? . . . My wife was very sick when Margaret was born and the doctor told her she had better not have any more babies because it wouldn't be good for her health. . . . So we just let that go right in one ear and out the other. . . . And there's the two other children we've had since the doctor told Ella to stop bein' a mother! . . . Nothin' the matter with them, is there? . . . That's Alice sittin' in my lap! She's four. I call her 'Sweetheart,' because she's a bit of a vamp. . . . You know? Makin' eyes at everybody? . . . And then there's Charles Junior in his high-chair, at the age of one and a half. . . .

"My name is Charles Joseph, but we called the baby Charles Bernard, because my wife has a fourth cousin named Bernard that's a priest in Foreign Missions. He's in China tryin' to tell the natives about the Catholic Church. My wife thinks that's great, so she insisted on calling the baby Bernard for his middle name after her fourth cousin, the priest. . . . As a matter of fact I don't believe this priest is a real relative of hers at all except distantly, but you know the way Catholics start in claimin' relationship with a fellow as soon as he becomes a priest. . . . Of course Ella hopes Charles Bernard will be a priest too, I don't need to tell you that. . . . Only I say to her, 'Now listen! I don't want any undue influence brought to bear on him! There'll be nobody in the world prouder than me to have that kid a priest, but I want you to let him make up his own mind about it. If he wants to become a priest himself, all right. But let him choose for himself. The worst kind of a priest in the world is one whose mother got the vocation. . . .' So of course I never say anything to the youngster about bein' a priest or anything like that. And I told Ella I wouldn't stand for any of this showing him holy pictures and sayin', 'And when little Charles gets to be a big man, what's little Charles going to be?' I don't want any of that stuff! . . . I want the kid to stand on his own feet. . . . He'll be a year and a half old next Tuesday and I haven't mentioned the word priest to him once yet. . . . Ella wants to buy him a little altar to play with. And I says, 'You mean as a toy?' And she says, 'Yes, as a toy. . . .' So I said, 'All right. You can get him a little altar to play with as a toy, but don't start lightin' any candles on it or the kid'll get burned to death. . . .'

"It'd be kind of funny, wouldn't it, Father, if he did grow up and become a priest? It'd be kind of funny, wouldn't it? . . . I met a Bishop once! I shook hands with him, that is to say, I kissed his ring! . . . Wouldn't it be funny if my kid grew up an' became a Bishop with a ring? . . . It's possible, ain't it? . . . 'The Right Reverend Charles Bernard Maloney, D.D.,' that's right, ain't it? . . . Gee, wouldn't that be funny? . . . Imagine that! . . . And then all the folks in our town'd be sayin', 'Gosh, and HIS old man used to go around the country sellin' gelatine to Jew bakers! . . .'

"By the way, do you see that fellow sittin' down at the end of the car . . . smokin' a cigarette? . . . Well, he's a great friend of mine. . . . He's one of my pals. . . . He's a hardware salesman. His name is Shmitty. His right name is Smith, but I call him Shmitty. . . . He's one of my pals and a darn nice fellow. . . . But he don't know beans about religion. . . . He ain't got NO religion. . . . If you ask him, 'Who made the world?', he don't know; see what I mean? . . . He don't know! . . . 'Search me!' says Shmitty if you ask him who made the world. . . . He don't believe in anything. . . . If you ask him, 'How many persons in God?' he's just as liable to say, 'Two'; see what I mean? . . . He don't know what it's all about! . . . I'd like to call him up here and have you give him a little talk on religion. Would you mind? . . . I wish you would. It'll do him a lot of good. . . . I'll just call him up here and introduce him and then you can give him the works. It'll do him a lot of good. . . . Oh, no, he won't mind! . . .

"HEY, SHMITTY! . . . SHMITTY! . . . COME UP HERE. . . . COME UP HERE. I WANT TO TALK TO YOU! . . .

"Sit down, Shmitty! . . . Father, this is my friend Shmitty! . . . This is one of my pals. We travel around the country together. . . . He sells hardware and I sell gelatine, but we're good friends just the same. . . . Shmitty, this is a Catholic priest. You know, Catholic, just the same as me! . . . And I want him to give you a little talk on religion. Because I think you need it. . . . Now wait a minute, Shmitty! . . . Listen, Shmitty! Wait a minute! . . . Just a minute, please! ... . Don't start talkin' that way! . . . Give Father a chance to talk! . . . Bible? . . . Bible? . . . What do you know about the Bible? . . . You don't know beans about the Bible; what are you tryin' to talk about the Bible for? . . . Listen, Shmitty! . . . Listen! . . . Don't be talking to Father about the Bible! Why, Father knows the Bible upside down, inside out, don't you, Father? . . . Why, Father knows the Bible in Latin, don't you, Father? . . . He can read it in Latin, the language Our Lord wrote it in, can't you, Father? . . . Listen, Shmitty, don't be talkin' about Our Lord that way! Don't call Him Christ, call Him Our Lord! . . . What do you know about Our Lord? . . . Well, who was He? . . . Yes, who was Our Lord? . . . The King of the Jews? . . . The King of the Jews? . . . He was NOT the King of the Jews! . . . Listen, Shmitty, He was *not* the King of the Jews! . . . No, He wasn't! . . .

"He was the King of the whole world, wasn't He, Father?
. . . Certainly! He was the King of the Irish and the Germans
and the French and everybody! . . . He was the King of the
whole world! . . . He WAS NOT the King of the Jews! . . .
No, sir! . . . Listen, Shmitty! . . . Listen, please! . . . Lis-
ten! That's what they said to Him when they put Him to
death, when they wanted to insult Him. They said, 'You are,—
Thou art the King of the Jews!' And Our Lord said, 'I AM NOT.
I am the King of Everybody! . . .' No! . . . Listen, Shmitty!
That's what the fellow said who condemned Him to death. He
was the one who said, 'You are the King of the Jews! . . .'
The fellow who put Him to death! . . . Was it Herod,
Father? . . . Oh, yes, Punches Pilate! . . . Punches Pilate, the
fellow who put Our Lord to death, he was the one who said
'Write on His cross: The King of the Jews. . . .' Punches
Pilate! . . . Do you know what a punch is? . . . Well, a lot
of them! Bing! Bing! Punches! . . . That's right, Punches!
. . . Well, he was the one who said, 'Call Him the King of
the Jews! . . .' Listen, Shmitty Who wants to be King of the
Jews? . . . Nobody does! . . . Battling Levinsky and all
those guys? Who wants to be King of them? . . . No, Our
Lord is King of the whole world! . . . He's the King of
Kings! . . . Certainly! He's the Good Shepherd! And all the
world is His sheep! . . . And furthermore on the Last Day
the sheep get saved and the goats lost, I'll bet you didn't even
know that, did you, Shmitty? . . . Well, Our Lord is the
Good Shepherd, because He said He was, didn't he, Father?
. . . And He said, 'I am the Good Shepherd and I lay down
my life for my sheep!' didn't He, Father? . . ."

"Yes, Charlie, He did!"

LITTLE SLIPPER STREET

THE SISTERS of Saint Pancratius (you may be sure I am inventing them a name) at RUE DE LA PETITE PANTOUFLE in Paris, had the distinction of having me as their chaplain for a six weeks' spell one summer. I was really not a full-fledged chaplain (my French was very much too bad for that); but it was my privilege to say Mass for them every morning, and to go twice a week in the late afternoon for Benediction of the Blessed Sacrament, which they call by the succinct and majestic name of "LE SALUT."

Saying Mass in a convent is a consolation and a joy, first because of the attention and inspiration of the worshippers, and second because of the flawlessness of the altar appointments. Vestments are loveliest, amices are whitest, cinctures most delicately braided, chalices most cuplike and golden, in a convent. Mass-cards are most artistically scrolled, linens are smoothest and most immaculate, carpets are plushiest and cleanest, marble is shiniest, lavabos glisten, flowers are most fragrant, in a convent.

Albs fit you in a convent. The book ribbons of the missal are most colorful, bells give their most ethereal tinkle, candles burn straightest and most purely, Mass-breads are baked nearest to the shade of snow, the texture and odor of wine is closest to perfection, even incense is faintest and most spicesome in a convent. The consummate order of a nun's life and the spotless purity of her heart find their completest outward expression in her chapel, where wood and fabric and foliage and metal and stone are raised to their utmost grandeur, and made as fit as material substances can ever be, to associate with the Sacramental Body of Our Lord, which His love has forged for our sacrifice, our worship, and our food. And nobody but her Guardian Angel knows the hours upon hours little Sister Sacristan puts in every day with her feathers, her wax, her soap and her rags, cleaning and scouring and scrubbing and airing and making God's House beaming and bright, and driving the dust and the devil out the window.

There is something exquisite about every nun, no matter how physically unbeautiful or shriveled or sick or old or feeble she may be, because her expression and her movements are bound to assume, in some way or other, the elegance of her aspiration and her desire. But I hope I am not disloyal to the wimpled friends of my childhood, and the best-beloved sisters of my school days, when I say that a French nun has a rare and almost piquant exquisiteness all her own. Margaret Mary Alacoque of Lhautcour, Teresa Martin of Lisieux, Jane Frances Mary de Chantal of Dijon, Madeleine-Sophie Barat of Joigny, Bernadette Soubirous of Lourdes, from the loam of such a garden does she spring, from the pattern of such a spindle is she spun. She is not as versatile in a human and sisterly way as are our American nuns, and I doubt (though let me be subject to correction) if she is quite as serviceable as they are in the hospital, the asylum, or in the classroom. But she *is* exquisite, continually eager and nervous and alert, elusive as a squirrel and sudden as a shadow, more naturally adapted to mystery and the heights of mystic contemplation, always on the point of bursting her bonds and exploding into an angel.

And her quality of other-worldliness is most revealed when she prays out loud. The sound of a French community of nuns singing or reciting their prayers is a low wind of melody, compact and perfect, with a rhythmic roundness and softness that outrivals all music and tests the ear's capacity for esthetic pleasure. There is a common fallacy that the French voice is nasal, because a series of sounds called "nasals" are recorded in French grammars. It is completely not nasal. It is, if anything, "roof-of-the-mouthal," performed with the best parts of the oral structure (parts which we Americans never bring into use) and approximating a state of pure vowelism, wherein consonants are ever so lightly touched, tail syllables often left

unpronounced, and negligible e's muted in order to give the
throat a full fling at tonal beauty pure and undefiled.

But French is decidedly not a language spoken through the
nose. And what are called "nasals" have really been devised
because the Gallic ear does not relish the abruptness of an
open tone quenched and closed by the lips or tongue. It is for
this reason that they have put a-e-i-o-u effects into terminal
m and n.

And the French voice is loveliest when it is feminine. And it
is most feminine when it is virginal. And most virginal when
it is cloistered. And most cloistral when it is praising God. You
may have your stringed symphony, your operatic ensemble,
your extravagant choral society with an Italian maestro beating
it into excellence with a baton, but for music give me LES
RELIGIEUSES of Little Slipper Street in Paris when they are
saying farewell to Jesus after "LE SALUT," and I am lifting Him
in His gold lunette and putting Him in His silver cradle behind
the tabernacle door, and the sweet chant of "DIEU SOIT BÉNI;
BÉNI SOIT SON SAINT NOM," in seraphic unison and breathful
adoration, thanks Him and bids Him good-night.

Besides the consolations of saying Mass in Little Slipper
Street, there were difficulties and humiliations as well. Espe-
cially when one had to read (with an American voice) prayers
in French for the First Friday devotions; and especially when
one had to say a few words of enquiry to Sister Sacristan
(who trembled like a divine butterfly) and that at a time when
one is extremely nervous, as I always am before Mass. For if
there is one inch of you not at ease, it is impossible to set your
body at the proper angle for speaking French correctly. I can
do it moderately well if I am not hurried, but if I am hurried
I do it slitheringly, as on a banana peel. And Sister Sacristan
spoke her native tongue with such celerity and elegance, that I
forgot my simplest grammar rules in trying to give swift (S'IL
N'Y A PAS DE VITESSE CE N'EST PAS FRANÇAIS) answers to her
easiest questions.

I remember distinctly the evening when I had to recite the long Prayer to the Sacred Heart at the First Friday devotions. I wanted to ask Sister Sacristan how many hymns were to be sung at Benediction, and where I was to insert the prayer. Endeavoring to gather speed as I spoke, I bombarded her delicate ear with the following barbarism: "MA SOEUR, EST-CE QUE LES RÉVÉRENDES DAMES CHANTERONT TROIS CHANSONS PENDANT LE SALUT? ET APRÈS LEQUEL FAUT-IL PARLER LA PRIÈRE?" Which, translated from broken French into broken English, would go (and must have sounded to her) something like this: "Sister, is it that the holy girls will sing three songs during the Benediction? And after which one ought I to talk the prayer?"

But my holy memories of six weeks at Little Slipper Street and its consecrated ladies who sing and sigh and suffer and pray for the salvation of the world, are most focused, not on the nuns themselves, but on Peter, their inimitable and exotic altar boy.

As everyone knows, a nun is not allowed to serve Mass. No woman is. She may, in an emergency, answer the prayers from the other side of the altar rail; but the ritual of the sanctuary and everything connected with it in public worship is hopelessly masculine. There is no such thing as a "priestess" in the Catholic Church, and no such person as an "altar maid." In this usage there is absolutely no question of the superiority of my sex over the other. There is question merely of a liturgical function to be performed according to the prescriptions of Christ, and He, for His own reasons, has assigned the rôle of levite and clerk to us. Women are probably God's best saints, and certainly the Blessed Virgin Mary is His greatest human achievement. But for all that we are runaways at a Crucifixion, the sacerdotal prerogative is one with the sex of Peter, and the keeper of the Holy of Holies must bear the physiognomy of the fisherman. It was fitting therefore that the Sisters at Little Slipper Street, anxious to have their Holy Mass rubrically (and therefore masculinely) perfect, should have scoured the neigh-boring streets and lanes and supplied themselves with a Peter for their daily altar boy.

In choosing Peter (the nuns called him "Pierre," but I called him Peter because it amused him) to be Little Slipper Mass-boy, it was obvious that Reverend Mother Superior and her Council (who are always discreet) outdid themselves in dis-cretion. For of all the wheezy, one cylindered, shop-worn and moth-eaten human beings I have ever witnessed, little Paris Peter of PETITE PANTOUFLE takes the golden apple.

He had the construction of a ventriloquist's doll, the expres-sion of a snow-man, and the individuality of a suit of clothes on a coat-hanger. He smiled as though something were continually hurting him, and walked as though he were riding a bicycle. His hair was the color of dry hay, his eyes the color of canned salmon, and his face the shade of butter-beans. His voice was something terrible and eerie to listen to. It was bass and un-natural beyond his years. He spoke as though he were garg-ling the low notes of a xylophone. He was fourteen years of age, five grades behind schedule in school, had flat cheek-bones and wide ears and was possessed of that awful accouter-ment of an overgrown boy, a pre-razor mustache.

Mother Superior, when Peter was made "warden of the cruets" in Little Slipper Chapel, specified that he should come to Mass every morning with a clean shirt, his shoes shined, and his hands and face washed. Peter observed these regulations scrupulously. But anything Mother Superior left unsaid he left undone. And it seems she had made no direct mention of a tooth-brush, or of that other extreme of personal fastidiousness, soap-and-water behind the ears. He also left his hair uncombed until he arrived in the sacristy. Sister Sacristan was sure to re-arrange it to her own satisfaction anyhow, when he came in (always a minute late) and she greeted him with her usual "BONJOUR. TSUH, TSUH, TSUH, PIERRE! TOUJOURS EN RETARD!" so what was the use of a fellow going to a lot of extra bother?

It was a small pageant to see Peter, abetted by pullings and twistings on the part of Sister Sacristan, getting into his altar clothes. First a big yawn. Then a lurch with your right hand. Then a lurch with your left hand. And, presto! you were inside the gorgeous white cassock which the champion needle-worker at PETITE PANTOUFLE had made for the priest's attend-ant. Then came the buttoning of interminable buttons. There were thirty-two down the front, all the way from Peter's chin to Peter's shoe shine. Peter began at the top, and Sister Sacristan began at the bottom. Theoretically they should have bumped thumbs at Peter's middle, but Peter wasn't as fast a buttoner as Sister Sacristan. His record was ten buttons to her twenty-two. When he was fairly spry and awake, he did about eight or nine of his share. When he was extra tired (as he usually was), he let her do thirty. I remember distinctly a cer-tain morning when Peter did only one; and that eventually came unbuttoned and had to be rebuttoned by Sister Sacris-tan, which gave her the score of thirty-two—love, the world's record in a button contest.

After Peter's cassock came his investiture in the surplice. This meant another disheveling of hair, and was an added reason why Peter should comb his with his fingers on the way to Mass. The surplice was a bit of dream work in lace, done by a tubercular nun in the convent infirmary before she coughed herself to eternal sleep. It was riotous with chalices and wheat stems and grapes, with a full figure of Our Lord in the front center, and twelve tiny apostles fringing the edges, a masterpiece of daintiness and devotion. When Peter had sur-rounded himself with this garment, one almost expected to hear him bark, he looked so much like the wolf playing at Little Red Ridinghood.

But he was not through yet. Next came a gorgeous cape with white ribbons and golden hooks-and-eyes, and fitting Peter (as far as anything could ever fit him) with regal perfection. And last of all, white gloves! (Foolish to wash your hands, but

Mother Superior said . . .) And so appareled, half urchin and half angel, Peter squiddled the uncomfortable parts of him, looked seraphically at me, and said silently with his eyes: "ALLEZ-OOP! HEY? Let's go! Huh?" We bowed to one another and walked out of the sacristy.

At the Mass proper, Peter was adequate, but no more. He enunciated properly about one-tenth of the Latin, and had not the slightest notion why I should wait for him to finish his part in the spoken prayer. He folded his hands unevenly, and seemed fascinated at times by the wavering of a candle, so fascinated that he invariably came late to move the book, and always slipped and juggled it when making the genuflection.

At Offertory time he sometimes (not often) gave me the water for the wine; and sometimes (very often) went back to the credence table without the lavabo cloth. But one thing Peter could do magnificently, and that was ring the bell. A good, solid, substantial jingle came out of the hand-chime whenever Peter operated it. And his bell work was always timely and decisive and suited to my word or movement at the altar.

If Mass seemed long to him (invariably it did), Peter went over to the side of the sanctuary and sat down. Mother Superior, for all her meticulosity, never seemed to object to this. I believe the reason was because when Peter sat down, a pillar hid him from the view of the community. In that way the sanctuary was well rid of him while still possessing him rubrically.

When Mass was over Peter gave me a low bow and a nod of approval, whisked off his vestments, dropped them on a chair before Sister Sacristan could come in from clearing the sanctuary, and scooted out of Little Slipper sacristy before the smoke had left the quenched candle tops on the high altar.

You see there was and could forever be only one Peter. I hope I have done him full justice and no injury. And now let me crown him with a single laurel and grace him with one encomium. Peter was master of one accomplishment, he was

radiant with one divine quality, he had one supreme title to
his office: he was innocent. There was in his expression that
heavenly sheepishness that smolders in the eyes of the stupid
who know no sin. He was the cow who looked at little Jesus
in the stall and borrowed enough intelligence to love him.

My blessing on you, Peter, so blithe and baptismal, so dear
and dumb. Not I to oust you from your grandeur and your
glory. I would I were as little God's enemy as you are. I would
I were as worthy as you to walk into a sanctuary. It was fit-
ting that you should lead me thither mornings when we had
Holy Mass at Little Slipper Chapel. It was fitting that you
should tell me at the foot of the stairs to go to the altar of
God, "to God Who giveth joy to your youth." It was fitting
that you should answer "MISEREATUR" to my "CONFITEOR."

Now it so happened (and this is where my story hopes to
beguile you) that during my term at Little Slipper Convent,
Peter, my curious clerk, took desperately sick. It was, if I
remember rightly, the twentieth day of my tenure of office at
that institution. Altar boys have taken desperately sick before
and stories have not been written to commemorate the sad
affair, but oddly enough it was precisely the occasion of Peter's
illness that made his mystic significance at MAISON DE LA
PETITE PANTOUFLE fully manifest to me.

I heard later that Peter's malady was a combination of fever
and colic, caused by eating seven green apples (including skins
and seeds) at the CIRQUE D'HIVER where he went one afternoon
with a street companion to see LES DARIO, the funniest clowns
in Paris. But whatever was the extent of his indiscretion, Peter
came home that night dizzy and in a panic. It did not help
matters any, either, when, in his mother's absence, he went to
the wrong bottle in the pantry (not the essence of rhubarb
which his mother always administered for sick headache or
pains in the stomach) and blithely swallowed a tablespoonful
of furniture polish.

At six o'clock that night he was writhing in agony. At

seven o'clock he had a chill. At eight he had a chill, a fever and the gripes. At nine o'clock he had the doctor, and that in the life of a poor French family is an event disparate by a hair's breadth from a summons to the undertaker.

Next morning, fully vested, I stood in Little Slipper sacristy and waited and waited for Peter to come. It was time for Mass, the bell had rung, the nuns had long since assembled, the organ was playing (for oh! the irony of it, it was a feast day), the candles were lit, Peter's altar garments were all fluffed and waiting for him on the vestment case. But the bridegroom tarried, and we listened in vain for the sound of his shuffle on the stair.

Sister Sacristan kept circulating like a bat from the door to the vestment case, trying to control her disappointment and her desperation. When fully five minutes had passed, we realized that Peter was not coming to play his important rôle in the Holy Sacrifice that day.

At this point, Reverend Mother Superior protruded her wimpled head through the vestry door, to see whether it was I or Peter who was missing. The two nuns exchanged little silent shrugs of perplexity. Sister Sacristan pointed to Peter's empty clothes on the table; and Mother Superior gave me the signal to go on with the Mass alone. Sister Sacristan went speedily ahead of me, transferred the cruets, the dish and the handcloth, from the credence stand to the altar, so that I might serve them to myself, carried the Mass bell to the other side of the altar rail, and when I launched out on my solitary way into the beautiful liturgy of the Holy Sacrifice, it was a strange and feminine voice, soft and indefinite and in the distance, that proclaimed how God, to Whose altar I desired to go, was a God "Who gaveth joy to HER youth."

When Mass was over and I was back in the sacristy, Sister Sacristan was very much constrained to reveal to me the extent of her anxiety concerning the mysterious defection of her ENFANT TERRIBLE. "MAIS VOUS CROYEZ BIEN, N'EST-CE PAS,

MON PÈRE," she said, "QU'IL SOIT TOMBÉ MALADE?" "Nonsense,
Sister," I replied (and I do forget what word I used for "non-
sense"), "he has merely overslept this morning, that is all. It is
a common affliction with altar boys."

"But no, MON PÈRE," she insisted, "he never oversleeps.
When we first got him he used to oversleep, yes. But I taught
him to say a prayer every night before he goes to sleep to
his Guardian Angel, a prayer to be wakened on time in the
morning. It has never failed. He has not been late, more than a
minute or two, ever since that day."

"Very true, sister," I rejoined with skeptical persistency,
"but is it not possible that Peter, before retiring last night, for-
got his prayer to the Guardian Angel, and so exempted that
celestial gentleman of his morning obligation?"

"Even so," she replied, "our community also says a prayer
every night to Peter's Guardian Angel. We also remind him to
wake Peter in time for our Holy Mass. And WE did not forget
it last night."

There was no gainsaying this argument. And so I was forced
to admit that Peter's absence must be due to some more serious
cause than a mere refusal to get out of bed this morning when
his faithful Angel shook him, called in his ear, and tickled his
toes with a feather.

The loyal and solicitous nuns were not long in finding out
what ailed Peter and why he had deserted them. After break-
fast Reverend Mother Bursar, or somebody equally august and
important in the hierarchy of nundom, was deputed to go with
her companion to Peter's home and investigate the matter. It
was she who brought back the story of the circus, the seven
green apples, and the furniture polish. And it was through her
that I was informed next morning of Peter's serious predica-
ment.

During the next few days, when Peter's fever hovered
between one hundred and one hundred and three degrees (the
greatest amount of vital activity that had ever taken place

within him), Little Slipper Convent was a place sad to visit and pitiful to behold. Big nuns and little nuns, fervent nuns and tepid nuns, nuns ecstatic and nuns matter-of-fact, old nuns in their wheel-chairs and radiant young postulants were, one and all alike, cast into the depths of unconsolable gloom.

Their solitary knight, their one virile possession, their lonely Lazarus, their Peter, their rock, was trembling on the verge of another life, and was about to leave them stranded in a dismal world of monotonous femininity. And out of the secret corners of their chaste hearts, the slumbering love they bore their little comrade was discovering itself for the first time, and rising up to plead for him, and asking God to give him pity and protection.

For stupid Peter, slovenly Peter, Peter the mule-eyed, Peter of the horrid grin and the unkempt hair, was linked in their imaginations with the tabernacle. He was part of the furniture of their altar. He was God's little page-boy who walked in the penumbra of Divine Light. He moved in their memories like a small moth that played and gyrated around the Flame of the Sacred Heart. In his absence everything symbolic and beautiful and ideal about him was remembered, everything unlovely and ugly and uncouth was forgotten.

In two or three short days Peter began to take on the wonder of a legend in Little Slipper household. Tales were being told of him that never happened. Secrets were being whispered in convent cell and corridor about his prowess in holiness, his gallantry, his sweet expression, even (God save the mark) his "nice eyes."

Sister Beatrice of Our Lady's Coronation, whose ailment had hitherto been analyzed by the charitable as "simple-mindedness," and by the literal as "out and out softening of the brain," was beginning to be half believed when she declared that she had been told in a vision that Peter was a heavenly messenger sent to the world in disguise, a Raphael parading as Toby, one of the Seraphim masquerading as a buffoon. At any rate, it was "little brother, the ragamuffin," who got tangled up in woman's love, and was eddied and whirled about in its crystal stream as it left its pure source in Little Slipper Convent and started its long journey to the stars.

The longer Peter remained sick abed, the more mythical and alluring became his souvenir. Sister Eloise, the convent artist, was already making a draft of him for a holy card, and had already schemed him out in her mind as sprouting with wings and aureoled with a halo. Sister Rita Celeste, expert at knitting and embroidery, was threading her needles with yarns of many colors, and preparing to do him in a tapestry for the relics chamber.

Each morning on top of my vestments I found a note of memento from the community. Monday it was "LE RÉVÉREND PÈRE VOUDRA BIEN RECOMMANDER AU BON DIEU LE PETIT SERVANT QUI SOUFFRE." Tuesday: "PRIÈRE DE NE PAS OUBLIER L'ENFANT GENTIL QUI NE VIENT PLUS POUR LA MESSE." Each day it was the same plaint, the supplication of Mary and Martha: "Lord, he whom Thou lovest is sick!" One morning there was an envelope with a ten franc note in it and a message (nicely phrased and calculated to relieve me of any simoniacal scruple) begging that I should offer up the whole Mass on that day for Peter's recovery.

It happened that on the same day the ORDO allowed me to say a votive—and therefore, if I chose, a requiem—Mass. Only I noticed how scared Sister Sacristan looked when I made a false motion in the direction of the black vestments. The very thought of them made her shudder. She rolled them up fearsomely and with dispatch and hid them out of sight. And so we had a Mass in white for little Peter, a MISSA PRO INFIRMO, and when I came to the special prayer in the Collect, I enunciated the words "PRO FAMULO TUO PETRO" with special feeling and emphasis, because I knew that seventy pairs of ears were, with awful attention, listening under their linens.

But I shall keep you in suspense no longer. Peter did not die. Prayer prevailed over the colic. Novenas, votive candles, hours of watching before the Blessed Sacrament, aspirations, promises of greater fidelity to religious discipline, and all that holy artillery that nuns train on the rampart of Heaven when they seek to sway the mighty Will of God, were once more successful. The doorpost was sprinkled with the blood of the lamb. The avenging angel menaced, but did not smite. Peter got better and better. And finally he got all better. And Little Slipper Convent was spared its most woeful tragedy.

As luck would have it (and I was very restless and in suspense in the meantime), Peter made his reappearance in Little Slipper sanctuary the very last day of my assignment there. To have been obliged to leave and not to have seen him again is such a withering thought that I shall dismiss it at once with a cold shiver.

Precisely at twenty minutes past six on the last day of my incumbency, the old familiar shoes came shuffling up the pebbled walk. We heard his twist on the door-knob. And in walked our Peter, a little thinner perhaps, and a little paler, but sound and substantial and ready for work once more.

Sister Sacristan swooped upon him like a mother bird who has found her stray fledgling under a hedge. She fairly cackled and cooed with delight as she shook him and felt of him and devoured him with her eyes. Mother Superior and her Council had to troop in to see him too and be witnesses to his resurrection.

Never did the summons bell for Mass toll so vigorously as on the day of Peter's revival. And indeed it had no need to toll at all, for rumor went like wild-fire through the convent that he was seen coming up the gravel walk, and every nun was in her place in chapel a twentieth of an hour ahead of time.

Mother Superior and her whole Council had to assist him to get into his altar clothes. Each one had a little tug at him in her own way. Sister Sacristan buttoned all his buttons, Mother Bursar tied his ribbons, and Reverend Mother Superior herself fastened his golden hooks-and-eyes.

Then came a solemn order from Mother Superior that he was not to kneel at all during the Mass, except for the few moments of Consecration. The bishop's throne and prie-dieu were arranged for him near the credence table. He must be weaned back to the altar little by little, and with no strain on the progress of his convalescence. It was sufficient for that day that he should just be there. The sanctuary must reassimilate him gradually. His physical reality was enough to begin with again, after the weeks of loneliness without him. Just Peter and his cassock and his surplice and his cape and his white gloves. On that foundation love would build again, and fancy would rest her slender ladder reaching to the sky.

When Mass was over (which Peter seemed to weather without any indications of a relapse) he was invited (and this was an unheard-of privilege) to take his PETIT DÉJEUNER with me in the chaplain's dining-room. As you know, the French PETIT DÉJEUNER is very PETIT indeed. It consists of coffee and a bun. There is sometimes a little butter and a little jam. On this eventful morning Sister Refectorian made it as fulsome as a PETIT DÉJEUNER is ever allowed to be and still retain its identity. There was a lot of butter and a lot of jam. There were reams of bread and dozens of buns, and the coffee was extravagantly hot.

During the breakfast I had many things to say to Peter. I said I was awfully glad to see him again. He grinned. I said we were so afraid he would die. He grinned at this too. I said we missed him very much when he was sick, and all the nuns prayed very hard for him. This remark made Peter grin once more. I told him it was lucky he got back on that very morning because I was leaving Paris in the afternoon, and I would have hated to go and not to have seen him again. Peter gave me another grin and went on eating. Then I told him an American kiddie joke. Peter grinned at it. I proceeded to tell him about the American Indians and Wild West and Buffalo Bill. This set him grinning again. It was time for me to be up and off, so I shook hands with Peter and bade him farewell. He nodded and grinned me a nice good-bye. I caught his face grinning in the mirror as I went out the door.

I left him in the chaplain's refectory dropping his fifth lump of sugar into his third bowl of coffee, and putting his ninth knifeful of butter on his fourth slice of bread. And if it will not be indecorous to mention it, during the course of our PETIT DÉJEUNER, a certain salivary teaspoon made thirteen separate journeys from Peter's open mouth to a bottle of orange jam.

I shall be forgiven for having counted such things accurately. For nothing Peter ever did seemed to me unimportant. And in my memories of Little Slipper Convent I wish no shred or part of him ever to be forgotten.

THIS LITTLE THING

MY BEING present at the final examination of Sister Bridget's First Communion Class was a mere formality. It was almost an impertinence. What Sister Bridget does not know about the art of First Communion instruction would about fill the vacancy in a ginger-ale bubble.

But the reverend pastor had been called away on business, and I, as his lieutenant, was deputed to go to Sister Bridget's classroom, and declare officially the presence or absence of the use of reason on the part of twenty-two innocents whom she had been preparing for the Holy Table.

On my way from the presbytery to the school-house, I reviewed quickly my canonical obligations. My duties, as far as I could determine them, were two-fold: first, to look very important; and second, in the name of Giuseppe Sarto, D.D.

(of childlike memory, who expired in the Vatican bearing the title of Pius the Tenth, and may be found at present in the nurseries of Heaven), to award the degree of T.T. (Tiny Theologian) to any six or seven year old dogmatist who could answer two questions on the Blessed Eucharist without falling into patent heresy.

I walked pompously across the school-yard. I opened the door and strolled pontifically in. I marched, not without a flourish, down the first-floor corridor, came to the kinder-garten classroom, knocked and demanded entrance in the name of the Holy See. Sister Bridget opened the door.

I shall not allow a description of Sister Bridget to delay my narrative. She is an incident, not an episode. She merely opens the door of my story. I can only say hurriedly that what small fraction of her face the holy habit of her Order allows the world to look at is amazingly beautiful. I should hazard a guess that she is in her middle thirties; but the evidence is too slight to warrant my being certain. The youthful sparkle of her eyes and twinkle of her mouth are not enough. Too much of her head has been shrouded in linen and veiled in mystery; and, furthermore, these wimpled secrets of youth and age are too sacred for any idle conjecture.

But this much is certain, whether Sister Bridget be goose-girl or octogenarian, she blushes like a child when you arrive for the examination of her First Communion Class. She is far more nervous than any of her catechizable candidates. And she seems suddenly relieved of an infantile misapprehension when she finds that you have not brought the Sacred College of Cardinals trooping after you.

I gave her an academic bow. I walked in my doctor's robes to the front of the room, and came to the pastor's armchair which had been transported from the convent parlor for the occasion. I sat down. I achieved a solemn clearing of the throat. I leaned forward in my seat (by way of assuming an *ex cathedra* posture), rested my elbows on the desk, and, in lieu of a gavel, tapped in proper ecumenical fashion with my spectacles.

"Are they ready?" I said to Sister Bridget.

She stiffened apprehensively, as though the proceedings were to begin by my firing a gun; but recovered immediately, and replied, "Yes, I think they are ready."

Then reassuring herself, obviously by an aspiration sent Holy Ghostwards, she repeated, "Yes, I think they are *quite* ready"; and lowered her long eyelashes by way of indicating that though *she* had instructed them, it was really *God* who had given them the use of reason.

"Very well, children," I said magnificently, "I have a few questions to ask you before you receive your First Holy Communion. Now think carefully. . . . First question. What is the Blessed Sacrament?"

Their reply, uttered in swift and perfect unison, startled me. It was a dissyllabic shout, a moan, a song, a whisper, and a prayer.

"Jesus!" they cried.

"And whom are you going to receive in Holy Communion?"

"Jesus!" They thundered it again, reverently and lingeringly, with even more meaning and emphasis.

The examination was finished. The degrees were awarded with a wave of my hand. We could now turn our thoughts to the theological implications of white slippers and stockings, blue jackets and Sunday boots, lily-colored veils and neckties, and a kiss for mummy and daddy when they met you after the great event in the church vestibule, and found your body so new and strange and sacred, and lifted you adoringly in their arms.

But Sister Bridget was to put a crimp in all this fine anticipation. She walked over to my chair with an air of misgiving. She was unmistakably struggling with a scruple.

"They're all ready," she whispered sadly, "all except This Little Thing." And she pointed to a small feminine object sitting in the second row, black-haired, black-eyed, crimson-frocked, who was chewing her thumb and focusing her gaze on infinity.

"And what's the matter with This Little Thing?" I said, looking with mingled surprise and concern in the direction of the entity indicated.

"She's seven years old," said Sister Bridget with a sigh, "and her parents wanted her to receive First Communion this spring, but she doesn't seem to comprehend. I'm afraid she hasn't quite reached the use of reason." And she lowered her long eyelashes again, to indicate that it was *she* this time, and *not* God, who was responsible.

I spoke a word of congratulation to the rest of the class, a word of comfort and hope to Sister Bridget, and dismissed them and her. They went off merrily, and could be heard scampering and laughing as they passed through the schoolyard. And she, belike, soft-footed and lonely, went to kneel unconsoled in the convent chapel where the bell was summoning her to evening prayer.

All alone in the deserted classroom, still chewing a thumb, still looking at some object beyond all distance and finding interest in some reality immeasurably far away, sat This Little Thing. I walked slowly up to it. I wanted to examine it closely, and see what it was, and why it couldn't comprehend.

"How old are you?"

"Seven."

"And what is your name?"

"Marjorie."

And sensing that there must be some reason for being especially selected and catechized when all the rest had gone, and wondering if there were some mysterious blame attached to having seven for your age, and Marjorie for your name, she put her hand in mine, laid her head against my cassock, and two little coal-black eyes began their pretty business of manufacturing each a crystal tear. She was so repentant. She would ask my pardon if there were any fault connected with having an identity.

I could not refrain from studying that little head as it lay against my gown. I raised it reverently in my hands. It was tiny and oval, flawlessly structured and fragile as a cup. It was crowned with hair, black and lustrous and clean as oil. Twinlet pools of wonder indented it, restless even in their repose, eyes timorous and trustful and unfathomably innocent. It was clothed with skin as smooth and fresh as the fabric of rose petal. And all the while it drank in air and color and odor and sound, transmuted them into thought, and riddled silently the meaning of all that is or ever can be.

Pleasure and pain beat against this tender globe of mystery. Noises knocked in these dainty ears. Perfumes were snuffed into these pretty nostrils. Lights swam through these soft windows and disappeared. And yet somewhere in the chambers of this lovely citadel a spirit waited to receive them, stripped them of all dimensions, and grafted them into the substance of a living soul. This little head was somebody's universe, peopling itself with realities, creating its own cosmos, outside the frail barriers of whose consciousness God Himself must plead for entrance and wait for existence. It housed the terror and loneliness of a human personality. I had not pity enough to comfort it. Its secret eluded the reaches of my tenderness and my love. I could only stand and look and marvel at its desolation, bounding it with my fingers and holding it like a ball.

"Who made you?"

"God."

"Where is God?"

She pointed to the sky. And that, I could not deny, was an adequate and excellent answer.

It was the last week in May. But Sister Bridget kept, for purposes of Catechism instruction, a seasonal remembrance of all the feasts of the year in the form of pictures and symbols and pious objects scattered about the room. There was a very small Christmas crib standing in the corner. I took This Little Thing over to the toy manger. We could discuss our theology by means of an object lesson.

"Where is Our Lord?"

She pointed to a lamb sleeping at the foot of the crèche.

"Where is His Mother?"

She pointed to an angel hanging on a golden wire.

Ex ore infantium, perfecisti laudem; but I am not sure that even Giuseppe Sarto, for all his leniency, would allow a skill at metaphors to do service for the Canonical use of reason. Poetic theology is very pretty, but we must have a little straight theology first. Only a little, but it must be straight. And our poetry afterwards.

I shall remember shudderingly until my dying day that I should never have asked my next question. May the Incarnate Word of God, the dust of whose foot-prints I am not worthy to kiss, forgive me.

"Whom do you receive in the Blessed Sacrament?"

"You!" said This Little Thing. And a ripple of white blasphemy went fluttering like fine lightning through the whole span of God's universe. The Sacred Host in the tabernacle quivered in Its golden cup. And the angels, who see Eternal Beauty face to face, covered their eyes with their wings and moaned.

"And now I think we had better go home," I said quietly.

I led her down the dark corridor and out through the schoolyard. I walked her safely past the traffic policeman. Her elder brother, who had been sent to fetch her, met us, luckily, on the street corner. I put This Little Thing in his safe keeping. He took her by the hand and led her home.

.   .   .   .

That night when This Little Thing lay in bed, somewhere about twelve o'clock, she turned in her sleep and awoke with a start. She awoke because she heard a noise inside her pillow. Something was throbbing very softly inside the pillow. Marjorie could hear it distinctly when she pressed her ear against the pillow-case. *Tup-tupp. Tup-tupp.* Was it something *in* the pillow or *under* it? *Tup-tupp. Tup-tupp.* Something mechanical or something alive? *Tup-tupp.* A clock? *Tup-tupp. Tup-tupp.* Maybe her Angora pussy-cat had got into bed with her and was hiding in the bedclothes!

Marjorie sat up in bed. She lifted the pillow and looked under it. She pressed it, squeezed it, punched it, shook it. Nothing wiggled. Nothing dropped out. No clock, No pussy-cat. The tup-tupping had ceased. But the problem remained: a noise in the dark uninterpreted, effect without cause in its most desperate form.

There was moonlight coming in through the window, and that intensifies matters when matters are mysterious. A little downy owl in the orchard hooted and seemed to say, "I know!" The midnight air in the garden, heated and abandoned by yesterday's sun, came to its ultimate cooling point. The garden grew hot and stuffy and signaled for aid to a squadron of winds scattered on the lake. They martialed themselves into a breeze and blew.

There was a great fuss in the tree-tops, and a rush of sounds like the spraying of many hoses. The flower-beds reveled in their cool refreshment. Poppies spin-wheeled on their stems, primroses shivered with delight, caladiums wagged their long ears in approval. The wind struck the house broadside. In every crevice and cranny from cellar to shingles it went "whee!", like the squashing of a giant accordion with none of the stops released. Window-frames rattled their glass. Lattices jiggled like skeletons. Everything shakeable shook. And the tassel of a curtain string, pretending to be a rat, sneaked along the window-sill, leapt into the air, and hung suspended by a long squirming tail.

By this time Marjorie was thoroughly awake. Her eyelids were heavy, but her ears were terribly open. Her sense of touch became acute in the darkness, ready to recoil at the feel of anything warm and hairy or of anything tinny and cold. She wanted to scream. There was every reason for screaming. Indeed, there was no reason for not screaming. And yet somehow she could not scream, even though she knew it meant waking daddy, who was sleeping in the next room, and who would be glad to come and comfort her. Something inside her kept telling her not to. A little thought seemed to come from nowhere and lodge in her head, and kept saying, "I'd rather you wouldn't scream. I think it would be much nicer to lie down again and listen. Nothing can harm you. And it's better not to be afraid." Marjorie had no notion where that little thought came from. It was a new kind of little thought. But it seemed to be quiet and kind, and so terribly sure of itself, that she thought it best to obey.

And so it happened that a small dark head went back again to the pillow to explore once more with courage and confidence. She smoothed back her hair with her hand. *Tup-tupp. Tup-tupp.* She found it again, the curious little noise, cupping her ear on the flat surface of the pillow cover.

Tup-tupp, tup-tupp. It really wasn't a dreadful sound anyhow. There was something soft and musical and velvety about it, even though you didn't know where it came from. It was much nicer than a clock. It was much slower than the purring of a pussy-cat, and much sweeter. *Tup-tupp.* Funny how intimate it was. It seemed to be coming right out of the pillow, crawling into your ear. You found a little bit of it in your throat. It was getting right inside you. You began to like it. It was a friendly little *tup-tupp.* You seemed to be breathing it, swallowing it. You *had* swallowed it. It was rolling in your blood, tingling in your feet. It was down in your stomach. And yet some of it had got into your head. You could feel it when you pressed your temples with your hands.

But after much turning and twisting and exploring there was one place where you managed to locate it exactly. If you should draw a line with your finger, beginning with your left eye and down your cheek and across your throat, and keep on going a little way down your breast, and then stop,—you would come to the seat of the mischief precisely. Right under the pocket in your nightdress. Not *in* the pocket, as you thought first of all, but right under the spot where the pocket rested when you lay on your back and smoothed your night-gown straight down in front.

That? *But that was your heart!* That little noise was *you*. You were alive! That's why something went on ticking inside you. Fancy not knowing you were alive! Fancy not remembering you had a heart! Now weren't you glad you had not screamed? Now weren't you happy because you had solved that dreadful mystery all by yourself?

It was funny being alive. It was funny realizing you were somebody. Somehow or other you liked being yourself for the first time, and it was pleasant to lie there with your head on the pillow listening to yourself live. It was so new and so interesting. Except that it was such a lonely business. With nobody to enjoy it but yourself. And nobody to talk to about it. In fact, nobody paying attention to it but you. Mummy and daddy didn't know, for they were sound asleep. Nobody in the whole world knew, for it was midnight and everyone was sound asleep. Everyone but you. You were the only one in the whole world who was awake. And nobody in the whole world knew you were awake but yourself. . . . You were just keeping yourself all to yourself in the darkness. Just lying there and living inside yourself where nobody could ever reach you. So terribly surprised. And so terribly happy. And yet so terribly unhappy. And so terribly alone. . . .

And a little heart continued to go *tup-tupp, tup-tupp*. But eventually nobody heard it. Nobody at all. And the moon kept sending in its second-hand light through the window. But some hours later the cock crew. And the sun came over the hill to do a decent job at brightening up things.

. . . .

A little mind is like a little bird. It requires time and patience to coax it out of the nest. But once aware of its wings and sure of its balance, it will not be long in exploring and possessing the open sky.

On the morning after her delectable, dialectical nightmare, Marjorie came to school as usual. As usual she sat in the second row, and proceeded, as soon as class had begun, to establish a far-away look in her eyes. She chewed her thumb as usual. And when Sister Bridget undertook, by additions and subtractions of oranges, peaches, apples, and bananas, to get a fruity hold on the unpalatable science of mathematics, This Little Thing paid her, as usual, the tribute of a complete and absorbed inattention.

It was not until a day or two had passed that Sister Bridget became aware that inside that tiny, oval and rebellious head thought was happening a little differently. There was more wonder and less bewilderment in This Little Thing's expression. And several times during Catechism lesson two small cherry lips fluttered, and were on the verge of asking a question.

It helped matters considerably when it was learned that the reverend pastor, during his visit to the city, had been seized with a splendid attack of sciatica (an old complaint of his), and was obliged to go to the hospital to have his aches analyzed. This delayed by a fortnight the First Communion reception, for the reverend pastor (in his arrogance) considers any First Communion invalid which he is not there to administer; and it gave Sister Bridget and me ample time to discover This Little Thing's new potentialities and to prime her hopefully once more on the fine points of penny theology. And now that she had a problem to settle—and though I have embellished her little heart experience in the telling, it is, without my interpretation and adornment, not too unlike her childish recital of it to me—it was less difficult to focus her small thoughts with sufficient accuracy on the meaning of the Bread of Life. For the problem of physical loneliness is precisely that for which the Blessed Sacrament was instituted. And the mystery of Love in the Sacred Host does not cloud or conceal the intimacy of Love therein, not even for the minds of children. Indeed, I wonder if they do not appreciate best of all the companionship of Love that melts in your mouth and flows in your veins, of Love that is near as nourishment and familiar as food.

And so when ten little boys and twelve little girls knelt at the altar rails on a bright June morning, This Little Thing was among them. The boys went first, manly and brave, small and silent, clean and young, each with a white band on his arm, a squeak in his new shoes, and a terrible surety and hunger in his eyes. I had hoped that it would be my privilege to give Holy Communion to these children. Having seen them safely through the perils of their final examination, I felt it was no more than right that I should say their First Communion Mass and welcome them to the Holy Sacrament. I suggested the idea to the reverend pastor with great tact. But he ridiculed and rejected it, and gave me such a withering and belittling look, you'd think I had asked him to ordain me to the priesthood for the occasion. Of course, I always have to excuse the reverend pastor on the score of his sufferings and his painful sciatica; but I think an equally painful but less egotistical form of sciatica would win him quite as much merit in Heaven.

After the boys came the girls, as fresh and light as lilies, all airy and white and hostlike as their mothers could make them. They drifted and dropped like doves on the altar steps: twelve little substances swathed in snow. As the golden ciborium passed and paused at each open mouth, I wonder if the ghost of Giuseppe Sarto stood behind them and counted them and added their ages and chuckled? Take them all together and they would not make one respectably old lady.

During the service This Little Thing behaved admirably. I stood and watched her from the rear of the church. Of course, I could not judge accurately from a back view of her head what was happening on the front of it; but certainly her movements and her posture, from where I could observe them, gave every indication of complete recollection. She took her place in the procession to the altar with great grace and dignity. And on the way back, in humble adoration, she covered her face with her hands. This last gesture was not according to Bridgetine instructions (one was supposed to fold one's hands in front of one's breast); but it was so obviously sincere and natural and made such an edifying picture for the lookers-on, I am sure it did not fail to gain a Bridgetine indulgence after the ceremony.

It was after the ceremony that This Little Thing had a complete reversal to form, and made it quite clear that though she had learned to think all by herself, she had no intention, not even on her First Communion morning, of allowing the mere use of reason to interfere with her individuality. She was to continue to be, as heretofore, a very decided personality, unique, precious and altogether unpredictable.

It was the custom of the girl First Communicants, after their Mass, to go to the school classroom for one last word with Sister Bridget while they were having their veils and rose-wreaths removed. Sister Bridget always managed a tear or two at this occasion (for there is always a sense of sadness attending the completion of any task, however agreeable), supplemented by a kiss, a holy picture, and a plea for prayers in behalf of those dreadfully desperate and indefinite desires all nuns possess in the form of "very special intentions."

But This Little Thing would not take off her veil. Nor her wreath of roses. She wanted first to say something to Sister

Bridget. She wanted to say something to her alone. All alone. When the others had gone. It was a secret. She wanted to whisper it. And the door must be closed. And nobody else must be there.

Eventually, when all these stipulations had been satisfied, the little whisper was whispered. And Sister Bridget was amused. Very amused. Because it was a very funny secret. And a very unusual request.

"All right, darling," said Sister Bridget, "I'll be glad to listen. There! . . . Now I can hear it. . . . Hmmmm! . . . Yes, indeed. . . . It's beating away as happy as can be. . . . And we know why it's beating so happy today, don't we? . . . What's that? . . . Do I what? . . . Do I hear two hearts beating inside you? . . . No, darling. . . . Of course not. . . . Oh, you mean Our Lord's Heart too? . . . No, darling. . . . Because Our Lord's Heart is concealed in the Blessed Sacrament and when He is hidden like that we don't see or hear Him at all. . . . We just believe in Him and love Him and know that He is there because He has told us. . . . And that's all we want is His word for it. . . . So now you had better take off your veil and . . ."

But Sister Bridget had listened a second too long. "Oh," she cried as a slow cold chill ran through her blood, followed by a quick wave of hot excitement. Was she imagining something? Of course she was. But how could she be imagining it? As clear and definite as the striking of two bells or the patter of two footsteps she heard inside that small bosom against which she pressed her ear, the beating of two hearts. Nonsense! But there was no mistaking it! Both kept a distinct and regular rhythm. One was a light and delicate throb, the other was heavy and labored. There were two heart-beats unmistakably. They did not even keep time with each other.

Sister Bridget's hands grew cold. Perspiration came out on her forehead and moistened the white band of her wimple. Her long eyelashes fluttered half in ecstasy, half in terror. She dropped upon her knees. And covered her face with her hands.

When This Little Thing had gone, Sister Bridget went quickly out of the school, ran across the convent yard, hurried through the door and up the stairs and along the corridor in frantic haste, and into her cell. She closed the door and threw herself on the bed. And buried her face in the pillow.

Why did she not go to the chapel? She kept asking herself this question, but she dared not go to the chapel. This was too terrible to pray about. She had no notion of how to thank God for this. It was so new and weird and unexpected. Maybe it was an illusion of the devil. But how could the devil have any power over a little body on its First Communion morning?

Sister Bridget reviewed her faults and her sins; her distractions at prayer; her moments of impatience; her moments of frivolity. Could a miracle be compatible with all this infidelity and perversity?

Now she would have to readjust her whole life and her whole psychology. The beautiful world of Faith where God was trusted and served for His own sake was now forever closed to her. No more Communion classes to prepare in the way she used to, a child among children, unspoiled by favors and seeking no reward save God's unspoken pleasure. She had asked her Father in Heaven for no sign. But a sign had been granted. Everything would be different from now on. She would always feel queer and self-conscious and unnatural.

No one must be told of what had happened. And yet the other nuns would be sure to notice a change in her. The Sacred Heart had beat in her ear. Clearly and unmistakably. But what a price to pay in the future! There might be a trial and investigations and canonical inquests. Maybe there would be more miracles and more revelations. Notoriety. And doubt. And fear. And obligations multiplied. And no peace. Sister Bridget clinched her hands and bit her fingers and wept unrestrainedly. She kept muttering short ejaculations. She was trying to be grateful. She was trying to be worthy of what had happened. And yet she was trying not to wish that it had not happened at all. . . .

It was some hours later in the morning, shortly before the bell for dinner, that Sister Bridget, lying weary and exhausted on her cot, with her handkerchief rumpled in her hand and her eyes fixed on the wall, became conscious of a strange noise throbbing in her ear. When she raised her head from the pillow it disappeared. When she pressed her ear tightly against the pillow it revived again. She opened her eyes in astonishment. And suddenly her expression changed. "Oh," she exclaimed. And the world turned over and came up right again.

Oh! So that was it! And Sister Bridget, listening enchantedly to a thumping pillow, made, like Newton when he heard enchantedly the thump of a falling apple, a great discovery. She discovered the law of pectoral acoustics. It is based, so the scientists say, on the simpler law of "pillow acoustics" (discovered by Miss Marjorie X., T.T., U. of R., aet. 7), and will be formulated in the text-books this way: If you press your ear very tightly against a slightly hollow object, you will hear your heart-beat. If it be the heart area of a living object, you will hear its heart-beat, as well as your own.

Sister Bridget arose. And dried her eyes. And bathed her face in warm water. And then in cool water. And put on a fresh linen coif. And arranged her dress with the proper creases. And her veil with religious precision. And went quietly down to dinner, with a chastened spirit, and a wise appetite.

COUSIN WILLIE

IF I COULD draw, I would introduce Cousin Willie by drawing you a picture of his shoes. And then you could probably guess what the rest of him looked like. But unfortunately I cannot draw, and much as I should like to describe Cousin Willie economically, I despair of ever being able to indicate the character of his shoes by mere words and sentences. I should exhaust myself finding them epithets.

They were typical old man's shoes, with broken in-steps and tattered linings, having neither tongues nor laces, but extending uninterruptedly up to his shins. Many seasons of wear had squashed them out of their original shapes and re-laxed their textures till they wore as many wrinkles as a naked turtle. They made little pleasant noises when Cousin Willie walked, like percussions from a cushion or squeezings of wind through a sponge. "Plosh! Plosh!" they whispered as they slithered along in the service of their master's feet, each an unpolished, unpresentable integument of pliable, adaptable leather, in which Cousin Willie's heel snuggled contentedly, his great toe swiveled luxuriously, and his sole was at peace.

Some dictionaries (not The Oxford) call the kind of shoes I am describing "romeos." I balk at the name. But not because I cannot find it in The Oxford Dictionary. For if Cousin Willie wore the certain variety of low shoes I wear myself, I should insist (albeit by a narrow New England provincialism) on calling them "oxfords," even though there are no oxfords in The Oxford Dictionary.

Nor am I afraid of the word "romeo" because it sounds sentimental. I believe nothing is worth writing about which is not sentimental. But because it might sound a bit ludicrous. After all, the subject of this story is seventy-six years of age. And he is not ludicrous. He is intensely exquisite and dignified. I am taking a liberty in calling him Cousin Willie. To go further and stick his feet in a pair of romeos would be facetious. It would be disrespectful. And I should rather cut my old gentleman's legs off, and send him rolling through the rest of this story in a wheel-chair, than have you take him as a joke. This is not a humorous story. On the contrary it is going to try to be pathetic. And because I, who write it, know beforehand how it is going to end, I shall fail to see anything funny in what you, who read it, may want to laugh at before you bid Cousin Willie good-bye.

And now, having abandoned my protagonist at the bottom, let me begin with him at the top. And if I am not delayed too long in describing the upper and middle parts of him, I may gradually work down to his shoes again. But it is imperative at this point in my prelude that I say something about Cousin Willie's hair.

Cousin Willie had white hair. He had *lovely* white hair. At least so Miss Lucy said. But again I see I am in difficulty. I dare not allow a certain frail spinster to enter this narrative until her proper time. And this is *not* her proper time.

"Not yet, Miss Lucy!" I whisper, as I see her trying to tip-toe out of my typewriter ahead of her cue; "I am sorry, but I must shoo you out of my sentences for the present. I want to save you till later if you please. I shall let you know when my story needs you, and then you may come back again. . . ." Her ghost hesitates for a moment on the edge of my paper, shrugs its shoulders bewilderedly, floats back and disappears behind the rubber roller of my lettering engine, and evaporates in a *zing!*

And therefore, because I cannot think of (and much less write about) Cousin Willie's lovely white hair without at the same time thinking of Miss Lucy, in order to avoid her now with security, I feel I must leave my hero with only his extremities described, and get on to telling you how I happened to meet him.

I knocked him down on a sidewalk in Lourdes, that's how I happened to meet him. It was Our Lady's Lourdes, of course, Lourdes of the Pyrenees in Southern France, whither I had gone on a fifteen dollar excursion from Paris.

I remember the street and the sidewalk vividly. It was the first small street to the left as one, going towards the Grotto, walks away from the bridge across the River Gave: a narrow, dingy by-way, famous for its statue stalls and pious knick-knack emporiums; bristling with trinket tinkers and medal merchants, crowded with rows of small shops devoted to semi-sanctimonious enterprises like "the rosary-bead business" and "the holy-water-bottle industry."

The afternoon had just passed twilight and was darkening into nightfall. Cousin Willie came shuffling along carrying a candle and a jug. He was on his way to deposit the jug at his *pension*, and thence to join his lighted candle to the torches of a thousand other pilgrims, already gathering in the main thoroughfare of Lourdes, and soon to march to the Basilica in one of the magnificent night processions.

The street in which I encountered him was not a street accurately. It was more of an alley, congested with noisy traffickers and jostling pilgrims. Cousin Willie was trying to find his way out of the alley, and I was trying to find my way into it. It may well be that the contrariness of our thoughts was the reason why each failed to notice the on-coming of the other. We collided. And he, the craft of lesser tonnage, collapsed, slipped, and sat down with a thud. His candle blew out. His jug exploded on the curbstone. And a precious pint of miraculous water splashed on his trousers and trickled sacrilegiously into the gutter.

Cousin Willie, subsiding on the pavement, looked up at me without the slightest sign of resentment. "Sorry!" he explained, promptly and politely. "I'm extremely sorry. Very stupid of me not to have looked where I was going."

I knew at once, even apart from the language and the soft-palate tones of his voice, the nationality of my opponent. He was most surely an Englishman. No one but an Englishman could have regarded a grave embarrassment so lightly and commanded such immediate composure and courtesy. This is his breeding, his tradition.

Naturally when I scrutinized my victim I became deeply

humiliated, both at having injured one so helpless, and at having obtained forgiveness so cheaply. If Cousin Willie had scolded me, I should have felt the situation less keenly. I tried hard to think of something decent to say by way of apology. Finally, after an awkward silence, I managed to enunciate this much: "My dear sir, I cannot tell you how sorry I am. It was my fault that you fell. I insist that you admit it was my fault. And unless you do, I shall leave you sitting there in the gutter."

Cousin Willie smiled. "Very well," he replied quietly, "suppose we share the blame? We'll each take half of it. I should have looked where I was going. And you shouldn't have knocked me down. And now, will you please give me a hand and help me to arise?" Whereupon I picked him up, straightened him, stretched him, brushed and investigated him, sponged his clothes with my handkerchief, examined his joints, patted his back, shook his hand, and asked his name.

I discovered that, in my rashness, I had bowled over the following distinguished personage: Colonel William Burrows, sometime of Her Majesty, Queen Victoria's, South African Legion, now retired . . . returning from a farewell holiday with old friends in England . . . journeying back all alone to his home in distant Rhodesia, in order, as he said, to make his will, settle his estates, and die . . . a University man (Downside, and Balliol College, Oxford), and, matrimonially as well as academically, a bachelor . . . a cavalier, and a devout Catholic, who had arranged to stop at Lourdes en route to Zululand, and visit the Rock of Massabieille, and see the famous field and the holy fountain, and chivalrously pay his respects to the spot where Queen Mary, Mother of God, once held her rendezvous with little Miss Soubirous . . . desirous incidentally of recommending to Her Majesty's kind intercession his soul's salvation, and a few temporal annoyances, chief of which he wished to mention his aching feet, which were crippled with rheumatism.

"I have a most intolerable rheumatism in my feet," said
Colonel Burrows, as he went on introducing himself to me.
"Look at the miserable shoes I have to wear!"

I did look at them. Very carefully. And I think the reader
will find in the early parts of this chapter sufficient indications
to show that I have not forgotten them.

The outcome of this unfortunate incident was nothing but
good fortune. For Cousin Willie and I, after a short but in-
tense scrutiny of each other, decided to become good friends,
such good friends that, during the three days of our mutual
sojourn in the little Village of Miracles, we became inseparable.

It was well that Cousin Willie found me, because he needed
me. He turned out to be even more helpless than I had at first
imagined. He was really very feeble and managed to keep his
body active and erect only by sheer will-power and effort.
What devotional folly had led him to take the long journey
to Lourdes alone, I could not at that time decide. Anyhow,
while he was with me, I became his cicerone, interpreter, valet,
and guardian angel all rolled into one. I woke him in the morn-
ing, steered him down the right street to Mass, steered him
back the right street to breakfast, walked him to and from
the Grotto in our intervals of prayer, pulled him out of the
way of trolley cars, bought him tobacco, matches, pipe-
cleaners, medals, post-cards (and wrote them), and was in gen-
eral most handy and indispensable.

In return for these services it was my privilege to explore,
through the medium of walk-chats, tea-talks, and coffee-con-
ferences, the interior life of an old gentleman of beautiful
culture and exquisite sensibilities; wise, witty, spiritual, peril-
ously near to being holy; simple in his prayers, soldierly in
his faith, boisterous in his courage, and gentle in his thoughts
towards God and man.

On our second afternoon together, Cousin Willie and I went
to the great square in front of the Basilica to watch the solemn

blessing of the sick. This ceremony, held in the open air, marks the crowning event of a visit to Lourdes. It is the pilgrims' hour of most fervid intercession, when the blind, the halt, and the maimed are taken from the hospitals, arranged, litter to litter, in a large quadrangle, and wait for the public prayers in their behalf, and for the procession of the Blessed Sacrament. During this service occurs, under Our Lady's auspices, the final appeal to God to relieve these poor sufferers of their infirmities.

The sick pilgrims, upon their arrival at Lourdes, are carried from the train to the Medical Bureau, where the doctors examine them and make records of their ailments. Then they are assigned to the infirmaries for care, food and shelter.

After this begins a series of devotional observances lasting two or three days. The invalids are brought to the Grotto for a personal dedication to Our Blessed Mother. They light candles at her shrine. They drink the water that flows under the Grotto from the wonderful spring which Bernadette was directed to discover during one of the apparitions. The water from this spring is piped to bath-houses and gathered in stone basins, and in these the sick are bathed. It is to be noted that nobody who bathes in these waters ever carries away from them any contagion, despite the fact that one and all are immersed therein, irrespective of the virulence of their sores or the unpleasant character of their diseases.

It may happen in the course of this preliminary ritual, that someone's malady is either alleviated, or even entirely cured. If so, the then-called *miraculé* (a delightfully appropriate word, utterly French, and uncoinable in English) is examined again by the doctors for a verification of the cure. If it is found to be authentic, the client is requested to come back again in a year's time for a confirmation of the completeness and permanence of the recovery.

But the statistics show that it is during the last festival, namely the solemn procession of the Blessed Sacrament, that

Our Lady's intercession is likely to be most potent and a miracle most likely to occur. And little wonder that this is so. For the solemn blessing of the sick may be called, not irreverently, a "challenge" to God's pity. His suffering children are made a spectacle to Him as He passes in Eucharistic guise. He is constrained to pause at each cot and bless each sufferer, and to acknowledge each human affliction by individual recognition. Thousands are watching, and the honor of His Virgin Mother is at stake. Our Lord will be heedless to cure at His own peril.

The preparations for this general benediction begin an hour ahead of time, with much hubbub and confusion. Bells ring. Men run in the streets. Dogs bark. Birds twitter. The whole town gets alive with excitement. Villagers and pilgrims hurry from their homes and their hotels. They march in crowds to the gate of the Basilica enclosure.

The commercial element in Lourdes (and it is considerable) is kept sedulously outside this enclosure. The candle hawkers (old ladies in black shawls) stand at the entrance to the precincts reserved for prayer, and emit their stream of mercenary mumblings as the pilgrims pass in. Just outside the gate too, one is surprised and amused to find rows of hucksters selling —of all things in the world—*sticks of vanilla*. Why vanilla? Everyone asks this question. And why here? What connection can such an article of food have with either miracles or Mariolatry!

Cousin Willie, whose mind is both reverent and inventive, settled this problem immediately, by deciding (and whispering to me) that there must be some mystical significance attached to vanilla: a spice symbol perchance, borrowed from the prophecies of the Old Testament which foretell the glories of the Virgin Mother. But later in the evening when we procured a Bible and rummaged through odds and ends of Scripture texts, and examined hagiographical tidbits referring to balsam, myrrh, aloes, and the like, we had to abandon his theory.

Neither he nor I could find any mention of vanilla in Holy Writ, nor any passages containing the slightest vanilla flavor.

My distraction in regard to these vanilla vendors was more profane. I had never known, till that day, that vanilla could exist other than in liquid form. I remembered it only in terms of a semi-fragrant bottle in my mother's pantry, a drop from which, stirred into a cake or a pudding, made it either smell better or taste better, I forget which. I now began to take a deep interest in vanilla, and to wonder in what category of food elements to place it. Was it a nut? Or a plant? Or the by-product of coal-tar or molasses or something of that sort? And for pity's sake, how did they manage to solidify it and shape it into sticks? . . .

I paused in my orisons (Cousin Willie and I were reciting the Rosary as we marched through the Basilica Gate) to make a mental note of vanilla as a problem to be investigated further. Characteristically, I have not since bothered to look it up in any book of information. And so vanilla, even today, remains to me wholly unaccounted for, a substance as mysterious in its origins as terrapin or tapioca.

The parade of the invalids to their places is a touching sight. Some are borne in beds, some are wheeled in chairs, some are carried in arms. The *brancardiers* and *infirmières* (volunteer stretcher-bearers and nurses) transport the sufferers and care for them with the greatest love and tenderness. The faces of these attendants as they go about their work is a study in the beauty of Christian sympathy and compassion. There are other problems in the supernatural evident at Lourdes besides the cure of the sick. There is (a) the problem of their transportation, many with only a spark of life smoldering in their bodies. They come in stuffy coaches and rattling railroad cars from enormous distances, some from Northern France, from Belgium, Germany, Italy, Ireland, England, Norway. Some have traveled even from Australia and America. How do they manage such extravagant journeys in such states of exhaustion?

There is (b) the problem of affection, unbelievable affection, on the part of the well for the sick. Sickness is not attractive. Watery eyes, fetid wounds, foul breaths, twisted limbs, cancerous deformities are loathsome and repelling. And yet at Lourdes, by a strange perversion of natural values, one's infirmities become one's title to distinction. The sick pilgrims receive from the bystanders, not pity, so much as reverence, admiration and even envy. Lourdes is a place where one feels ashamed of being in good health and of having no physical hardships to bear with resignation for the love of God.

And finally, (c) there is the problem of the unwarranted patience and silence of the invalids as they lie in the open square, in the hot sun, waiting for the Benediction of the Blessed Sacrament. Surely in the course of these physically tiresome proceedings the pains of some poor unfortunate ought to become unbearable. Someone might be expected to shriek, to rebel, to leap from his bed and be overpowered by the attendants. This does not happen. They suffer, one and all, soundlessly, with scarcely any movement, and no complaint.

As the time for the ceremony drew near, the crowd became more and more quiet until, within five minutes of procession time, it was very nearly in a complete hush. There was a tightness in the air, as though masses of spirits were assembling to watch the spectacle. A few pigeons fluttered out of the steeple of the Basilica and circled about in the sky, as if on the lookout for the Dove whose arrival was expected at any moment.

Promptly on the stroke of the hour, two acolytes emerged from the church door, followed by candle-bearers, censer-bearers, a group of priests and monsignori, a bishop, and finally, under a canopy carried by four stalwart peasants, a priest carrying the Blessed Sacrament. We all settled on our knees, bowed our heads, and watched and waited.

The first person to be blessed was an old man with a stick, sitting in a chair. To those of us who were having "our first

Lourdes," this first blessing was a high-water mark in devotional excitement. *Benedictio Dei omnipotentis . . . Patris . . . et Filii . . . et Spiritus Sancti . . . descendat super te . . . et maneat semper*, spoke the priest as he elevated the Monstrance in the form of a cross. The poor old sick man blessed himself. . . . He gripped tightly on his stick. . . . Was he cured? . . Was he going to get up and walk? . . . Yes! . . . No, it seemed not! . . . Yet how did we know? . . . Maybe he was going to wait. . . . Maybe he did not want to shout out at once. . . . In order not to interrupt the procession. . . . Are you cured, old man? . . . Are you all well again? . . .

In the meantime I had paid no attention to the fact that the priest had advanced down the line and had already finished blessing a half a dozen more sufferers when I turned to follow him again with my eyes. The priest was a tall, thin man and looked very ill himself. Monstrances are heavy, and the physical hardship entailed in raising and lowering one several hundred times in the course of an afternoon is very great. I pitied the poor priest. There were lines of suffering and fatigue already in his face.

By this time the procession had passed all the semi-invalids and had arrived at the beds of the desperate cases. Men and women in skeleton form, wrapped in sheets and blankets, heard the sound of footsteps, saw the glare of candles, smelled the odor of incense, and knew in some sad, delirious way that the Blessed Sacrament was passing.

Inch by inch the procession advanced. Hopeless cases became such a common sight that one soon failed to be surprised at beholding humanity in any state whatsoever of degradation or misery. Occasionally some poor suppliant in the line of march stood out conspicuously: a young man with his head swathed in bandages through which his nose alone protruded; or a pretty little German girl of eight or nine years, with an ulcerated leg, wearing her First Communion dress, a white veil, and a wreath of roses.

There was no hurry and not the slightest sign of uneasiness on the part of the Benediction officials, despite the fact that the prayers for a cure were being defeated. The Blessed Sacrament moved on and on in its persistent, snail-like journey, and over and over again the priest chanted his monotonous incantation. Little by little our minds began to surrender all expectation of a miracle. We stopped thinking of these pilgrims as petitioners wanting to be made well, and began to contemplate them as holocausts being offered, as victims brought here to be immolated.

At last, after more than an hour of continuous intercession, the ultimate bed was reached. The benediction prayer was recited for the last time. The priest retired to the steps of the Basilica for the singing of the *Tantum Ergo* and the final blessing. He then marched with his attendants into the church; the door closed after him; and the festival of faith was over.

Not a single cure had been obtained, as far as we could see. Not one. Slowly and patiently the sick were wheeled back again to the hospitals. The crowd dispersed, the villagers to their homes, the tourists to their hotels. And the Grand Esplanade was left deserted. The pigeons might now return from the steeple and flutter again on the ground unmolested. . . .

"Are your feet any better?" I said to Cousin Willie as I took him by the arm and proceeded to lead him home to supper, though I could see from the way he walked that they were not.

"My feet!" he replied with amazement, as though he had never owned such appendages. "Why of course not!" He hesitated for a moment and then added: "But what a travesty of mercy it would have been for Our Lady to have cured my feet and have let those real sufferers go unanswered! Surely it would have been caddish of me to kneel and watch that spectacle and think of my own private infirmities. Don't you think so?"

I did not answer. But later in the evening, as we rested on the bridge on our way home from our night walk, I told him my true reaction to the afternoon's proceedings. I cannot remember at the present writing what I said to him in full, but I recall that I ended my oral meditation in his presence somewhat in this fashion: "What a revelation it was of the power and dignity and value of the human spirit! Think of the heroisms to which man can be inspired for the love of God! If anyone was humiliated this afternoon, it was God who was humiliated. For He stood in the presence of those poor sufferers, showing not one trace of His omnipotence, bearing them no gifts but the naked gift of His divine love. And yet that was enough for them. And they went on trusting and believing and adoring Him just the same, excusing and forgiving Him, rejoicing only that He had passed in their midst, even though it was only to pass them by. We are wonderful creatures, Colonel Burrows. With all our helplessnesses, we are a great people. May God be praised for making us what we are and for giving us a share in a humanity which, even at its zero point, can achieve such splendor and sublimity in the sight of the Most High. May His Kingdom come. For His Kingdom is surely not of this world."

Cousin Willie did not reply. But as he turned to look at me in the darkness, I saw by the quiet light burning in his eye that he was in possession of deeper and better thoughts of his own.

"Ahem!" said Cousin Willie to me at breakfast on the last day of our stay at Lourdes; and then "Ahem!" again. My sensitiveness to his moods was by this time so highly developed that I knew this twofold throat-clearing was the preface to some startling announcement. It was likely to have some of the significance of the double "Amen" in Holy Scripture by which weighty and important statements are introduced: "Ahem, ahem, I say unto you."

I sipped my coffee and waited patiently. Ahem what?

"Would you—" said Cousin Willie, making precise motions

with his lips, "would you like to take a little tram ride with me this afternoon?"

"Tram ride?" I inquired, with an affected lack of interest, seeming only to be amused at the un-American name for street-car.

"Yes," he replied, and I thought I noticed him redden considerably.

I paused to sip my coffee again, and before I committed myself, indulged in a few private speculations. . . . Yes, surely there *were* "trams" in Lourdes. . . . And one could go tramming through the countryside in many directions if one wished. . . . But Lourdes itself was so intensely interesting, why lose any of it when our time there was so short! . . . It was like traveling to the Holy Land in order to make a balloon ascension, or running away from the Pyramids in order to get a good view of the sand.

Cousin Willie decided that I had paused long enough and continued: "I should like very much to take a trip to Bagnères-de-Bigorre this afternoon. Ever hear of it?"

"No."

"It's about ten miles from here, a pretty little village up in the mountains."

"What's there to see in Bagnères-de-Bigorre?"

"Well, I'll tell you." And Cousin Willie removed his spectacles and began to clean them. "There are some friends of mine stopping there for the summer. English people. I haven't seen them for forty years or more. Not since I left England to go to South Africa. They are distant relatives of mine. At least they say they are, though I've never bothered to investigate the relationship accurately. I imagine they're third or fourth cousins or something of that sort. At least they have always called me 'Cousin Willie,' and I let it go at that. . . . Well, they know I'm here at Lourdes, and they are most anxious to see me. A lot of bother, and I dislike going, but one can't offend people. I hate to drag you away from Lourdes on my account. But it would be an awfully great favor if you would come with me. You see, these people are all ladies, old ladies, spinsters!" (And he blew his nose.) "You know it's the devil trying to keep a conversation going with that sort. And of course I'll have to take tea and answer questions about my stay in Rhodesia and all that sort of rubbish. And there are four of them, four unmarried ladies. I could never manage them all alone. I feel like a cad in asking you to sacrifice any of your time here by coming with me. But will you?"

"All right," I said as I proceeded to garnish my empty coffee cup with ringlets of cigarette smoke, "I'll go." And lucky for Colonel W. Burrows those same little smoke ribbons didn't sky-write my thoughts at this juncture. Else he would have seen two silky, pale blue spirals of tobacco wriggle sarcastically out of my mouth and silently arrange themselves, letter by letter, into the words *you faker!* as they sailed upwards, struck the ceiling, and melted into whitewash. For I was beginning to suspect for the first time the full reason why Cousin Willie had come to Lourdes.

The little tram that elevates passengers from Lourdes to Bagnères-de-Bigorre is unable to manage the whole journey by itself. It requires the assistance of another little tram that meets it half way up the mountain. The first little tram climbs as far as it can, until it contracts an electrical wheeze and falls into a state of mechanical exhaustion: whereupon its gallant companion, the second little tram, takes over the travelers and baggage and carries them upwards for the rest of the trip. It is a roller-coaster route all the way, up hill and down dale, and only after some minutes of this lark-like manner of ascent does one realize that the valley of Lourdes is retreating in the distance and that one is getting nearer and nearer to the summit of the Pyrenees.

The scenery all the way is attractive; for fixtures there are quaint cottages, pretty fields, a brook, two bridges, and some interesting rock formations; and for incidentals, a flock of sheep, an old woman feeding a hen, and a little girl flying to and fro on a swing. But most fascinating of all the sights en route are the white cows which we saw grazing far above us on the crest of the mountain. The tram conductor pointed them out to us. These white cows, he said, remain on the heights all the year round, and the farmers must climb with their pails to milk them. Nor may they be brought down to lower altitudes without injury to their health. For if they are pastured for any length of time too near sea level, they contract asthma and die. The white cows of the Pyrenees entranced me. I watched them for nearly the whole journey, half specters and half clouds as they moved along the skyline jingling their bells. And I marveled at their heavenly genius in selecting as their favorite indisposition, asthma, the most ethereal of all diseases.

"There!" said the second little tram with a sigh of relief as it rounded the last lap of our ascent and rolled us into the station. "There! This is Bagnères-de-Bigorre at last, my dear passengers. At least I hope it is. And if it isn't, you can get out and walk the rest of the way, for I'll climb no more mountain this afternoon. I am in a state of collapse. My joints have become disorganized, my batteries have run down, and I feel cardiac murmurings in my motor. Whatever place this is in reality, its Bagnères-de-Bigorre as far as I am concerned."

We all got out and looked at the sign on the station. And, sure enough, Bagnères-de-Bigorre it was.

With the aid of a little kindergarten French, we secured a *renseignement* from the station master, and a short walk brought us to our ladies, sitting on their veranda and rocking impatiently. They became excited when they saw us, arose in unison, and amidst a cackled confusion of "Well Wells!", "My Mys!", "My Goodnesses!", and "My Goodness Graciouses!", we were welcomed. Cousin Willie, their lost one, had returned, their prodigal from Rhodesia, their hero from the land of kaffirs and cocoanuts. Unfortunately there was a little extra confusion entailed in finding out who I was. And, to be honest, I do not think I was ever satisfactorily explained.

As we sat down to tea, after a cup and saucer had been added to the tea things in my honor, I could see that my presence amid such a galaxy of old people was a bit disconcerting. For that reason I tried to make myself as neutral as possible in order not to add any false juvenile note to this long-waited-for reunion. I kept all my social graces under cover. I answered questions in the briefest possible manner, and asked none. I was determined not to steal the show from its rightful leading man nor to hamper his performance in any way. Every time the conversation threatened to include me as a topic I steered it back at once into Cousin Willie's territory. Every time I got the ball I punted.

And yet I do think I served Cousin Willie, after a fashion, to a very good purpose. For while one pair of spinsters was vacuum-cleaning him with questions, I kept the other pair distracted with small talk at another end of the room. And thus the odds against him were only two to one for the afternoon, instead of four to one as the ladies had anticipated. And by a judicious and well-timed change of seatings, on the excuse of getting a book, or a letter, or a photograph, or some more tea, etc., it came about that each of us entertained a different brace of spinsters every quarter of an hour. And this method, after the manner of a well-regulated bridge-game, gave our hostesses great satisfaction, as there was no time when some one of them was not occupying a full half of Cousin Willie's attention.

The youngest of the spinsters was about fifty-five, though she did not quite look it. Indeed there were times when, save for the heavy lines under her eyes, she managed to appear an excellent thirty-five. Her personality resented the burdens imposed on it by a half a century of existence and fluctuated continually in the area of bygone birthdays. She was fifty in her wrinkles, forty in her enthusiasms, thirty in her dress, twenty in her coiffure, and up and down her teens in ideas. Her name was Miss Clara, and we learned that only the afternoon before she had played and won a set of tennis.

Miss Harriet I guessed to be the next youngest, and very charming she was in a purple frock and a white shawl. She was an amiable and sensible sixty, and unashamed of it, in fact insisted on it, somewhat to Miss Clara's displeasure.

"You know," said Miss Harriet to Cousin Willie, as she waggled one of her loose-fitting house slippers, "next February I'll be actually sixty-*humph!*" and she stopped short when Miss Clara gave her a good poke in the back.

Miss Harriet did not resume her revelation after this rebuff, and so I did not hear what integer in addition to sixty Miss Clara's elbow had destroyed. But I am glad to leave Miss Harriet at a flat three score, assuring her that I should be prepared to like her at any age.

Miss Alice was indubitably the oldest of the sisters, and even as a spinster she was definitely out of the running. She was edging on to eighty, prim, puckered and picturesque, had interior ailments, loved hot tea, and hated cold draughts, and was wrapping and rewrapping herself up in a warm blanket all the while we were with her.

Miss Lucy, whom I mention last, was somewhere in between Miss Harriet and Miss Alice, nearing seventy I should say, though not imperiled by it. Instantly I liked Miss Lucy best of all. She was a lady of great delicacy, with a lovely face, spiritualized by illness and still retaining memories of its youth. She had gentle blue eyes that shone wistfully and seemed to say to everyone they looked at: "I forgive you!"

So much for our *dramatis personæ*. And now for our dialogue. My part in it, as I have said, was purely distractive. I talked of Lourdes of course, of Bernadette, and the shabby little cottage where she used to live with her frightened mother and her drunken father. I talked of the pilgrims of all sorts whom one meets in the streets. And I filled out my lines with some stock remarks about Europe in general as it appears to the eyes of a foreigner. Once I laughed out loud at having been forced to make a good joke, the point of which I alone could see.

"And how did Cousin Willie happen to pick you up?" inquired the voluble Miss Clara when she was seated as one of my partners.

"Oh!" I replied with a heavy chuckle, "we ran into each other purely by accident. And it was really *I* who picked him up."

Cousin Willie (for, although he was separated from me, I never became engrossed in my own conversation to the extent of losing him with my ear) was truly magnificent. A little stiff perhaps, and somewhat matter of fact, and excessively modest, but on the whole very impressive. He would not allow his African exploits to be lionized, as though he had gone there as a big-game hunter. And he threw cold water on all attempts to sentimentalize his hardships, as behooves a good soldier. And whenever a pair of feminine eyes attempted to melt him with adulation, his favorite deprecatory expressions were: "A mere trifle!", "Nonsense!", and "Tut, Tut!"

And was it *lone-ly* away off in South Africa all these years? . . .

Nonsense. Of course not. Too much to do.

And did he really associate with *real* Zulus? . . .

Zulus? Of course. Fine people. A lot of nonsense about their being dangerous. Made the finest servants one could ever imagine. Kept three of them on his property all year round.

OooooH! But wasn't he *sometimes* sorry he had left England? . . .

Tut, Tut! Never missed it. Would have liked to return once

in a while for a holiday. But certainly not to live there again. Had lost all attraction for the stupid English climate. Preferred by far the warm sun and blue skies of the Indian Ocean.

But why didn't he write oftener and let people know how he was getting on? . . .

Tosh! Never was much at correspondence. And besides had too many new interests. Had long since passed his rugger and cricket days, and now had new problems to engross him, the civilization and government of the natives for instance, and the problem of their education, physical and mental.

But didn't he *really* wish he had never gone there in the first place? . . .

Damn it, no! He didn't! What a foolish question!

But didn't he realize that his old friends missed *him* a lot? And didn't he remember the happy times they used to have when he was a school-boy and came to visit them for the vacs? . . .

Yes, of course he remembered. But! But one can't be a school-boy *all one's life,* can one? One has to get out and *do* things, hasn't one? One has *obligations* to fulfill, hasn't one? And *enterprises* to undertake? And one can't get things done by thinking in terms of *mere sentiment, can one*?

No, I suppose one can't. . . . And each spinster when confronted with this unanswerable dilemma indicated her resignation to fate by making a gesture of futility, and sibilating each an individual kind of sigh. Heigh-ho! In four different keys. Three sharps. Five sharps. Four flats. And an A-flat minor.

During one of the many shuffles that occurred in our seating arrangements I drew as my companions: Miss Harriet, the communicative one, and Miss Alice, the sleepy one. I began to discourse on my newly acquired object of interest, the white cows of the Pyrenees and their strange susceptibility to asthma. Miss Alice obliged by yawning and falling asleep. This gave Miss Harriet a full chance to communicate to me a secret I saw she had been anxious to reveal for some time past.

"Oh, I don't suppose you heard," she began with a furtive look around the room, "but Lucy and Cousin Willie were once . . . *you* know!", and she crossed her fingers. And drawing her rocking-chair a little closer she said in a staccato whisper: "They were practically engaged. But it broke off when he went away. Later Lucy planned to go to South Africa and marry him and settle there for good, but it never came about. He wouldn't let her go there to live, and he said his duty wouldn't let him return. It nearly killed Lucy, though she never speaks about it."

Thank you, Miss Harriet. You have completely solved a great mystery. How grateful to God we ought to be for the garrulous. They disentangle so many of our problems with their tongues, quite as many in the long run, I believe, as they complicate.

Heaven knows that, once I became armed with this information, I tried by every ruse in my power to wheedle the three incidental spinsters into my corner and give Cousin Willie and Miss Lucy a few moments together. I nearly made a fool of myself trying to do so. But these old lovers would *not* seize an occasion.

I even suggested that I should be glad to wheel Miss Alice out into the garden for a ride in her rolling chair if Miss Harriet and Miss Clara would help me. But this suggestion also went for naught. It turned out that I *did* give Miss Alice a ride in the garden, but it was Miss Lucy who volunteered to help me, leaving Cousin Willie alone in the house to be grilled further by the remaining Clara and Harriet.

It was in the garden, however, while pushing Miss Alice between a row of high hedges, that Miss Lucy disengaged me for a moment from my task and whispered the significant line I have commemorated earlier in this story. "Don't you think Cousin Willie has *lovely* white hair?"

It was nearly five o'clock, and we had to leave. There was

dinner waiting for us at our hotel, and there was an Italian pilgrimage, four hundred strong, coming in that night from Genoa, and we did not want to miss seeing its colorful arrival at the station.

Good-bye, Miss Alice! Good-bye, Miss Clara! And Miss Harriet! And Miss Lucy! But Miss Lucy was putting on her hat and coat and was coming with us to the station!

"Nonsense, Lucy," said Cousin Willie. "There's no need of your coming. We can find the station quite well!"

But Miss Lucy's hat had been put on at such a determined angle, one look at it showed us that it had no intention of coming off again under pressure of an argument.

"A lot of bother, Lucy," continued Cousin Willie. "Entirely unnecessary for you to come." And I believe he would have kept up this sort of grumbling and whining all the way down to the car if I had not interposed, "We think it's awfully nice of you to come, Miss Lucy. In fact we *want* you to come. . . ." That settled *him* for a while.

So off we marched to the station, myself, my drooping Romeo, and my faded Juliet. My tactics I quickly decided on the way. Upon arriving at the station I should beg leave to go and buy some cigarettes, of which I happened to have at the time a great plenty. And I should take lots of time to procure them. And in my absence, God willing, something decent might occur in the way of a farewell.

So I made them hurry, Miss Lucy in her light coat and hat, carrying an umbrella, and Cousin Willie shuffling along in his shoes. And as we crossed the main street of the village I had the privilege of taking his arm with one hand and hers with the other, and rushing them out of the way of a passing motor car. It was a moment of high excitement for me, and I had great difficulty in not imagining that some of love's electricity flowed through me on that occasion and found its rightful terminals in the two aching hearts with whom I was in contact.

Whether or not anything tender did happen when I left them

at the station and went to make my bogus purchase, I do not know. At least I allowed plenty of time for it to happen, and even read a nocturne of my Breviary in the tobacco store for a good measure of delay. Let us hope and pray some word was spoken, some look given, of which this story can make no mention, some little token that eased if it did not eradicate the pain of a forty years' separation.

I only know that when I returned I found them chattering about matters most unromantic, some insipidities about the rain and the weather, things damp and uninspiring and miles away from any subject savoring of affection.

Meanwhile our little tram, having had a good rest in a neighboring shed while we were taking tea, was ready to transport us downwards again. *All aboard!*

"Good-bye, Cousin Willie."

"Oh, good-bye! Good-bye!"

"Safe journey!"

"Thanks awfully."

"Write and let us know that you got home safely, won't you?"

"Yes, I may drop a card sometime."

"I suppose this is the last time we'll ever see you, isn't it, Cousin Willie?"

"Yes, I suppose so."

"Give my love to Mrs. Marshall, won't you?"

"Yes, I will. Good-bye!"

"And give my love to Adelaide?"

"Yes. Yes. Certainly."

"And give my love to David?"

"Yes. Yes. Yes. Good-bye."

"And give my love to . . ."

And that, dear reader, was the last of Miss Lucy. The last of her forever. Standing on the hilltop. Waving her umbrella.

Cousin Willie never waved back. But I did, as long as I could see her through the tram window.

As we rattled down the mountainside, Cousin Willie and I sat for a long time in silence. I knew he had been deeply moved, but I could not understand why he had been so deliberately frigid and irresponsive to all the overtures of farewell Miss Lucy had offered him. I hoped he was not an attitudinizer, capable of turning an unfulfillable affection into some mean form of spite like a school-girl. No. Surely this could not be so. I thought it best, therefore, to leave him alone, ask him no questions, and attend to my own business. After all it was *his* heart that was involved, not mine, and he could be counted on to be the best arbiter of its destinies. Only I was sorry, so sorry, Miss Lucy was not there to hear the reverie with which he finally decided to reopen the conversation.

"That was awfully decent of her to come down to the station with us, wasn't it?" he said at last.

I nodded.

"She's really the nicest one of those four, did you know it?"

Of course I knew it. And I was delighted to notice that he was employing in her regard a more gentle tone of voice than I had heard him use heretofore.

"And when she was a girl," he went on, "she was awfully pretty."

Bumpety! Bumpety! Bump! went the little tram, adding hideous, unmusical discords to the flow of this fine poetry.

"And I suppose I was an awful fool to leave England, eh?"

But how was I to answer that question?

"Oh, by the way," I said, watching him from the corner of my eye, "I had a nice talk with Miss Lucy in the garden."

"Oh, did you? What did she say?"

"Nothing in particular," I replied, pretending to yawn, "except she made a rather amusing remark about you."

"Oh, I say!" he answered quickly. "What did she say about me?"

"She said she thought you had *lovely* white hair," I said with great emphasis.

"Go on. Did she really?"

There was another interval of silence.

"I suppose she meant she was surprised to find I had any hair left at all. Wasn't that it?" he questioned at last.

"Yes, I guess so," I murmured casually. But I knew I had hit my mark.

"Well, to be honest," he went on, "I really don't know how I kept my hair. Never did anything for it in my life, except cold water. And come to think of it, I still have quite a lot, haven't I? Quite a mystery to know just why some men lose their hair and others keep it, isn't it?" he added, running his hand across the top of his head.

"Yes, it is," I answered, reaching and taking hold of my own to make sure it was still there.

But the incident in our whole afternoon's excursion which was to be most memorable and significant happened in the little village half way down the mountain while we were waiting for a change of trams.

"Would you mind," said Cousin Willie, "if I ran over to the chemist's shop to make a small purchase while we're waiting for the other tram to come?"

The idea of his *running over* to any place amused me. "I'll go with you," I said.

"No, you wait here and watch for it."

"I'll go with you," I repeated.

"No. You wait here. Please."

So I let him go. Which was nearly a disastrous permission. For he was gone well over five minutes. The alternate little tram began to appear in the distance. If we missed it there would be no getting back to Lourdes that night. I ran across the street and into the chemist's shop.

"Hurry up! Hurry up!" I shouted. "What are you doing? What's keeping you?"

"I'm buying some of this stuff," he answered sheepishly, seeing there was no way to make a subterfuge, "eau de quinine. It's wonderful for the hair. They make it here in France. And I just remembered I wanted to get some, as it's hard as the devil to buy it in Rhodesia because the duty's so high. . . ."

Nor was that all. In the hotel that night it was necessary, so he told me, to pour some eau de quinine out of the bottle, just a little, so one would be able to take it through the customs free of assessment. And part of the "little" poured out was replaced by a spoonful of Lourdes water, just to help matters on supernaturally as well as naturally.

And thus ended the history of what I believe to be the most interesting temporal favor ever requested at Lourdes, the case of an old Englishman who came thither with foot trouble and went away petitioning Our Blessed Mother to safeguard his hair, under the double auspices of her humble servants, Mlle. Bernadette Soubirous and Monsieur Ed Pinaud.

Cousin Willie and I parted on the train while we were en route back to Paris. He was to go to Marseilles and take the boat for South Africa by way of the Suez Canal. And he left me at a terminal station in Southern France, called Dax. Or maybe it was Pau. I am hazy about the name for my eyes were a bit misty when I looked out to see the name on the sign-post. Maybe it was Dau, or even Pax.

"Good-bye," he said. "Good-bye!" as we stood in the corridor of the train shipping his baggage out to the porter. "Don't forget to write to me. Here!—I'll write you my address on this envelope!"

"And I'll write mine on this," I said, procuring myself a piece of paper from my pocket-book.

But in the wild confusion, here's what happened, I put *my*

address back in my own pocket, and he put *his* address back in his, thus making us unattainable to each other for the rest of this earthly pilgrimage. I did not discover this awful mistake until I got back to Paris.

"Been to Lourdes?" asked an American tourist of me when I returned to my compartment in the train.

"Yes," I replied glumly.

"See any miracles?"

"Yes, a dandy."

"A real cure?" he inquired with great interest.

"Yes, sir, a very real one. An old man with foot trouble."

"But was he actually cured?" he persisted. "Did you really see it?"

"I did," I replied, giving him an enigmatical look. "Of course Our Lady had a little difficulty in managing it."

"How's that?"

"Well, first of all she had to stand him on his head."

He stared at me in blank amazement. Whereupon I took out my Breviary, arranged my prayer-ribbons, and began the task of reciting what is known in sacerdotal circles as our *onus diei*.

INSTRUCTIONS FOR MEETING
MRS. NOLAN

IF YOU wish to meet Mrs. Nolan, you must go to the Babson Memorial Hospital between the hours either of ten and eleven in the morning, or of three and five in the afternoon. I suggest that you go in the afternoon: first, because the visiting period is longer, and, second, because Mrs. Nolan's windows have a westward exposure, and—supposing it to be a pleasant day— her room will be filled with sunlight when you enter. For although it is a delightful experience to meet Mrs. Nolan at any time of day, I am in favor of your seeing her for the first time when she is at her best, which is between the hours of three and five, when her bedroom is brightest, when there are flowers on her medicine table, and when the nurse has just finished grooming her for afternoon callers.

Mrs. Nolan is a young woman, only twenty-eight years of age, but is afflicted with spinal trouble. A dozen doctors have examined her but none has been able to declare just what sort of spinal trouble it is; not even two medical specialists who were imported from a great distance and remunerated with extravagant fees for not being sure that Mrs. Nolan is not suffering from *Paraplegic Syringomyelia*. Following this examination, which was long and painful, Mrs. Nolan collapsed, and it was feared for a few hours that she would die; whereupon her confessor was summoned, and he successfully absolved in Latin her who had failed to be successfully diagnosed in Greek.

But I am presenting Mrs. Nolan to you altogether too abruptly. Although you are meeting her now only in your imagination, I insist that you suppose yourself going through the preliminary annoyance of trying to get to Babson Memorial Hospital by trolley-car, on a hot summer's day.

First, I should like to have you stand in Central Subway Station for twenty-five minutes, waiting for a car marked *Upsala Street*. Central Subway Station in mid-July is a perfect oven; and while you are walking up and down the platform, mopping the sweat-band of your hat, and having plush collisions with fat persons (who seem always attracted to the most congested areas during a heat wave), you may amuse yourself by speculating on the correct pronunciation of Upsala Street. Has it second-syllable emphasis like La Scala, umbrella, vanilla? One would think so. But no. The trolley starter who calls out the names of the cars as they swing around the loop into Central Subway Station, is indignantly in favor of giving "Upsala" a violent stress on the antepenult. "UPS-ala!" he shouts, as though he were urging a Japanese balancing artist to take a jump, or saluting with a hiccup the sacred prophet of the Mohammedans.

When you board the Upsala Street car, you will be sure not to find a seat. A crowd of expert rushers, shovers and elbowers will have managed to get all the vacant places ahead of you. Avail yourself immediately of the leather straps which are supplied for the support of the standing passengers. I advise you to get hold of two of these straps, one for each hand, because the journey is long (three-quarters of an hour), and the day (remember) is hot. You can make the trip seem less tiresome by looking down with pity on the seated passengers, rigid, tight, uncomfortable, who may not sway to and fro as you do on your leather trapeze. Or, if you prefer diversions which are on a level with your eyes, the Upsala Street car contains some tenderly solicitous advertisements concerning throat ailments, a splendid lithograph of a tomato, and an incontrovertible argument in behalf of floating soap.

You get off the Upsala Street car at Harrison Square; and if you cross directly in front of the car before it starts again, you will be standing beside the open-air pulpit of a traffic policeman. "Where is Babson Memorial Hospital?" you will say to him, or words to that effect. He will not answer you. He is a pointing policeman. He will point up the hill at your right. "Thank you" you say; and as you proceed to follow the conjectured direction of his index finger, a motor truck will almost knock you down in mid-street, because you will have made the mistake of thinking that, having just spoken to a policeman, you were entitled to cross to the sidewalk before the traffic lights changed color.

The sullen policeman will quickly become articulate upon his whistle; but there will be no sense in trying to go back to him again. Instead, some magnificent profanity on the part of the truck-driver will speed you to the curbstone, and several of the bystanders will giggle. One of them will kindly retrieve your straw hat, which has fallen in the gutter; and while you are attempting to thank him, it will be well to ask again: "Where is Babson Memorial Hospital?" "Right at the top of the hill" he will answer; "This is Highland Street—the hospital is right at the top of the hill." (It is so nice to have directions repeated twice; and it is so vulgar to point.)

You are now on Highland Street, climbing the hill, very tired and very nervous, for you have not as yet met Mrs. Nolan, and you have no idea how much she is going to refresh you after all this weariness. On your way up the hill a small dog will run up and sniff you and bark gently. Your humiliations thus far have made your brain so bewildered that you will be tempted to stoop and pat the dog and ask: "Am I right? Is this really the way to the hospital?" He is a friendly little animal, and will know how you are suffering, and will seem to tell you with his tail that you are on the right road at last.

Babson Memorial Hospital is a non-sectarian institution, excellently constructed, clean, airy, efficient—defective only in the quality of its architecture. Mr. Babson, when he lived, was one of those vague, though not unlovable, Christians called philanthropists, who believe that suffering is very bad for people and leave money in their wills in order to have it exterminated. All diseases, Mr. Babson maintained, could be done away with if folks would only take themselves in hand, cooperate with the hygienists, get enough fresh air. The idea of some form of sickness being inevitable to human nature he scouted most vigorously. He himself had lived to the ripe age of seventy-nine without an ill or an ache. Why couldn't everyone? And as for appendicitis, that mainstay of hospitals, and in its heyday when Mr. Babson died, he had dreams of a time when science might grow babies who had no appendices, just as Burbank had grown oranges which had no seeds. It might even have been a fond hope of his that one of the first sans-appendix infants might see the light of day in one of the

B.M.H. delivery rooms, and be promptly opened, inspected, affidavited, and reported by telegraph to the American Medical Association.

Mr. Babson was a kindly man, but there was no nonsense about him. He had a horror of incurables. He wanted people who insisted on getting sick to get well, and get well quickly. If this purpose could be achieved, he was willing to treat them generously, solicitously, antiseptically, within the walls of an institution which he had erected as a perpetual monument to his own good health. With such a motive behind it, it is not strange that Babson Memorial Hospital failed to achieve a notable architecture. It always felt too sorry for itself for having had to be a hospital at all.

Upon entering the main corridor of the building you will go immediately to the information desk, behind which are: a) two bookkeepers drowsing over their charts; b) a telephone operator, with assiduous elbows, pulling electrical snakes out of a rack and pushing them head first into small electrical tunnels; and c) the hospital superintendent. Let us not neglect the hospital superintendent.

She is a woman of about forty, distinguished in bearing, but without a touch of warmth in her manner. She is dressed, half as nurse, half as laywoman, her main professional emphasis being a puckered white cap, shaped like an inverted teacup and circumferenced at the bottom with a strip of black velvet. She has squirrel-grey eyes, and a sharply pointed nose that looks as though it felt very cold; and she continually purses her lips so as to seem always on the verge of expectorating a fruit pit.

When you first see the hospital superintendent she will be patrolling up and down behind the counter, obviously waiting for some problem to arise over which she may exercise her authority. Her air of proprietorship in the place makes one believe that she is more than an official: possibly a grandniece of Mr. Babson's, for the philanthropist died in 1919, and it would not be wrong to accuse him of having left his affairs in charge of his descendants. Furthermore, one feels it would be very much to his taste to know that the institution is now in charge of this ominous, germ-proof lady who might be counted on to perpetuate the Babson theory of illness: "an unnecessary, economic nuisance" (I quote from the old gentleman's address to the Kiwanis Club) "afflicting the thoughtless members of our community, and which ought to be got rid of as thoroughly and expeditiously as possible." (Loud applause, cheers, etc.)

If you happen to be a Catholic priest (and I hope for the moment you are not), your first encounter with Miss (?) Babson (?) will not be pleasant. She does not like Catholic priests. Doesn't she? Or am I too sensitive on this point? Why do I seem to be able to tell whenever anyone looks at me whether or not they have aversions for my religion and profession? I am not good at suffering for the Faith. I thrive on affection, and can never cope with a smoldering enemy. When I am disliked I lose all powers of social intercourse. Interruptions occur in my digestion. I become rigid, cautious, frightened, ungrammatical.

If you happen not only to be a Catholic priest, but are, in addition to that, a coward, you will resort to a subterfuge when the hospital superintendent approaches you with that machine-gun look in her eye. In order not to be shot down in cold blood, you will try to pretend by your manner that you are some sort of Evangelical minister. And how is this done? The method is twofold: feign deafness, and put on your pince-nez glasses. I have not the slightest notion why this formula works, but it does. I am not aware that the Protestant minister-hood is conspicuously deaf; I know many Catholic clergymen who are addicted to pince-nez glasses. But this juncture of afflictions will completely protect you against the hospital superintendent, especially if you embellish it with a cultured air of absent-mindedness and begin turning over the pages of the hospital register with the blithe insolence of a child.

"Can I help you?" the hospital superintendent will snap as

she eyes with annoyance the liberties you are taking with the hospital register.

"I beg your pardon?" (Stop fiddling with the hospital register and put your hand behind your ear like a shell.)

"Do you wish to see one of the patients?"

"Yes it is. But it's nice and cool in here just the same."

"What is your business? What do you want?" (Her voice becomes refreshingly feminine when it is pitched high, and makes one believe that in her youth she may have taken singing lessons and have been a very charming little girl.)

"Is this the Babson Memorial Hospital?" (Remove your pince-nez glasses and begin to clean them.)

"Yes. Whom do you wish to see?"

"Oh, excuse me. I thought you were one of the nurses."

"One of the *nurses*! I . . . am the hospital . . . *superintendent*!"

This last statement, dictatorially enunciated, has reminded her that if she lets this situation get out of hand, it will hurt her prestige before the rest of the personnel at the information desk. Whereupon, she wheels about and says sharply to the telephone operator: "Miss Lyons! Take charge of him, please; and find out his business here!"; and then clicks her heels and disappears defiantly into an adjoining room.

The telephone operator now takes "him" in hand and approaches smilingly.

"Can I help you, Father?" (Disguises henceforth will be useless. There is a kinship of spirit between Catholics and an almost instantaneous recognition. There is not the slightest danger of your being mistaken by Miss Lyons. You might as well make the sign of the cross and give yourself away.)

"May I see Mrs. Nolan, please?"

"Certainly, Father. She is on the fourth floor, room number forty-six."

"Thank you. And by the way—is that lady's name Miss Babson?"

"No, her name is Miss Fussfield," and, in a whisper: "She's a Ku-Kluxer, Father, if you ask me."

"I see." (It's marvelous how you can hear whispers when you want to.)

On your way up to Mrs. Nolan's room you will have no trouble with the elevator boy.

As you alight from the elevator and walk quietly along the fourth corridor, you will pass a pantry out of which will come floating a nurse, appareled like a white butterfly. She is not Mrs. Nolan's nurse—Mrs. Nolan's nurse is absent for the moment, having gone to the supply room for bandages and other paraphernalia—but she will be glad to confirm your remembrance that number forty-six is the room you are seeking.

Mrs. Nolan's door is open. Evidently she has been prepared for visitors. Stealthily you approach the threshold and look in.

Your first reaction to Mrs. Nolan's predicament will be one of horror. Everyone is, somehow, frightensome in a hospital. We wear our bodies so lightly when we are in good health that we often fail to notice what grotesque substances they are, until we see one like this, stretched on a bed and dejected with a disease. For what could be more grotesque than an exhausted animal with long hair . . . five feet eight inches in length . . . partially paralyzed in its movements . . . wrapped in sheets and propped upon a pillow . . . the daily subject of experiment by puzzled doctors who are endeavoring to correct defects in its mechanism and overcome poisons secreted in its chemistry?

Can this wretched object be Mrs. Nolan, whom one has been anticipating so eagerly? Has this tragic makeshift the power to laugh, sing, dream, pray? Does it possess qualities like intelligence, innocence, patience, reverence, resignation? Is it conscious of Mrs. Nolan's personality, and does it answer to her name?

Look! Those light-blue mirrors under its forehead have unveiled and are regarding you with attention. Those delicately structured instruments at the ends of its arms are beckoning. Those waxen features are achieving a unity, assuming an expression, asserting their spirituality. Some mysterious lightning has flamed behind that oval mask and suffused it with a sudden loveliness. Thought—abstract, angelic, undimensioned—has taken place inside that gracefully turning head. It opens its mouth. It speaks.

"Good afternoon!"

"Good afternoon!"

"Won't you come in?"

"Certainly."

(There is a pause.)

"Are you Mrs. Nolan?"

"Yes, I am."

Let the materialists take this miracle to their laboratories and solve it as they may.

THE PROBLEM MIND

I

I SHALL make it my business to go back nine or ten years, as the movies can, and I shall figuratively plant my camera and sound-machine on the deck of an Italian liner, three days out from Naples and en route to New York, just passing when we board it, the last fringes of shore on the outposts of the Azores.

Let us not blame the boat for the dreary individual I shall describe traveling thereon. He simply *happened* to take an Italian liner at Naples. He might, if he had cared to, have gone to Cherbourg and come home on the *Ile de France*, or the

Berengaria. The same situation would have occurred, and the tale now being told would be exactly the same.

Now that we are on the boat, a good way to get a *locale* will be to go to the B deck (the fashionable one in the *de luxe* section) and follow Chico, the deck-steward, as he passes down the line of steamer chairs, dispensing to blanketed sea-gazers their afternoon rations of crackers and tea. (There's chicken soup, too, if you wish it, and an uncountable variety of pastries.)

Chico wheels a wagon, and each customer is expected to stop him and select from an assortment of trays whatever delectables or drinkables may suit his fancy. As we go along with Chico we see people sprawled on deck-chairs in all attitudes of repose, proving what an infinite number of designs the human body can assume when the will abandons it to the law of gravity. In that long procession of distorted figures you will observe a rhombus, a rhomboid, a truncated prism, a parallelopiped, and will be tempted to poke each with a stick to see what sort of human personality emerges from the diagram. Let us examine one.

That right-angle triangle with its feet stuck out in front of it and a folded blanket on its stomach, is Mr. Wells, a thin, sad-faced little man of middle age, possessed of a moustache and an evident dyspepsia, who looks during journeys as if he wished he had never taken them, and who is particularly pitiable at sea. Mr. Wells has been asleep, but wakes up when Chico confronts him, and after a bewildered conference with himself selects a cup of tea with lemon and no sugar, and an innocuous cracker unviolated by any icing. Mr. Wells stares at his food, and when he has assured himself that the tea is really tea and the cracker really a cracker, he smiles a tired smile, indicating not that he is too tired to smile, but that he is tired of trying to find something worth smiling at.

Mr. Wells could easily be dispensed with, but, now that I have stopped to notice him, I must not in charity leave him unexplained. His pitiableness cannot be all due to dyspepsia. Indeed, one wonders if some of his dyspepsia is not due to his pitiableness—a vicious circle in the physio-psychological order, for soul and body can get at each other in this way and undigested ideas will often cause a good dinner to be badly assimilated.

Mr. Wells is suffering from—I feel certain of it—ocean trouble. Ocean trouble is not to be confused with seasickness; the latter is an affair of the intestines, the former of the intellect. If I may put it boldly, Mr. Wells is mentally unable to digest the ocean. You see, he has assumed that the ocean is a problem, and it is not, it is a mystery.

There is a great difference between a problem and a mystery. In the one you expect ultimately to find a solution, although you are in darkness about it when you tackle it for the first time. In the other you never expect to find a solution, but keep on getting more and more light as you go on. A problem is exhaustible, a mystery never. A problem is meant for one's scientific mind, a mystery for one's poetic and religious mind. A problem caters to one's sense of curiosity, a mystery to one's sense of wonder. A cross-word puzzle is a problem, and so is a detective story (erroneously called a "mystery story"), and the fact that such diversions are taken so seriously in our day is a sign that our sense of religion and poetry has begun to decay. In solving a cross-word puzzle you begin with a maximum of perplexity and proceed through a maximum of annoyance until you come to a maximum of light. And then what? And then nothing! No truth has been acquired, the mind has enlarged in scope not one inch. A disorder deliberately planned by the cross-word puzzle maker has been untangled. Interest in the subject ceases immediately and permanently. For there is nothing in the world so uninteresting as a completed cross-word puzzle, unless it be a completed detective story when the last chapter has been reached and the "mystery" solved.

This question of problems would be innocent enough if it were confined to the realm of recreation and entertainment. Puzzles, charades and make-believe murders serve their purpose in refreshing the mind when it is tired. But in the ethos of which Mr. Wells is a product it is assumed that the mind is always tired, incapable of ever grappling with thought in its own right, and needing constantly to be fed formulas that promise ultimately to do away with the necessity of thinking altogether. Through a mass of informative literature, compendious in content, ranging all the way from prophecies (about the past) to histories (about the future), Mr. Wells has managed to touch spots in the whole field of knowledge. But unfortunately he has studied each subject with the wrong side of his brain. He has learned theology from a mathematician, ethics from a physiologist, metaphysics from a novelist, and psychology from a breeder of rats. He has studied chemistry theologically, theology biologically, biology sociologically, and sociology paleontologically. He is already on the verge (with the aid of a Sunday magazine Messiah) of studying his own existence fourth dimensionally, which offers difficulties when one has only a three-dimensioned head. Problems are sometimes not fun.

And yet, confronted on a sea voyage with that large, importunate item, the ocean, Mr. Wells feels faint rumblings in his conscience, more poignant even than the rumblings in his stomach, warning him that all is not well when one tries to dismiss the ocean as a problem. For the ocean is, as far as the imagination goes, an infinite thing. True, the ocean is in fact limited, and conceptually we know that it has boundaries, and that navigators and surveyors can mark them. But our imaginations can never stretch as far as our numerical calculations. A thousand miles of water, two thousand miles of water, are all the same to the imagination. Add the Atlantic Ocean to the Pacific Ocean, and *imaginatively* you have the same ocean, because the picture-making faculty in man's mind is incapable of snap-shotting even a millionth part of either. It is the same way with the stars. A million stars or two million stars, though mathematically vastly dissimilar, make exactly the same imaginative and emotional impression on the mind.

God intended it this way, and wanted, as far as was possible, to represent His own infinity in the magnitude of the created things He sets before our eyes. *Benedicite, sol et luna Domino: Benedicite, stellae coeli, Domino: Benedicite, maria et flumina, Domino.* From the imaginary infinity of the things we see we are intended to rise to the actual infinity of Him Whom we cannot see. This is the ocean's chief purpose—compared to which its secondary purpose as a usable thing is almost nil—namely, to be a religious symbol proclaiming its Creator's immeasurableness and everlastingness. But to a non-contemplative intelligence like Mr. Wells's, filled with the rubbish of tinkerism and problemism, the ocean is merely a bulky absurdity, an extravagant squandering of water, ceaselessly swishing and swaying, put there by nobody, serving no purpose and making no sense.

To one in this frame of mind (and the steamship companies assume that all their passengers are in this frame of mind) there is only one thing to do about the ocean when it confronts you, surrounds you, overwhelms you on all sides. Ignore it. Turn your attention to those distractive enterprises abundantly supplied by the steamship companies for the diversion of passengers to whom earth's wonders have no spiritual significance. Go in heavily for hoop-throwing, ping-pong, shuffle-board, or horse-racing with wooden horses. You may not enjoy yourself—recreation is never enjoyable when it is made a career—but at least you will avoid that mental *mal de mer* that comes from being stumped by the too-muchness of the Atlantic.

It is to Mr. Wells's credit that although the ocean bores him, he is even more exasperated by the skittishness of steamship entertainment. He has already told his wife what profane terms he wishes to apply to ping-pong as a way for a sensible man to spend an afternoon at sea; and she has also learned that he prefers to be polysyllabically damned rather than dress up in his pajamas, come down to the dining hall, and compete for a prize in the masquerade.

I admire Mr. Wells in these matters both for the strength of his aversions and the strength of his epithets. And so I leave him, sitting on a deck chair, gazing blankly at the briny deep, with a cup of tea gurgling in his stomach, and a couple of sea waves slopping in his head.

2

But, if the reader insists, there may be a certain amount of pleasure in seeing this little gentleman in action before I leave him forever. I offer him in an altercation with his wife, at the point in their voyage when they are passing the islands of the Azores.

In the course of their argument it will be convenient to refer to him as Edgar, and to Mrs. Wells as Eleanor. She is a large, pleasant-faced woman, who has endured this waspy little bozo for well on to thirty years. Her patience is as inexhaustible as her stupidity is innocuous and as his conceit is acid. They begin:

ELEANOR *(dropping her knitting and pointing in the distance)*: Edgar, is that island way over there an *Azore*?

EDGAR *(awakening from a drowse)*: Is what a what?

ELEANOR: That island! Is it an *Azore*?

EDGAR: My dear, you don't say *an Azore*. The islands are called *The Azores*. But you don't call one of them *an Azore*.

ELEANOR: What do you call one of them?

EDGAR: You call one of them *one of the Azores*.

ELEANOR: Oh, what's the difference!

EDGAR: My dear, there's a lot of difference. *An Azore* is a solecism.

ELEANOR: It's a what?

EDGAR: It isn't said. People don't use the expression *an Azore*.

ELEANOR: I don't see that it matters what expression you use as long as you make yourself clear.

EDGAR: But that's the point! You don't make yourself clear. Furthermore, you made the same sort of silly mistake when we were in Switzerland.

ELEANOR: What did I say in Switzerland?

EDGAR: Don't you remember in the hotel in Interlaken, when you were pointing out the window at one of the mountains, and you asked Mrs. Featherstone: *Is that an Alp?*

ELEANOR: Well, it *was* an Alp, wasn't it?

EDGAR: It was *not* an Alp. The term is incorrect. It was *one of the Alps*, do you see? . . . It was *one of Thee Alps!*

ELEANOR: I don't see why you have to say *one of Theee Alps* in order to speak about a simple Alp.

EDGAR: Listen, my dear! Will you *please* listen? . . . There are certain nouns in the English language—I mean the English language as intelligent people speak it—there are certain nouns, I say, which we call *collective nouns*, and they have no singular form.

ELEANOR: Oh, don't bother going into details.

EDGAR: I *will* bother. I have to go around with you constantly, and listen to your asinine mistakes . . . and I have to suffer shame because of your ignorance. And I want you to correct it. I am trying to explain the whole thing to you in a nutshell. Can't you see what I'm trying to do?

ELEANOR: Well, go on.

EDGAR *(becoming very professorial)*: Now, we call our country *The United States of America*. Is that correct? . . . Eleanor! Am I right in saying that we call our country *The United States of America*?

ELEANOR *(yawns by way of saying)*: "Yes!"

EDGAR: Very good. And that's a collective noun. *United States of America* is a collective noun. . . . But you wouldn't say of one of the States—let us say Michigan—you wouldn't say of Michigan that it was *A United State*, would you?

ELEANOR: I don't see why not, if they're *all* United States.

EDGAR: Wrong, my dear. You'd say of Michigan that it was *one* of the United States.

ELEANOR: Yes, but there are forty-seven others!

EDGAR: There are forty-seven others? What the devil has *that* got to do with it?

ELEANOR: Edgar, you're getting all excited about such a simple little thing.

EDGAR: Good grammar, my dear, is *not* a simple little thing. It's a necessary adjunct of correct thought. And when a man has to go around, as I do, listening to his wife perpetrate the most outrageous barbarisms . . .

ELEANOR: I *don't* perpetrate outrageous barbarisms. I made two teeny little mistakes, *an Alp* and *an Azore*, and now you're flying off the handle.

EDGAR: I'm *not* flying off the handle. . . . I am talking to you very calmly, very, very calmly. But I am going to explain this matter to you if it takes me all night! Do you hear?

ELEANOR: Please hurry. The bell for dinner will be ringing soon, and you know I must go down and dress.

EDGAR *(getting back to work again):* Listen, my dear! You've heard of a disease called *the mumps*, haven't you? You remember Gladys had the mumps when she was a child? . . .

ELEANOR: Of course.

EDGAR: Well, when Gladys had the mumps, would you ever think of pointing to one of the swellings on her neck and saying: That's *a mump*? Would you ever think of saying such a thing?

ELEANOR: No, I'd call it a lump!

EDGAR: Eleanor, please! Don't be so tantalizing. . . . Will you please stick to the point? . . . Would you or would you not call one of Gladys' mumps *a mump*? Answer me!

ELEANOR: A mump or a lump, what's the difference?

EDGAR: The next thing you'll be wanting to do is to call me, your husband, *a Well*. I'm not *a Well*. I'm *a Wells* and you're *a Wells:* and together we're *the Wellses*, do you see? We're not *the Wells*!

ELEANOR: Why not?

EDGAR: Because *Wells* is a singular noun.

ELEANOR: It sounds plural to me.

EDGAR: My dear, it is not plural.

ELEANOR: Every noun ending in s is plural; I learned that when I was a little girl at school.

EDGAR: Damnation, Eleanor! Listen! There are *thousands* of nouns ending in s that are not plural. *Thouuuuusands* of them!

ELEANOR: Name one!

EDGAR *(he cannot think of one at the moment, which annoys him greatly; finally, after an intense cerebration he breaks out with):* Well, how about *basis?* Ha. Thought I couldn't think of one, eh? Well how will *basis* suit you? That ends in s. Is it singular or plural?

ELEANOR: I don't know.

EDGAR: You don't know!!

ELEANOR: It sounds just as plural to me as it does singular.

EDGAR: My dear, it is *not* plural. The singular is *basis*, and the plural is *bases*. You've often heard me say I'd like to put my business on a sound *basis*, haven't you? You never heard me say I'd like to put my business on a sound *bases*, did you?

ELEANOR: Oh dear, you give me a word with so many s's in it that the singular, if there is a singular, sounds just as plural to me as the plural does.

EDGAR: All right, I'll give you a word with only one stinking s in it and see how that satisfies you.

ELEANOR: I'm afraid there isn't any such word, Edgar.

EDGAR: And I'm afraid there is, Eleanor. And I've got it. *Dais! Dais!* Do you know what a dais is?

ELEANOR: What did you say?

EDGAR: I said: do you know what a dais is?

ELEANOR: Flowers?

EDGAR: Flowers!!

ELEANOR: Aren't they?

EDGAR: Aren't who? Aren't what? What the devil are you talking about?

ELEANOR: Daisies.

EDGAR: I never mentioned the word daisies. I'm not asking you what are daisies. I'm asking you if you know what a dais is? A dais is a throne, or rather a little platform that elevates the throne. "The Queen stood on the dais." That means she stood on the little platform that elevates the throne. And the word is singular, do you hear? And it ends in s. And there is only one *s* in it! (*He sits back triumphantly in his chair, and draws a deep breath.*)

ELEANOR: You can't expect me to use a word I never heard of.

EDGAR: I'm not asking you to *use* it, my dear. I'm merely asking you to *acknowledge* it. *Dais* is the word we have both been looking for.

ELEANOR (*candidly*): I haven't been looking for it. And I think you made it up.

EDGAR (*sitting up rigidly again*): Made it up! Do you mean to accuse me of dishonesty?

ELEANOR: You're losing your temper. I think it's silly of you to lose your temper. Why can't you smile once in awhile?

EDGAR: Do you expect me to smile at your ignorance, your *crass* and *astounding* ignorance, in not knowing that there is a word in the English language called dais. It's spelt d-a-i-s, and pronounced *day-iss*. There's a diaeresis over the i. . . . There's another word, by the way, *diaeresis*. That ends in s too. But, damnation, if you don't know what a *dais* is, how can I expect you to know what a *diaeresis* is?

ELEANOR: I'm willing to let the matter drop.

EDGAR (*firmly*): And I too, if you are convinced. Are you convinced?

ELEANOR: I'll be convinced when you give me a word, a sensible word that people understand, that ends in s and is singular.

EDGAR: I *gave* you such a word, my dear.

ELEANOR: You said there were thousands of such words. You had an awfully hard time to think of even one. And it's a word I never heard of.

EDGAR: There are thousands. And if you'll be patient, I'll be glad to give you another one. *(suddenly.)* Asparagus! Just thought of it! Fancy my not remembering dear old *asparagus*! Don't tell me you don't know what *asparagus* is?

ELEANOR: Yes, but it's plural.

EDGAR *(stumped)*: *Asparagus* is plural?

ELEANOR: Isn't it?

EDGAR *(he sees he had better watch his step)*: It *can* be plural, Eleanor. It *can* be, my dear. But it can *also* be singular. *(And then petulantly.)* It counts for *me*, my dear, just as much as it counts for you. You can say *asparagus* of a quantity, or an *asparagus* of a single item.

ELEANOR: Edgar! You know right well you ought to say *a piece of asparagus* if you're talking of only one.

EDGAR *(completely on the defensive)*: I maintain you can say both, my dear; *asparagus*, for a number, and *an asparagus* for one. The word *has* to have a singular form, and if it hasn't a singular form, you have to invent one. Otherwise, you can't talk about the thing intelligently.

ELEANOR: Oh dear! That's why I said *an Azore;* and there you go blaming me and starting such a quarrel.

EDGAR: Ugh! *(It has been the knock-out blow; he subsides in his chair, folds his hands on his stomach, and is in evident intestinal distress.)*

ELEANOR *(genuinely repentant)*: There now, Edgar! The last thing I wanted to do was to make you cross. And I'll bet you'll get indigestion again from becoming so excited. . . . I'll go and get you a glass of water and a soda-mint tablet.

(She gets up and covers him with a blanket; he moans slightly and peers at her through the slits of his eyelids. She bulks large in silhouette against the horizon; and as she proceeds to waddle down the promenade deck, like something inflated in a Mardi Gras procession, he is seized with a sudden inspiration. . . . He throws the blanket to the floor, leaps to his feet, cups his hands about his mouth and shouts after her):

EDGAR: Hippopotamus! Eleanor? Hippopotamus! Now try to argue *that* away!!

Mr. Wells, flushed with satisfaction because of this final, palpable and uncharitable hit, stretches his legs, exercises his arms, buttons his coat, and decides to set out on a constitutional walk around the boat. Nothing like keeping fit for future arguments, future problems. So off he goes, jauntily, with exalted nose, inhaling deep lungfuls of air, restored, it would seem, to a normal function in his digestive processes.

Meanwhile the Azores vanish in the distance, the sky begins to be dotted with early stars. The great expanses of the thunderous Atlantic encircle the ship on all sides. Nature, in the wonderful simplicities of sky and sea, pleads for attention, begs to be assumed for the mystery she is and to be used in symbol for purposes of adoration and prayer; and gets in return only a series of sniffs from Mr. Wells's nose, as he whirls around the boat.

A SYMPATHETIC SUMMARY

I

ON EVERY big trans-Atlantic liner sailing from Europe to New York—save perhaps in the dead slough of the winter season —you will find a group of what are best designated "healthy, wealthy Americans." Where this inexhaustible supply of star-spangled-bannered folk who are both financial and fit comes from, and how they manage to be returning from Europe so frequently, I do not know. But there is a generous collection of them on every ship.

They usually travel in full or partial families: a father, mother, two daughters and a son; a mother, daughter and two sons; a father, son and daughter; occasionally a lone daughter or a lone son affiliated with some friends. The first thing one notices about these healthy, wealthy Americans is their indescribable sameness. They are so stereotyped in kind one could almost write a formula for them. I should like to undertake such a formula for the father in a family of four, which includes a vivacious, gaunt, over-painted mother; a rather handsome college-boy son (probably Princeton); and an athletic daughter who has been completely finished at a finishing school. Father's official title among his dear ones is *Dad*.

Dad: a moderately tall, smooth shaven, slightly bald banking or business man, between fifty and sixty; well tanned, white-trousered, fond of a cigar; with a full-toned, monotonously masculine voice, and a self-contented, deliberately sustained smile; whose main chore at sea is to point out things; to ask the family if they have seen this or that, report on the ship's log, sight objects on the horizon, whales, other boats, etc., and point them out.

Dad is always the first of his party to rise in the morning, usually eats breakfast alone, and never gets seasick. He reads through three books while crossing: the best-selling novel of the year; a detective story, and a popular book about sociology or finance. Of the first two books he invariably reports, "a darn good story"; of the third, "some interesting things in it, but I don't quite agree with him."

When the ship docks *Dad* is the first to spy friends or relatives standing on the pier, shouting "There's Laura waving to us!"; and then "Come on Ida. Come on children. Has everyone

got everything? Son, have you got the keys to the trunks?",
etc., etc.

Dad is intensely preoccupied with trying to keep fit, with
keeping young. Whenever he meets a stranger the very first
thing he wants to discover is the stranger's age, and even when
not bold enough to ask it, is always sizing it up, arriving at
some secret, plausible figure.

Dad likes nothing better than to be handled as though he
were a youngster, relishes nothing better than a good slap
on the back. He loves to be asked to go golfing, and always
has an imminent fishing trip memorandumed in the back of his
mind. He dances too, and is equally at home with young or old
ladies; dances well, indeed, but would dance much better if
he didn't try to be so "young" at it. For the past fifteen years,
while being perfunctorily kissed, hand-shaken or back-slapped
on his birthday, he has never failed to say "I feel as young as
a colt."

Dad is a persistent taker of turkish baths, devotes hours
weekly to being shaved, rubbed, manicured, pomaded, etc.;
has spent a small fortune on hair remedies, treatments, etc.
(some of them really gruesome). He gargles and tooth-brushes
faithfully, and washes religiously once an hour. Towels, other
than being slightly rumpled, look as clean after he has used
them as before. About a hundred times a day he flexes his
muscles to see if they are still working.

Dad is constantly on the point of "cutting down" on things,
on eating, smoking, drinking, and is capable in short spells of
acute acts of self-denial. He has read uncountable health books,
and is forever giving his family little therapeutic exhortations,
such as "Come on now, let's all get to bed!"—a remark in
which he is seldom if ever noticed; "Come on now, let's all
get some fresh air!" At table his almost perpetual incantation
into the ears of his daughter is "Eat slowly, darling!" "Darling"
looks at him alternately pityingly or annoyed, seems momen-

tarily protected against the ravages of indigestion, or else irritated at the thought of its possibility, and then goes on eating about as before. Yet in this phrase "Eat slowly, darling!" *Dad's* features assume for one flashing instant a benevolence, innocence, lovability. The maid who serves them dinner at home has often noticed this.

Barber-shop, brokerage and bridge: these are pretty nearly the high spots in *Dad's* life: sticking-plaster and stock-market reports, interspersed with a trip to Europe. In Europe as in America *Dad* is greatly annoyed at the slum areas in the large cities, at the faces of the underpaid and the undernourished. "Can't the Government do something for these people?" he always remarks in a sudden burst of charity. "Haven't they got any public welfare organizations?" Twice a year his conscience troubles him in these matters and drives him to his pocketbook. He never fails to contribute a generous cheque annually to the Red Cross and the Community Chest drives. *Dad* always purrs contentedly at dinner on the days of these donations, always sleeps better within the octave.

Though doctors have never been able to explain it, nor detect it in the prescribed six months' physical examination, *Dad* makes his departure from this world by one of two routes: apoplexy, or coronary thrombosis. He had been feeling "as fit as a fiddle" just before dinner. Shortly after dinner he swooned in his chair. *Son* ran to his assistance. *Daughter* screamed, *Mother* became tearful through smelling salts.

"Good old dad!"

"Oh I can't stand it. It's perfectly horrible!"

"Be sure to get the very best doctors."

The very best doctors come, three of them, so as to hold "a consultation." Sufficient drugs are administered so as to keep *Dad's* consciousness out of reach of all pain. It is invariably reported in the papers that he "died in a coma," which is not true. He was *put in a coma* by variations of veronal, luminol and morphine, as the day and night nurses can testify. "The very best doctors" like an unconscious patient when they're stumped, so that they can "consult" with greater professional quiet and report to the prospective widow unannoyed by the indecorous accompaniment of groans. A groaning man does somehow give the impression of not being properly attended to.

Son attends the funeral manfully, in dark clothes, with bowed head. A minister is resurrected for the occasion and reads a text that is more impressive than comforting. *Son* escorts *Mother* who *could* walk, but prefers to be carried mostly. She keeps pressing a handkerchief to her lips, and in the end all but swallows it. Something in her really wants to cry, if only to indicate that a vacuum of some sort has been arrived at; but she lacks any spiritual certitude toward the after-life capable of supporting tears. One can cry at a death, but not at an annihilation. One could rage; but there are sensible reasons for not becoming quite so forcible as that.

Daughter does not attend the funeral. Everyone agrees it is better for her not to. She spends a fortnight with friends at Greenwich or Darien, lives largely on stimulants and sedatives, and reads from end to end the year's volumes of *Liberty*, *Fortune*, *Time*, *Life* and other magazines with transcendental names. In the end she gets coaxed into a recuperation by some vigorous sets of tennis and by some good sound plunges in a swimming pool.

(N. B. A novelist, which I am not, and a Freudian, which I am neither, will complain that I have sent *Dad* to his grave without any mention of the complex determinants of his life, the chorus girl, manicurist, stenographer, who lurks in the background and in whose company the amorous deficiencies of his career were reconditioned and recompensed. I omit these ladies deliberately. First, because I do not think they were necessarily there; and second, because it would require little

art and no imagination to describe them. I stand on *Dad* as
sufficiently tragic as he is, without a single triangular move-
ment in his affections, or a single blot against his moral integ-
rity.)

2

But we have anticipated. *Dad* is not yet dead, and *Mother*
is very much not yet a widow. You would not think so to see
her prancing about the boat. I hesitate to call her *Mother*, not
on my own score, but because *Dad* never does, though the
children do, *Son* with some warmth, *Daughter* with none.
However, she can be *Mother* to us, provided we remember
that to *Dad* she is *Ida* (or *Ada* or *Eva*, as the case may be);
is "my dear" when he wishes to be particularly instructive or
sarcastic; and is sometimes not denominated at all, but only
implicitly included in such exclamations as "For God's sake!"
or "What the devil did you say that for?"

Mother has interests much like a butterfly. She hovers here
and there for instants, and likes nothing better than to alight
on the coat-lapel of a celebrity. Meeting celebrities is part of
the necessary business of her existence. Her social charms
have in a single season been exercised on everything from a
noted entomologist to a heavyweight wrestler, including, of
course, the usual sprinkling of violinists, poets, novelists,
actors, war generals and bankrupt British noblemen—at whose
stories one is "thrilled," at whose playing one is "entranced,"
at whose exploits one is "terrified," at whose verses one is
"fascinated," at whose manners one is "electrified." Where
perspective is lacking *Mother* can supply it, and is known to
have remembered a celebrated Russian cellist, at whose art the
Tsar was wont to be moved to tears, by nothing more than
"he had the most curious feet."

In literature, fiction is *Mother's* single fare, and the sum of
culture enjoyed by Mr. Somerset Maugham and Miss Fanny
Hurst conjointly would constitute for her a millennium. In

the drama and cinema her preferences are all for actresses who play their parts in such a personal way as to extinguish entirely the character they are portraying. She enjoys seeing Lynn Fontanne as Lynn Fontanne in Lynn Fontanne, or Greta Garbo as Greta Garbo in Greta Garbo. As for her spiritual life, you would pity *Mother* in conflict with, let us say, an ethical principle from which she has chosen to vary. She has in reserve a much nicer God than the traditional one where sanctions for sin are discussed and where the indecency of Eternal Punishment is brought into question. This temporary Deity vanishes as soon as *Mother's* conscience conflicts are over, nor does she ever pray to Him or thank Him, not even for His niceness in not having created Hell.

On shipboard it cannot be denied that *Mother* has one marvelous moment in the day. It is on the way down to dinner in the evening. Unsuccessfully juvenile in her mornings and afternoons—sweatered, scarfed, short-stockinged, all out of proportion with her age; overemphasized in her wrinkles, her yawns, her efforts to jack herself up by constitutional walks, facial treatments (in the manner of the Swedes), and even little divertissements in the gymnasium—there is one golden hour when *Mother* overcomes these handicaps and emerges like a queen. Promptly at five o'clock she goes to her stateroom to dress for dinner. It takes a long time. It takes nearly two hours. It never terminates until her door has been knocked upon, pounded upon, banged upon by *Dad* with successively firmer implementalizations of his fist. A kick on the door is sometimes added for good measure, and *Daughter's* voice is enlisted to implore through the key-hole: "Mother, will you *please* hurry?"

But *Mother* cannot hurry. Why should she? Dinner is the one affair of the day when that inherent quality of good-taste, which is hidden in every lady and never dies, induces her to assert her feminine charm in the manner of the matron which she is, rather than in the manner of the manikin which she is not. Whatever else *Mother* does to disconcert her hus-

band, she marches down to dinner as his wife, not as his stenog-
rapher.

After a nearly two hours' bout with powder, cream, rouge,
perfume, pins, things dropped and picked up again, things
mislaid and recovered, much marveling in the mirror, surveil-
lance in all attitudes, selection of gown, slippers, flowers, ad-
justment of jewelry, *Mother* throws a silk shawl over her
shoulders, puts a final crimp in her hair, slips the lock in the
stateroom door and steps daintily into the corridor, so
resplendent that even *Dad* forgets his temper and must mo-
mentarily acknowledge her beauty. *Daughter*—too athletic for
aesthetic decoration—is a perfect slattern beside her. *Daughter*
looks like something picked up on the beach and embellished
with a temporary ruffle.

Mother, on the other hand, seems to have out-flowered
from fairyland. And all the way down the aisles, smiling and
sparkling to everyone including the sailors, she proceeds to her
nocturnal conquest of the dining hall. *Son* joins them in the
foyer. There may or may not be cocktails, depending on the
gentlemen's endurance without them up to this point. The
main stairway is reached. The descent is made royally down
the plushy steps. And into the lights, the tinkles, the music,
the murmurings of the grand refectory, *Mother* floats. Heads
turn. Eyes enlarge. Little gurgles of appreciation follow her
on all sides. The waiter adjusts her in her chair. And then
follows, with excited delight, the matter of the menu.

But alas for the briefness of this triumph!

Men grow handsomer as a dinner progresses. Women de-
cline. If they are young, their charms can be revived later in
the ballroom. Not so if they are middle-aged. *Mother's* fas-
cination manages to survive the appetizer and the soup, and
stands up fairly well through the entrée. But it begins to wilt
at the roast, and is all but exhausted at the salad. Coffee in the
lounge after dinner is for *Mother* not a stimulation but a
restorative.

At eight o'clock *Mother's* hour is definitely over. At eight-fifteen there appears the first fatal yawn. At eight-thirty she is more yawn than not. At nine she must leave the company and go into the open air. This she usually does alone, humming a little ancient tune, that sounds very intimate, small and discordant beside the strains of the orchestra blaring through the dance-hall window. After this airing there can be a restful talk with some quiet person, if such can be found. And it is noticed that *Mother's* efforts at being fascinating definitely cease before ten o'clock. And just about this hour she begins to take a decided interest in people older than herself. She will possibly like to slip over to some elderly group and say: "Good evening! I've really been anxious to meet you ever since we got on the boat!"

At ten o'clock *Daughter* and *Son* are whirling in the dance hall. *Dad* is at his bridge, or in the bar. And here is *Mother* all alone in the moonlight talking to strangers. Her shawl is wrapped tightly around her, for the breeze is strong. At ten-thirty more yawns begin, despite such interests as dyspepsia, diabetes and the Civil War. *Mother* is solicitous, kindly, sympathetic, but the yawns persist. Eventually they become violent. It is so nice to be, in these late-night seizures, in the company of people whom one is not trying to impress. The bell tolls forward which announces that the waves are high and the boat pitching. It is time for *Mother* to go to bed. "Good night! Good night! Oh, yes indeed! Good night!"

Mother stumbles into her stateroom and quickly locks the door. Clothes come off much quicker than they went on. There is some ritual with face preparations to be undergone, but it is unenthusiastically fulfilled. Close to eleven she slips into bed having been preceded by a hot-water bottle. *Mother* seems very shriveled and small and cold as she slides under the coverlet and stretches out for the night. She takes up a novel and makes believe to read it for ten minutes or more. Then she switches off the light. Some memories of her dazzlingness in the early evening come back to her, but most of the relish is it is gone. For a long time after this she makes believe that she cannot go to sleep. But finally does. And the little purr of her breathing is soon lost in the thunderous susurration of the ship's motors.

*

MARY FAVORITE

I

MICHAEL COSTELLO is a young author who is always on the verge of writing a book. It is a pity he doesn't write one, because some of his ideas are stimulating. But, as is often the case with young authors, Michael has so many theories on writing they get in the way of his performance. He spends far too much time being displeased with the way other writers write.

Let us take, for instance, his criticism of John Galsworthy, the great English novelist.

John Galsworthy, so Michael maintains, died of exhaustion, from having tried to be in sex, singularity and sentiment every member of the Forsyte family. No artist, according to Michael, should attempt to be so fatuously vicarious.

A poet, willing to submit his observations, sympathies and insights to the purifying disciplines of meter and rhyme, might have given us the whole of the Forsyte saga in a few discreet stanzas. A dramatist, grouping the family on the stage, and arranging them around a central incident capable of eliciting a sufficiently varied and valuable number of human responses, might have settled their complications and told us all we ever needed to know about the Forsytes in less than three hours of acting time. But the novelist by whom the family was fabricated required hundreds and hundreds of pages, sequel after sequel, in order to show us that he could eat, walk, sleep, dream, even bathe like one of his characters.

Michael insists that all personality, even in literature, resists such intrusions. For personality is the principle of uniqueness in us that will allow us to savor in detailed experience no ego but our own. How one of the Forsytes felt when he looked up at the stars, or listened to his mother's voice, or was told some very bad news, even Shelley or Shakespeare might have guessed. But what he was thinking of when he picked his fingernails, gargled his throat, or digested his dinner, nobody else ever realized, not even Mr. Galsworthy. And so his death marked the end not only of his fiction, but also of his pretense.

Michael Costello warns his readers-to-be that when he writes *his* book, he will make no novelist's effort in it. And if he dies before it is finished, it will be of his own diseases, not of his heroine's hypertension or his hero's heart-trouble. Every single thought expressed in Michael's book is going to be his own. And if he agrees, as he does, with Aristotle's dictum that each individual soul is somehow all things (*anima est quodamodo onmia*) Michael insists on the *somehow*, lays stress on the *quodamodo*, even wanting to include in this disclaimer the strength of the Latin sound.

There follows a brief account of how Michael almost wrote one of his books.

2

"I beg your pardon!" said Michael to an attractive young girl who was coming out of Symphony Hall in Boston at the close of a concert by its celebrated orchestra.

It was late afternoon in April, very near to the end of the official season of full programs, chief conductor and complete personnel. The young lady was twenty years old, or thereabouts. She was tall and marvelously molded. She had a sure head, an abundance of unhindered hair, a notable neck, conspicuous elbows, and feet large enough to be worth standing on. Hers was that unique mixture of majesty and athletic made famous by the almost mythological daughters of th first families of Boston. She was dressed in blue and white, with the first touches of summer in her attire. She wore a suitable hat. Her ears, and eyes, were filled with music as she walked out of Symphony Hall, only to have her reverie rudely interrupted by the voice of a male stranger, saying to someone whom the circumstances demanded to be herself:

"I beg your pardon! Are you a Unitarian?"

She stopped and put her hand to her head, as if to discover with which of her powers she might cope with this situation. Finding it to be a problem of insolence, pure and simple, and beyond the reach of her lighter social graces, she dropped her long arm to her side, stretched herself to full height, and proceeded to give her questioner a sustained devastating, aristocratic stare.

"I know your name," he went on quickly and nervously, "because I heard someone say it as you went in for the concert. Your name is Mary Favorite. I think it is the loveliest name I ever heard. I was wondering about your religion. Because yours is a name just made for religion. Its religious overtones are tremendous. I am interested in such things because of the nature of my religious training. I am also a writer, and I sometimes fancy I can do a lot with a good idea if I ever get one. And you are a wonderful idea: you and your name. I am going to write a book about you. I do not need many details in order to do so, because an artist likes to create a person rather than copy one. But it would help if I knew your religion. I am making a guess that you are a Unitarian. Are you a Unitarian?"

She listened to this long apostrophe while breathing deep, indignant breaths. It must have seemed to her that it was some weird coda added to the concert, and that she had left the hall before the program inside was finished.

After another long stare, full of legitimate resentment and exquisite reserve, in which she fully established her credentials as a lady by not even letting it occur to her to call a policeman, she averted her head and stepped aside into the stream of exiting music-lovers pouring out of Symphony Hall. She departed, not by way of her limousine, which had been jacked up in a garage, as part of her contribution to the War effort of 1943. Instead, she walked resolutely, patriotically along the sidewalk, and disappeared in a nearby subway.

Michael has not seen or heard from her since.

And so his book, from there on, had to go on being a book about a supposed Mary Favorite, instead of about a real one.

But the slightest, most fleeting remembrance of the real Mary Favorite was going to be preserved in it, so Michael said.

For an artist, unlike God, cannot create out of nothing.

3

When Mary Favorite, in a state of calm consternation, took leave of Michael at the door of Symphony Hall, frankly he had no way of following her. To be sure, he had now seen her at close range, and would recognize her again in any crowd. To be sure, he had often traveled in the subway into which she had descended, and during the rush hours too. To be sure, he knew what it was like not to be able to find a seat, to hang on a strap, and, while making a vertiginous study of street-car advertisements, to be jostled by the swaying of the other passengers. He was even familiar with the route she would take: down to Park Street, and back again to Kenmore Station. Could he not throw all these disparate experience together and make one imaginary journey: that of accompanying Mary Favorite home the evening he had asked her that very pertinent, impertinent question?

Michael supposed he could; and by a judicious use of literary tricks he might make it seem that everywhere that Mary went her author was sure to go. But these detective tactics, other than to unearth what murders she had committed or what money she had stolen, would reveal very little of her intrinsic character. The problem Michael proposed to himself once he decided to launch Mary Favorite in literature, was to get inside her mind, listen with her ears, and see with her eyes, and try to discover why she was avoiding the celestial implications of her pretty name.

Identification of spirit with another Michael knew to be impossible. But union of spirit with another was achievable, it was said through love, and he often felt through prayer. Perhaps prayer, and the mutual amity of Michael's and Mary Favorite's Guardian Angels (neither of whom could fail to be interested in this fantastic, momentary meeting of their charges) might establish lines of communication between their thoughts, and turn them, for at least the space of a book, into a satisfactory heroine haunted by an author. *Perhaps* was all Michael could be sure of. But relying on that *perhaps* he was prepared to go on, in his own fashion, with the rest of her story.

4

And so, when Mary Favorite deposited her dime in the automatic turnstile through which one makes entrance to Symphony subway station, she did not hear the mysterious click of another little dime dropped in an instant later by Michael. It was a shame, thought Michael, to charge himself admission to his own subway, operating entirely in his own memory, built out of the masonry of his own mind. But even in matters of the imagination Michael felt it was better to observe all the routine procedures so as to keep the worlds of fact and fancy as closely allied as possible.

The platform on which they both stood in the subway station was packed. And so was the Park Street car when it came in. By dint of being pushed into it, they both got on. And, in the manner of vertical sardines, incarcerated in their own dimensions, pressed on all sides by various shoulders, elbows and shoes, they rolled, in a state of semi-suffocation, through a long tunnel of darkness held up by steel girders.

There was nothing to look at outside the window. Inside, one had a good view of a cross-section of someone's back, a portion of someone's chin, a number of bobbing, perspiring foreheads, and the rim of a lady's hat trying to protrude itself into one's eye.

Whatever else this journey was the time for, it was not the time for creative observation. And so Michael closed his eyes, held on to a strap for dear life, and proceeded to utilize the time till they got to Park Street, and thence till they reversed their direction in the forked route that leads back to Kenmore Station, by indulging in a serious and somewhat surgical reverie, calculated to pierce the religious smoke-screens which divided their cultures, his and Mary Favorite's, and which kept him from seeing his heroine clearly focused in the light of her divine destiny. It was fair business, Michael thought, for an author to do this objectively, honestly, and in the open; not insinuate it in a story, as a novelist would, and let it be all mixed up with emotional trivialities and petulant details. For Heaven comes clear when it comes at all. There are no nostalgias so great as those caused to a nation by religious confusion. And there is no loneliness so poignant as to be aware of an admired one who does not believe in your God.

5

The generic religion of the United States of America is meeting-house Christianity. Its ritual requires three items: a pew, a pulpit, and a preacher. Add to that a small organ, to assist in its single devotional indulgence: a hymn.

The meeting-house itself is a sacred edifice which looks something like a church, partly like a library, and a little like bank. It is often covered with ivy, and in more cultivated sections of our country, as in New England, is usually rich in historical reminiscences.

Meeting-house Christianity discourages an intellectual outlook on the subject of salvation, and thrives on sinceriti rather than on certitudes. Its theories in the field of Christian Doctrine are so diverse that its disciples have fairly run out of hyphens trying to link them all together. This program leaves it with a confused Christology, and even with a theology which is sometimes a matter of conjecture. The lifework of a devout meeting-house parishoner is to be a perpetual seeker after truth, whose proper chastisement comes from never being permitted to find it. Such asceticism, especially in the rural areas, has been responsible for untold heroisms: witness those shy-eyed farmers and sweet-visaged housewives, with countenances full of deep spiritual appeal, whose joyless humility and resolute resignation Grant Wood, the artist, has patiently commemorated in portraits as haunting as they are instructive.

Lacking system, even in its morals, meeting-house Christianity was bound to have an explosion of pride somewhere in its ranks, and it had one about a hundred years ago in the State of Massachusetts, by way of an eccentric doctrine known as Unitarianism. The Unitarians, many of whom were men of abstemious habits and great wealth, finding the Christianity they were experiencing too complex to be a reflection of God, delved into Deism and discovered a God too fastidious to become man. As a result the divinity of Christ went overboard in Boston as lightly as tea had gone overboard in an earlier revolt. But the genius of Christ, like the excellence of the flavor of tea, has never been questioned there. In Boston Christ continues to be quoted by Unitarians, more at tea parties than in church, and not for what He said but for what He "put so well."

Having unburdened itself of this lofty heresy, meeting-house Christianity went on at Biblical levels to evangelize the upper and lower middle-classes of our nation. But it was noticeable henceforth that its clergymen assumed their vocation to be less for the task of teaching than for the arts of preaching and edification. Texts from the Old and New Testament were chosen for their slogan value rather than for their inspired content, and if possessed of sufficient rhetorical resonance and literary allure, were mingled in sermons indiscriminately with the moralizings of good men. The hagiographer, the poet, the essayist, the historian and the statesman, all combined to supply the meeting-house minister with spiritual enthusiasm, and in communities in which there has been continuity and some sense of tradition, the result has been the best written and spoken English ever produced in our land.

In the more exclusive churches of middle-class Christianity the meeting-house exhortation offered at Sunday Service has, during the last half century, differed so slightly from the academic instruction offered daily at some nearby sectarian college that there have been mistaken vocations among parsons and professors, and satisfactory exchanges made later in life to the benefit of both pulpit and lecture platform. And whereas many a college curriculum has thereby been loaded with more disguised religion courses than it bargained for, many a congregation has reaped the reward of a much more liberal education than it contracted to receive in return for the slight tuition fee of a coin dropped on a collection plate.

Of liturgy, meeting-house Christianity (with the exception of one decorative outburst which is its own explanation) has none. Its liturgy has entirely escaped into subsidiary fraternal organizations, some with impressive names like the Knights of Pythias; some with curious names like the Odd Fellows; and others, under a more secular ritual, with nomenclatures held over from the hunting season: e.g., the Moose. One such movement went completely aboriginal and called itself the Red Men. But the majority of these sash-and-sword enterprises being unreliably religious and therefore not effectively fraternal, have disintegrated into mere groups of good-fellowship and many of them are now on the verge of becoming extinct.

The last loud echo of meeting-house liturgy subsiding among the elements, can be heard in the splashes of athletic Christian

SKETCHES 147

nakedly swimming in pools constructed in buildings where
Bible classes are held; or in the open-air cornet solos of over-
coated evangelicals standing on street corners in the middle of
winter and summoning the world to repentance.

Among remaining Americans, and on an indiscriminate
basis, a collective effort to revive the liturgical impulse of
Christianity was made some years ago in several semi-civic,
semi-convivial crusades, whose members were invited to dine
in community once a week, greet each other vigorously, and
submit to being called by their Christian names. The recent
War effort has somewhat curtailed the routine of these
brotherhoods. Their spirit remains undaunted; their members
continue to be fond of one another; but the caterers are com-
plaining that they do not lunch as often as they used to.

6

"At what point in your thoughts did you give up all further
quest of Mary Favorite?" Michael was asked by one of a group
to whom he had been expatiating.

"At Copley Station, two stops before Kenmore. I decided
it was no use to go on. So I got out at Copley, and went over
to the public library. And there, under one of the green
reading lamps, I settled with Mary Favorite for a poem.
Would you like to hear it?"

We said we would. And Michael took a paper out of his
coat pocket, his inside one, and read:

> Mary Favorite gives one the impression
> That God is both good and gay,
> But how she does it, or with what expression
> Is more than my mouth can say,
> But infinitely less than my mind can see
> Whenever I am in Mary Favorite's company.
>
> Thought after thought in beautiful interpretation
> Of human hardship and human frailty,

Store upon store of exquisite sensation
In things that are pure and free,
Have textured in Mary Favorite's eyes
Something I had no word for, were I wise.

"That girl haunts you, doesn't she, Michael?" said one of his listeners.

"Frankly, she does," Michael replied. "I'll worry about that lovely creature, worry a lot about her, with a name like . . . with a name like . . ."

"With a name like what?"

"Oh, if you don't know, never mind."

"Isn't her coldness part of her charm?"

"Frankly, it is," Michael again replied. "You know, blood tells, gentlemen, blood tells. It always achieves a chastity, the kind mongrels never dream of. Even when it goes to the dogs, it goes their aloofly, so to speak. *Patuit incessu dea.* . . . But what about my poem?" he added abruptly, looking more pleased about it than we thought he should be. "Didn't you like my poem?"

"Moderately good," said one.

"Fair," said another.

And a third added: "You'll have to do better than that, Mr Artist, before you start taking cracks at Galsworthy."

Outlines

———◆———

YOU'D BETTER COME QUIETLY

1

WE MIGHT begin by talking about nothing, but there wouldn't be much to say. Nothing is not a book, a rock, a snowflake, a meadow, a meadow-lark, a fish, a man, an angel. It isn't you or I or anything tangible or thinkable. All you can do with nothing is to abuse it by telling it what it isn't.

2

Let us pass, therefore, from nothing to the simplest order of something: the sheer material world, the world of stuff, extensioned, dimensioned, resistible, lying at the bottom of all creation, subsisting in the simple status of length, breadth and thickness, pitched one hop above the eternal void.

This material world is not dead, because it was never alive. And yet it is worse than dead, because it was never informed with the dignity of a living principle. I shall call this lowest order of being "the kingdom of thingdom," a fanciful phrase, but I am in the mood for it, because I am on the road ultimately to talk about the loveliest being God made.

The kingdom of thingdom is made up, so it seems, of little articles called electrons and protons, wreathed into a trillion fantastic shapes in the varied flux of the material world. These little entities are not immanent, they do not live, rather, their activity is *ad extra*; they work on one another; they revolve, interlock, combine into every sort of shape and substance, some for contemplative, some for practical uses, and God is very pleased with them.

It took infinite power to produce these little electrons, to raise them from the possible to the actual state, to throw them out of the realm of nothing into a simple, dimensional existence. No matter how insignificant they are in the order of creaturehood—they have neither intelligence, freedom nor reflection—they are tremendously more wonderful than nothing. And to prove their excitement at the fact of existence, they expand as water, evaporate as air, explode as fire, congeal as rock. In their congealed state (minerals) they are proletarian or aristocratic as the case may be: junk or jewels. I admire them very much massed in the magnificence of a mountain, diffused in the plume of a cloud, banked in the brilliance of a star.

A great darkness broods over the kingdom of thingdom: the darkness of unknowability (because matter ultimately resists being the object of thought, is stubborn to it, is nauseating to it, if I may use a metaphor); and also a great sadness: the sadness of essential complexity and change. You see, the inhabitants of the kingdom of thingdom are not *things* in the authentic, subsistential use of the word. They do not exist for themselves, they exist for other things. They are constantly reaching out for a permanent state of selfhood in "surrenders" which we call chemistry, in "conquests" which we call physics. Yet, because permanency is the prerogative of spirit alone, and not of matter, a true "self" is always denied them. No sooner has an "otherness" been attained than they abandon it for the sake of something still other, in variations of weariness and frenzy (again physics and chemistry—in reverse order) which exchange accounts for the perpetual maelstrom of the material world.

Into this realm of minerals there fall incessantly discarded relics from the soft world of life. These latter are not welcome in the kingdom of thingdom. The plow will ravage the loam the axe hew the timber, the scissors cut the cloth. Fights among themselves are fairest. And diamond cut diamond is a tournament *par excellence*.

Prodigious events happen in the kingdom of thingdom, all of their own accord: landslides, earthquakes, whirlwinds, tornadoes. Prodigious effects are also wrought in their midst under the guidance of the thought of man: skyscrapers, mortar-mixers, derricks, bridges, ocean liners.

But the most beautiful service offered to man by the mineral world is its adaptability in symbol to suit some whim of human emotion. Perhaps I shall express this idea best in a verse, before I leave this brief contemplation of creation's lowest world, to ascend, world by world, to the throne of God.

In the little kingdom of thingdom
That has no soul,
A pebble will tinkle and roll
In a bric-a-brac bowl.
By the brewing and brothing
Of silver and steel,
A knickknack is never not nothing
And a trinket is real.
By repulsion, attraction,
Devoid of all immanent action,
The length, breadth and thickness of stuff
Is existence enough
In the little kingdom of thingdom.

In the little kingdom of thingdom,
Where shells become pearls,
Where diamonds are princes and princesses,
Emeralds earls,
The well-fueled ruby will flash,
The coin on the counter will clash;
There's a lovely alarm for the ear,
Were there someone to hear,

There's a mineral meaning to find,
Were there only a mind,
In the little kingdom of thingdom.

In the little kingdom of thingdom,
Where hands are all handles,
The lady was pleased to put shiny white sticks under lily
    white candles,
With one of her fingers residing in ringdom:
A beautiful pledge evermore
That was bought in a honeymoon store,
One day in the little kingdom of thingdom.

3

Our next step on our way from the darkness of nothing to
the blazing splendor of the Deity, is to move from the king-
dom of thingdom to the first simple world of life: the world
of flower and tree (for a tree is only a wooden flower). Easy
as it is to take this step with the mind, it is required that we
traverse almost an infinite distance to take it in meaning. For
the difference between a rock and a rose is so tremendous that
it unveils a whole new vista of essence before the light of our
intelligence.

A rock and a rose are, of course, in many points alike. The
points in which they are similar: their dimensional activity, is
all too evident. They resist each other, attract each other, if
you drop both from a window they will obediently obey the
law of gravity and will, in the one case drop, in the other case
flutter, to the ground. But the points in which they are differ-
ent awake astonishment in the mind to the point almost of
fright.

For here's what a rose is which a rock isn't. It is a little unit
of being, each part succulently united to another in a way no
piece of rock could be to any other piece. It works in the
short space of what we are pleased to call its "life," as a small

pseudo-self in the realm of matter. It can grow, nourish itself, reproduce its kind. No rock can do that.

I once put the problem to a young University student, who had all his certitudes destroyed in college by an atheistic professor and who (remembering his textbook) was not willing to admit an essential difference between a living and a non-living being, this way:

"Now take this ink-bottle. Do you think I should ever leave it on my desk, and come back some day and find a brood of baby ink-bottles cluttering around it?"

He laughed—which we all do when our sanities are touched —but was not willing to admit that it could *never* be so.

"Do you think I should ever leave this small ink-bottle on my desk, and then come back some day and find (while knowing that nobody had entered my room in the interval) that it had grown to be a great big ink-bottle!"

Another laugh! Another tribute to the sense of what I was saying. For laughter is, in some way, an arbiter of truth. But still he "didn't know *for sure*."

And, finally, the third question.

"Would there be any need for me, ever, to keep coming in and watering and feeding this ink-bottle, in order to keep it in its present status? Does it, in other words, need nourishment of any kind in order to keep on being a good ink-bottle?"

Again he sniggered, humanly, but still didn't know academically. So I had to leave him in possession of the worthless assurance, "You never can tell what science will discover."

But to return to the rose and the rock. All the magnificence and power of the inanimate world packed into one display could not begin to adequate the wonderfulness of performance in one small rose, acting as a unified being, exercising itself in the marvelous functions of growth, nourishment and reproduction, putting forth its little challenge of thorns. Because the time will come when you can say of the rose, "It now is dead!" You cannot say that of any rock that ever existed, from the tiniest pebble on the beach to the Grand Canyon of the Colorado.

I may say that instinctively we notice—let us say on coming into a room—the superior excellence of being that is enjoyed by a flower or plant when we discover it in a melange of rugs, chairs, books and crockery. "Ah, a flower!" we exclaim, and immediately we want it placed in the sunlight, knowing the needs of its fragile, perishable nature.

4

We are now two worlds away from nothing in our progress towards Infinity. Many of my readers will have tired of the journey at this point, I daresay. But for those who have courage to climb with me, I shall climb with them. There will be constantly countless reasons for delaying as each superior degree of being is reached. But I have an impetus preventing me from delaying, as will later be shown. So let us climb, up from the world of flower to the world of animal!

5

Nothing! . . . Rocks! . . . Flowers! . . . And what then? . . . The fish, the beast and the bird! . . . Are they a new world? You would think so if you studied the behavior by which they surpass all operatives in the realm below them. Here are creatures which are not only dimensioned, not only immanently active, but equipped with five astounding instruments of knowledge. They are able to smell, see, hear, taste and feel. Not all the oceans and mountains of the world can approximate in such activity one fluttering butterfly. Not all the forests and field-flowers, one squirming worm.

Once arriving at the stage of animal in the hierarchy of creation, we are set in thought three hops away from nothing and are beginning to fumble for the first time with the profundities of the great mystery of knowledge.

Gorillas, gazelles, antelopes, tigers, seals, bluebirds, monkeys —is there any way to catalogue or classify all the fantastic forms and shapes which God the Father (who is the poet, the "maker" in God) has delighted to reveal Himself in symbol, once He has reached the world of sensitive creation? I stand —and so must you—astounded at what I behold in the jungle, the aquarium, the zoo. Think of what nerves must be arranged in order that one tiny mouse should smell a crumb of cheese! Think of what fibres must be devised and coordinated in order that a single whale should explode a jowl-full of salt water in mid-ocean!

And yet while lions crouch in their lairs, and hippopotamuses splash in their baths; while watch dogs bark in the night to protect their masters, and the skylarks soar aloft to sing their songs, we must be content to unify the marvelous ensemble in a category: the category of "sense," which distinguishes the third world above the void from the unfeeling world that lies just below it.

So remarkable is the performance of an animal in its five-fold assimilation of experience from the world through which it prowls, that a host of scientists (masquerading under the guise of philosophers) with minds which have been *drilled* in the ways of knowledge rather than *schooled* in them, have attributed human intelligence to an ape, human emotions to a baboon. This is not the time to refute this group. Let us climb to another world and then settle the score against them. But first let us pay tribute to God the Father, for the infinite display of His variety and humor in the world of animal creation. "I have made a lot of necks," He would seem to say. "Do you now want to see what I can do when I specialize in neck? Behold, the giraffe! Do you want to see me truly intent on the subject of nose? I give you the elephant! And for eyes, the owl. And for legs, the ostrich. And for belly, the hippopotamus." And so on.

6

It is humiliating for me to say so, but the next world into which we pass in our progress upward from nothing to God, is the world of *you* and *me*, the human world, the world of *man*.

Being still in the sphere of matter, we will find in the human world similarities of behavior with all the orders below us. I am like a rock in that I fall from a height. I am like a flower in that I nourish myself, grow, and can reproduce my kind, I am like an animal in that I can smell, feel, taste, hear and see.

The way to differentiate a man and a stone, a man and a vegetable, a man and a dog, is, by the way, not to study the points in which they are similar. That is the trick of Julian Huxley, Pavlov et al., a trick so subtle that it has in my presence sent a lady in a moving-picture house (while witnessing the presentation of Pavlov's picture "The Mechanics of the Brain") sprawling into the aisle in a dead faint.

"My dear lady," I said to her when she revived (since nobody else was willing to play the hero) "don't you let Pavlov worry you. You are neither a fish nor a monkey. I assure you, you are not. Pavlov has been trying to rub in the points in which you are like these animals. Let me tell you the points in which you are different. You can sing, laugh, read, talk, play the piano, draw pictures, say your prayers. Today you saw on the screen Pavlov making a study of an amoeba to discover its secrets of life. Now when an amoeba begins to make a study of Pavlov, then we shall both begin to worry. And, speaking of monkeys, monkeys have been eating bananas since the world began, but never in the world's history has a monkey ever been impelled to draw a picture of a banana!"

The lady began to feel a little better. And felt all better when she got out in the open air and saw people behaving pretty much as they did before she entered the cinema theatre

It is unfortunate that the philosophers have called us "rational animals." This is by way of putting us in a category of the *genera* devised by Aristotle. But these *genera* exist in the logical, not in the physical order. As a matter of fact we are not animals at all. We are men. Every single fibre of us is informed by a spiritual, indestructible soul, which gives even to our humblest functions an exquisiteness, a dignity, not enjoyed by any beast that lives. We are matter made fastidious to the utmost degree, by reason of the spiritual principle that keeps us alive. We do not eat, sleep, breathe, suffer, die in the same way as a beast does. Even a nurse in a hospital, caring for man in his most humiliating conditions, will realize that she is in charge (and that's part of the reason why she wears a white dress and a white cap) of a being infinitely more to be reverenced than an ox or a cow in the charge of a stable-keeper.

Still, we are partly material. This is our triumph as well as our shame; our triumph, because we can exercise in this lowly sphere such beautiful qualities as forgiveness, patience, purity, resignation; our humiliation, because we are subject to such indignities as nausea, rheumatism, sinus trouble.

Yet, there is a formula in regard to the human world which I shall now reveal. Our fundamental problems, it is true, are birth, love, suffering and death. But the situation can be summarized more succinctly. Everyone is sensitive. Everyone is lonely.

Think of our problem of loneliness! Eyes and mouth are, at rest, closed. Only the ears are open, through which we do not communicate, only receive. And how little we receive! I have found the sweetest voice imaginable (one which I knew well in my childhood) incapable of assuaging the insatiate human spirit desiring to know both why it is and why it is left so shut off from all comfort.

7

How beautifully, exquisitely the human body is apportioned and structured in order to meet the needs of an immortal spirit is shown by some statistics from the biologists. There are in the eye (each eye) in a space not larger than the head of a pin, twenty-one million little mirrors (twenty-one million reflecting substances, nine million rods and twelve million cones—or maybe it's the other way) showing how anxious God is to have His child equipped with vision, capable of appraising not only color, but every degree of shade, depth, texture. There are twenty-seven thousand harp strings in every human ear. (Think of a piano or an organ with twenty-seven thousand notes!) And so we become aware not only of outward noise, but of every grade and variation of sound. We recognize wood when it is knocked on, a saxophone when it is blown, a violin when it is sawed with a bow, we even discriminate exactly among footsteps, the impact of a voice friendly or hostile.

If I were to continue on through the various material faculties (take the taste buds, for instance, by which we so clearly discriminate between the savor of a lemon and an orange) I should be indefinitely preoccupied with nothing but the marvelous function of sense-knowledge in man. To close this paragraph with a bang I may say that in each human brain there are one billion cells. (A billion is a thousand million.) Each cell is connected directly or indirectly by flesh wires with every other cell housed inside a human skull. At a single moment, because of our unpredictable activity in the requirements of sense, the whole exchange is likely to be in operation. Imagine a telephone operator with a billion calls buzzing at the same time!

Into our world God came as a baby. He never entered the world of angel in personal life. There is an Incarnation, but not any Angelization of God. Why He became one of our kind, I do not know, except to put it down to the immeasurable extent

of His love. Let us not be too ashamed of ourselves, there-
fore. There is a dignity in having bones and flesh and blood
and limbs, and eyes and a heart, since Bethlehem gave us Jesus.
But if we are to accept the consolations of the Incarnation,
we must accept the annoyances as well. And Bethlehem was
chiefly a nuisance to Jesus and Mary as soon as Our Saviour
had been born. There was no room for them in the inn. The
stable was cold. There was no light. It smelled very badly. And
the crib of the Holy Infant was only a much-munched oats
box. No sooner had they settled in these ungracious quarters
than King Herod tried to kill the Holy Child. It was all bother,
borne for love of us.

8

After we leave the material world, of which we are the most
excellent, and perhaps the most awkward members, where do
we pass next? To the Deity Himself? Not quite yet. Not quite
yet by a large margin.

When we leave man, we soar into the world of angel. No
length, breadth and thickness now. All stuff ceases. No Law of
Gravity. No muscles and blood adhering to the bones of a
skeleton. Merely a clear, bright will and intelligence unham-
pered by dimensional hindrances, able to assert its selfhood free
of all our flesh-fetters, our stumbles and our falls. It must be
beautiful to be an angel and never know fatigue!

Yet we would be wrong in dismissing an angel with such a
simplified description. For though essentially simple in nature,
angels are marvelously complex in intensity and degree of
perfection. There are exactly nine worlds of angels, each order
surpassing the order below it similarly as the orders of life
surpass each other in the material sphere.

The notion of an angel will, of course, be obnoxious to a
mind not prepared to receive it. Angels are not for the bour-
geois, who lack any relish for hierarchy. Angels are for poets,
soldiers and saints. College professors, shop-keepers and butter-

and-egg salesmen are more suitably entertained with ghosts and ghost stories.

Angels cannot be photographed, or visualized with our material eyes. Therefore what? Therefore there are no such things as angels? To say this is to contradict God's sacred affidavit that there are. A disinclination for an invisible world, simply because it cannot be apprehended with a yardstick or measured like a pound of butter, is one of the sure symptoms of incipient savagery. Remember we are only one degree above the animals in creation's order, and if we do not give our spiritual intellect some concepts befitting its dignity, back into the jungle we will fall and quickly disintegrate in greeds, lusts and growls!

Let me tell you one thing about an angel that will impress you. Or rather two things. First he is launched into existence by a stroke of God's will, fully intelligenced for all his natural functions. He knows in the first flash of his existence all he ever will know, short of the Beatific Vision, which, of course, he must earn by some trial of fidelity. No angel ever went to school. Secondly, so powerful is his will that when he makes a choice he remains rooted, fixed in it by sheer force of spiritual drive, forever and ever. The angels who chose God in their trial-instant in eternity, stayed fixed in adoration of Him always. The angels who chose Lucifer and themselves for adoration, fixed themselves immediately in Hell and stayed rooted there. If there could be in us any sense of pity for a damned angel, or rather any sense of excuse—which there can not properly be—it would be at least to admit that God had made him so beautiful it were possible to apprehend in himself the mirage of divinity. If you were to want to ask what an angel could do in relation to the material world, I shall tell you. He could, by sheer force of will, without the aid of a slingshot or a fulcrum, hurl the planet Mars out of its orbit and disrupt the whole solar system. What wonder that Christ says part of an angel's care of us is to see we do not dash our foot against a stone! An angel could really make a cow jump over the moon.

If this be just an angel, I mean a simple, plain angel of the lowest order of pure spirit, what must an archangel be, a super-angel!

There are no pictures I can supply to enable my readers to climb visually the ladders of being that rise in the angelic order all the way from flesh and blood to God. But some intellectual apprehension of what it is to see one order surpassing another we have experienced in climbing from stone to flower, from flower to animal, from animal to man. Somehow in the same way we would climb as we went from

ANGELS
to
ARCHANGELS
to
PRINCIPALITIES

for so the lowest hierarchy in the celestial order is named. This hierarchy of angels is especially interested in human welfare. We each have, upon the assurance of St. Jerome, an angel to protect and pray for us—a Guardian Angel we call him. There is an Archangel set over large spiritual enterprises, such as a diocese, maybe even a parish, maybe even a large household. The Principalities concern themselves with human interests that rise to the proportions of national importance. It is possible that each state of the forty-eight in our United States may be complex enough in spiritual needs to require a Principality to protect it. Then of course the upper angels look always with especial care and interest on the order of angels just below them. Everything created participates in the providence of God whose care of things is boundless.

The second great hierarchy of angels is called by these mysterious, yet wonderfully impressive names:

POWERS

VIRTUES

DOMINIONS

Remember, please, as you advance towards God, through the ranges of excellence in intellectual and spiritual intensity bestowed on each of these ascending groups, you see a new revelation in the order of knowledge and love of the raging power of God written in the creatures of His hand. It is *on and on* with the angels, *more and more, greater and greater, wilder and wilder* beauty, *intenser and intenser* light as we follow an arrow-path to the Absolute.

Let me count the steps I have taken so far in going from nothing to God.

NOTHING

STONES

FLOWERS

ANIMALS

MEN

ANGELS

ARCHANGELS

PRINCIPALITIES

POWERS

VIRTUES

DOMINIONS

And now we soar into the last great hierarchy of angels, the mightiest, loftiest spirits of all. Ranged in a last breathless order of three (everything created seems to be threefold in some aspect, so as to image the Blessed Trinity of God Himself) are the top aristocrats of the angelic system. Their interests are far, far away from us, it would seem. Their concerns all lie Godwards. God is their ecstasy to such a point that they would swoon out of existence, with all their raging, blinding strength, if God did not support them. This last hierarchy of angels is called

THRONES
CHERUBIM
SERAPHIM

Even to mention them takes your breath away, for since an angel is invisible, he seems to bestow on his poor human brothers some little blinking awareness of what he is, simply as a reward for saying an angel's name.

The THRONES are the "foundation" angels, or so I like to call them. The CHERUBIM are the "knowledge" angels, that is to say, theirs is knowledge *par excellence*. The SERAPHIM are the love angels. They feed on the infinite adorableness of the Divine essence.

Creation's bonfire can, in nature's scheme, reach no higher. The topmost flame has been mentioned. The last soaring spark has been reached.

I don't see what more I can say, except to make another summary. Please bear that it should be repeated. Here's how it goes again, with all items accounted for.

NOTHING
STONES
FLOWERS
ANIMALS
MEN
ANGELS
ARCHANGELS
PRINCIPALITIES
POWERS
VIRTUES
DOMINIONS
THRONES
CHERUBIM
SERAPHIM

Make a little chart of this and put it on your wall. Think of it daily, no matter how little results you get. You'd be surprised to find, sometimes, how much you actually can get. Let the chart be called merely a series of signposts, if you will. They are the RIGHT signposts, not the wrong ones. And we've got into the habit of getting things so wrong these days, it will do no harm to get one thing at least verbally right. After all, the words of all languages and all literatures are potentially placed in the right alphabets.

9

After we have passed the last flaming seraph in the world of angel, what comes next? The Godhead itself? . . . In the order of nature, yes. In the order of Grace, no!

Strangely enough, in the dispensation of Grace, creation restores itself into flesh and blood once more, and we find human nature again at the portal of the Divine Reality. We find it in the form of a girl. Our minds, weary of climbing without pictures to assist us, through the tenuous droves of spirits that lie above us in the nine worlds of angel, are refreshed once more with an imaginative picture of something we know, love and have seen, before we step across the threshold of creation into the Ecstatic Essence of God. We find a girl again; with hands and eyes and hair, and a heart; airing her maiden-mother manners at the summit of all creation, constituted Queen of the Universe, with dominion over all angels and all men, more beautiful in her single reality, more pleasing to God, more full of Grace, than all the rest of creation put together. She is "beautiful as the moon, chosen as the sun, mighty as an army set in array." She is the Queen of Angels. She is the Mother and the Queen of Men. She originated on this little planet of ours, pertains to our race, our kind, is related to us not by the angelic ties of love and thought, but by the very fibres of flesh and blood.

She is still a woman, even in this awful majestic status bestowed upon her by God. And she likes compliments.

Tower of Ivory, Mystical Rose, Morning Star. . . . Such tributes please her.

Her alliance to God is threefold. She is the Daughter of the Father, the Spouse of the Holy Spirit, and the Mother of the Son. She presents all creation with a baby, whose name in Eternity is God, and whose name in time is Jesus.

She is the Mother of Divine Grace, powerful in her intercession. She is not God, she is the *Gate to God,* the Gate of Heaven. There is no passing to Eternal Life except through her. She is understanding, innocent, marvelously simple and unsuspicious, tender towards sinners. She takes us each by the hand and leads us to the Beatific Vision, and shares the radiant beauty of Christ's human nature begotten in her womb.

One cannot escape her. One cannot get into Heaven except through the Gate!

"You'd better come through the Gate!" God says to each of us. "Hesitations, incertitudes, nervousness, suspicions, doubts, what good do these do either a man or an angel?

"You'd better come through the Gate . . . !

"And . . . YOU'D BETTER COME QUIETLY!"

THE BLESSED SACRAMENT
EXPLAINED TO BARBARA

"FATHER, in order to be a priest you have to know a lot about bread, don't you, I mean if bread becomes the Blessed Sacrament?"

"Come to think of it, Barbara, you really do. You have to know a lot about bread if you're a priest. Not about preparing it, or mixing the flour, or baking it. That can be left to the nice Sisters who have charge of the hosts which are to be used in the Holy Sacrifice. But about bread as a *thing,* about what it *is* and what it can *become* when Our Lord asks it to, you really have to know a lot. And by the way, I like you, Barbara, because you ask such sensible questions."

"I ought to be sensible, I'm nine years old, going on ten."

"Yes, and I find more joy in discussing the Blessed Sacrament with you than with almost any person I know."

"Thank you."

"You're welcome."

"But, Father?"

"Yes?"

"In the Mass, where does the bread go when you say 'This is My Body'?"

"Where does it go? It doesn't go any place. It just ceases to be. It just vanishes. It just drops out of existence, not by becoming nothing, which we would call annihilation, but by becoming the Body of Our Lord."

"Doesn't it mind it, I mean, having to drop out of existence?"

"No, it doesn't really mind. Because, you see, it can't really mind anything, because it hasn't *got* a mind. It never knows what happens to it, because it doesn't know anything. But if it did know what was happening to it, it would be delighted."

"Would it?"

"Of course."

"Why?"

"Because there isn't anything it could do, is there, that would please it more than to give God its color, its shape, its taste, all its delicate little structure, to be used for the vesture of His most beautiful Body?"

"No. But do you think it would want to do that for anybody else?"

"Of course not. The only one it would ever want to obey in such a way is God. If anybody else stood over it and said 'This is a flower,' 'This is a stone,' or 'This is a bird,' the little bread would simply laugh. It wouldn't budge an inch. It wouldn't pay the slightest attention. But when Our Lord, through the mouth of the priest, says, 'This is My Body,' the little bread just has to give up. It hasn't got the strength to resist Our Lord's orders. So it just vanishes out of existence, and leaves its little shadow there, in the form of shape, taste and size, for Our Lord to clothe His Sacred Body within the Blessed Sacrament."

"Don't you think it's awfully nice of the little bread to do this for Our Lord?"

"Wonderfully nice. That's why the priest always treats it with such reverence, even before it has succumbed to the words of Consecration. To begin with, the Sisters take wonderful care of it when they are making it. They bake it until it is so white and fine and precious that you couldn't imagine anything more lovely in the way of bread than a little host is. Then when it is sent to the sacristy and is waiting to be taken to the altar, it always gets the most wonderful respect. It is kept in a little silver case, sometimes lined with gold. And at the Offertory of the Mass, when it is still only bread, the priest says the most beautiful prayers over it and tells the Eternal Father what an immaculate little host it is. And you know, if something happened to it after the Offertory, and it couldn't be used for the Consecration, the priest would have to take very good care of it and never could let it be used for anything else."

"Couldn't he?"

"No siree! The priest would have to put it away in a sacred place where nobody could touch it."

"But it wouldn't have become Our Lord's Body if it didn't stay on the altar until the Consecration, would it?"

"No, it wouldn't. But it would always be the little bread that was *ready* to become Our Lord's Body, and was *ready* to give Him all its whiteness and littleness and roundness; and so, you see, you would always have to respect it for that, and you could never treat it like any other little bread again."

"Did you ever see a host that was offered in the Offertory and then wasn't consecrated into the Body of Our Lord?"

"Yes I did, once. It was an awful pity. I had put it on the paten, and had offered it to the Eternal Father, and had told Him what a spotless little host it was, and then, when I looked at it closely, I found it was broken."

"Couldn't you use it when it was broken?"

"No, you couldn't, that is if you had another little host there that wasn't broken."

"But wasn't it bread all right?"

"Yes, it surely was bread, but there was something which Our Lord's Body wanted to borrow from it which it didn't have to give."

"And what was that?"

"Roundness and wholeness. You see this little host was jagged and broken. It could have given God brokenness, but He didn't want that at the moment."

"Didn't you feel sorry for it?"

"Of course. But there was no use asking it to give Our Lord's Body something it didn't have."

"What did you do with it then?"

"I dissolved it and dropped it down a little secret hiding place we have under the sacristy, called a *sacrarium*."

"Is that where all the little hosts go that don't become Our Lord's Body?"

"Exactly."

"Do you think they feel sorry?"

"If they could feel anything they'd be so sorry you could never console them."

"I hate to think of them buried under the church!"

"I do too. But it's best to forget them. They're really happy in their own way. They did the best they could. They were ready to give God all their little qualities to use in His Blessed Eucharist, if He had wanted them. And that's something to have been bread for, isn't it, Barbara?"

"Yes, it is."

"Well, what next?"

"Does the little bread make any struggle about leaving its appearances when you say 'This is My Body'?"

"No, it obeys promptly. It just gives up all it has in the way of whiteness, texture and shape, and vanishes immediately. Then Our Lord's Body comes in and takes its place, looking just like it, but being something entirely different, as you know. But the wine that becomes Our Lord's Blood makes a little bit of a struggle."

"Does it?"

"Well, you really wouldn't call it a struggle, because it is all unconscious of what is happening. But you have to talk to it more strictly than you do to the bread."

"Do you?"

"Yes. You have to give it a little sermon and let it know that something great is being done to it, that the Old Testament is being completed in the New, and that this new Substance to which it is lending all its fragrance and sweetness and taste and color, is the Blood of Jesus, which shall be shed for many unto the remission of sins."

"Why do you suppose it takes longer to consecrate the wine into Our Lord's Blood than it does to consecrate the bread into Our Lord's Body?"

"Well, it wouldn't take a second longer if God wanted to insist. But wine, you know, is a very fastidious substance. It is the nearest to a living thing of any non-living thing we know. It has an individuality (no two wines are the same), and when you bottle wine you always write the date on the bottle. It even seems to be sensitive about its age. And so God, in His nice way, sort of respects it at the Consecration, and in asking it to give up its taste and odor and pungency so that they can be used by His Precious Blood in the Eucharist, gives it, so to speak, a little sermon, so that it will have been respected in a reverential and holy way. God, you know, has a marvelous respect for every creature He has made, even for those things which haven't any minds or can't think. Before

He uses them, He blesses them and makes them holy, as He did, through the priest, the water with which you were baptized."

"The host looks the same after the Consecration as it does before, doesn't it, Father?"

"Exactly the same."

"But the bread is no longer there?"

"No. God takes the lookness right off the bread and uses it for His own lookness."

"Why doesn't He look like Himself in the Blessed Sacrament?"

"Don't you know?"

"Almost. But maybe you'll help me to know it better."

"Why, the reason God takes the lookness and the whiteness and the tasteness of the bread, is so that you can eat Him."

"Couldn't I eat Him otherwise?"

"Of course not. You could hold His hand or touch the hem of His garment. But you couldn't eat Him unless He became eatable. So in order to become eatable and come to us in the form of Holy Communion, He takes away the qualities of something that is eatable and palatable, and gives us His own Body hidden under this edible shape. That's why we can consume Him and let Him nestle close to our hearts; because He has become breadlike for love of us."

"Father?"

"Yes?"

"Wouldn't you rather see Him than eat Him?"

"I'd really like to do both. But if I had my choice, honestly, and had to take one or the other, I'd rather receive Him in Holy Communion than listen to His voice in a thousand sermons, or see Him in a thousand postures, however beautiful they may be. Because sermons are, after all, only His words, and sights of Him only His images in our eyes; but the Blessed Sacrament is Himself united to us as food. You can't get any closer to Him than that."

"But, Father?"

"Yes?"

"Isn't it lovely of the little bread to give Our Lord's Body all its whiteness, its taste, its smallness, so we can receive Him in the Blessed Sacrament?"

"Barbara, it is not only lovely of it, it is perfectly darling of it."

"Good-bye!"

"Good-bye!"

DO NOT GO TO BETHLEHEM TO FIND THE OBVIOUS

CHRISTIANITY is not the religion which holds that God exists. Every religion holds this dogma, whether it conceives God to be one or many. Christianity is the religion which holds that God became man, that He entered our ranks, assumed our nature, translated Himself into our idiom, "sifted Himself to suit our light," and was born in Bethlehem in a temporal generation, Who was born in eternity in an eternal generation.

When we betake ourselves to the crib on Christmas morning, it is not to see just another baby, nor even to see just another mother. This is the most different child and the most different mother who have ever existed. Nobody like them ever was before, or ever will be again. Take the mother.

Her child was born of the love of the Holy Ghost; sheer Love made her fruitful. She is the fulfillment of a thousand prophecies uttered in the Old Testament. As a special preparation for this most holy prerogative, she was herself conceived free from Original Sin, never tainted by the evil that beset our nature when Adam spoiled us all in Paradise.

A few brief notes in connection with the Lady who bends over her child with such awe and reverence on the first Christmas night, may be not unwelcome even to those who know in substance the details of the mystery. There was established between this young girl and God Himself, a sublime relationship which we call the state of Sanctifying Grace. This relationship was determined by God to be a permanent quality of human nature. Adam and Eve, the father and mother of the human family, were endowed with the gift of sanctification and were given the opportunity of establishing it as a permanent possession of mankind, and of handing it on as an heirloom to their children. God's plan was excellent and simple. By applying the gift of Sanctifying Grace to human nature at its sources, in the persons of the parent mother and father who contained potentially the natures of all human children, God could devise most generously and expeditiously to sanctify all mankind without compromising, as He never could, the gratuitous character of His gift.

But, by a most contemptible abuse of their liberty, this man and woman desecrated our nature and unsanctified it by sin. They were false to their trust and robbed the human race of the supernatural excellence which God had attached to it. We are the children of that sinful pair, and we pay the toll. We come into this world deprived of the heavenly adornment which would make us eternally desirable in the sight of God. There is a lack in us of something God's love had wanted to be there. Our nature is now crippled and unable to achieve its primal destiny. There is a void in us, a darkness, an incapacity for fulfilling our original purpose. We bear a wound, a guilt; we are soiled with a stain, a *macula*, which is called Original Sin.

To restore human nature to the Divine excellence it once possessed, God became man. He wanted to redeem us and adopt us back again into our original state of Divine childhood. Nineteen hundred years ago He came to fulfil this task. He took possession of a human nature and made it his own; He came to pay the price of our ransom and be our Saviour.

Please do not think I am attempting to exaggerate this mission of Our Lord in coming into our world. About Baptism, the normal means by which a Christian is restored to the state of Sanctifying Grace, Our Lord has said: "Unless a man be born again of water and the Holy Ghost he shall not enter into the kingdom of Heaven." And of Sanctifying Grace, the "living water" of which He spoke to the woman of Samaria, He said: "If thou didst know the gift of God." Sanctifying Grace is no catchword. It is the fundamental benefit Christianity has to offer the world through the Incarnation. Its realization and fulfillment in the souls of men is the only reason for the existence of the Catholic Church. A sanctifying Jesus Christ has been the Catholic Church's Messias from the beginning. God did not become man to make us contented with this world; He came to make us discontented with this world. He came to amaze us with a revelation about a world to come. He came to talk about a pearl of great price, a wedding garment of incomparable beauty which humanity could put on and thus enter the wedding feast of Eternal Life.

Listen to the way Christ prayed for us to His Heavenly Father on the night before He died:

Sanctify them in truth . . . that they all may be one, as thou, Father, in me, and I in thee; . . . that they may be one as we also are one: I in them, and thou in me; . . . and the world may know that thou hast sent me, and hast loved them, as thou hast also loved me. Father, I will that where I am, they also whom thou hast given me may be with me; that they may see my glory which thou hast given me, because thou hast loved me before the creation of the world. . . . And I have made known thy name to them, and will make it known; that the love wherewith thou hast loved me, may be in them, and I in them.

What is the meaning of this constant repetition of one . . . one . . . on Our Saviour's lips? With whom are we to be made one? With God? "Yes," said Saint Augustine, "God became man that man might become God." He became man to adopt us into the sunlight of His everlasting beatitude, to make us participators of the life of God, to unite us to the perfection of His single nature and take us to live in eternal ecstasy with the Blessed Trinity.

To the young Mother who stands in silence and wonderment beside the manger-box in the cave of Bethlehem, this gift of Sanctifying Grace was bestowed in its fullness.

Our Blessed Lady was a little Jewish girl. She lived in the northern province of Palestine, which is called Galilee, and was the only child of an aged couple, Joachim and Anna, and her name, as we know, was Mary. Nine months before her birth, Mary of Nazareth was conceived in the womb of Anna. Her physical conception occurred naturally, according to the manner of every other human child, through the humble processes of her father and mother cooperating as husband and wife. This much of her was usual and ordinary.

But being destined, as she was, to become the Mother of Jesus Christ, she was presanctified for this sublime function by being given at the first moment of her conception the gift of Sanctifying Grace. The darkness which exists in human nature in the first phase of its development was not allowed to enter the soul of Mary. As a beautiful gesture of Divine courtesy and filial respect, Our Saviour saw to it that this maiden from whose body He would one day derive the substance of His own, should enjoy the benefits of Redemption in a fashion all her own. At the first earliest instant when there was life in the womb of Anna, God sanctified it. He destined Mary at that moment for the Kingdom of Heaven. This is the Immaculate Conception.

The Immaculate Conception has nothing to do, as is commonly supposed, with Our Lady's chastity, nor with the chastity of her father and mother. The Immaculate Conception refers to Our Lady's *Christianity*. Its meaning is best studied, not in connection with the Nativity or the Annunciation, but in connection with the third chapter of Genesis and with the discourse of Our Lord at the Last Supper; for there is a world of difference between the doctrine of the Immaculate Conception and that of the Virgin Birth. The Immaculate Conception refers to Our Lady *at her own birth* and the sanctified condition of her soul in the nine months that preceded it. The Virgin Birth refers to her *at Our Lord's* birth, and to the fact that she conceived Him without the aid of man. The Immaculate Conception refers to Our Lady *as a child*; the Virgin Birth has to do with her *as a mother*. The Immaculate Conception has reference to the condition of Our Lady's *soul* at the instant of its creation; the Virgin Birth to the condition of her *body* before, during, and after the time that she became fruitful with the Divine Child. This is the woman, the miracle woman of all the centuries, who stands so quietly by her Infant in the cold of the first Christmas Eve, and at whose side stands meekly her husband, Saint Joseph, marveling at the Child of predilection which was not his own.

And now about the Child Himself. One does not go down to Bethlehem to see an ordinary child, for the little Jesus is the wonder child of our earth, fashioned and structured in a way no child has ever been since the human race began. To begin with, He possesses two natures, the nature of God and the nature of man: He possesses the Divine Nature because it was such that the Eternal Father gave to Him in Its fullness when He generated Him in eternity. He is true man because He possesses a human body and a human soul. But there is only one person in Him, the person who coexists in beatitude with the Father and the Holy Ghost in Heaven. The same "I" who says, "I am the Father's only begotten Son," also says in truth, once

Bethlehem has occurred, "and I am also Mary's Child." The theological implication behind this great mystery should not be ignored simply because of the strangeness of our Emmanuel. To love Him we must know Him, and we must know Him as He is, and realize that there is no one in this world like Him. He has two minds, two wills, two spirits (one of them a human soul), one body. From the very first moment of His conception by the power of the Holy Ghost, He was in possession of the Beatific Vision, and saw with His human mind the eternal beauty of God face to face. He was also gifted with infused knowledge to enable Him to fulfil His rôle as Messias and prophet; and lastly, there came through the medium of His little senses, through the windows of His eyes, and the doorways of His ears, human sights and sounds just as they come to any other child, and this we call His "experimental knowledge."

Having known the Eternal Beatitude in the bosom of His Father, it was most terrible that He should ever experience suffering in the temporal sphere into which He moved. This little Child should never have been cold, should never have been abandoned or neglected or forced to go into exile. No one should ever have been unkind to Him, or ungrateful. Never should His poor body have been scourged at the pillar, His beautiful head crowned with thorns, and nails impressed into His sacred hands and feet. He should never have been covered with mud and spittle, never been called a sinner and a fool; not even after His death should the Centurion, save for fulfilling the prophecy, have pierced His side with a spear.

But we will forget at Christmas time that such things are to happen in the course of His short life. We shall only be glad that a Child is born to us who is the salvation of the world, and we shall join our minds and hearts to some simple shepherds, adore Him, and be glad there is another Christmas.

DIALOGUE WITH AN ANGEL

MAN: It is impossible to hold a conversation with you.

ANGEL: Why?

MAN: Why? Because I must do both the talking and the answering. You never answer.

ANGEL: That is not true. I do answer.

MAN: I never hear you.

ANGEL: Do you expect me to make sounds?

MAN: A little sound wouldn't hurt.

ANGEL: But I am a pure spirit. I have no dimensions, no body, no mouth, nor hands, nor any instrument of noise. Do you want me to stop being an angel?

MAN: You might accommodate yourself to me as a man. I have a body. I have ears.

ANGEL: Why should I stay outside your ears when I can go straight to your intellect? What good to knock at a door which one can pass through?

MAN: It might let the occupant know that you have arrived.

ANGEL: In which case the arrival would not be an angel . . .

MAN: But something very much more satisfactory. Something one could see and feel and hear, not simply guess at, as I am now doing with you.

ANGEL: You will simply have it that I must stop being an angel if I am to continue to exist. Is that not it?

MAN: No, that's not it. But why not materialize, assume some shape, and appear to me? It would make this conversation less nonsensical. . . .

ANGEL: And likewise very much less angelical. An angel with a shape is a nonsense. Would you prefer to know me as I am not, rather than to know me as I am.

MAN: But do I know you at all?

ANGEL: You seem to know me well enough to abuse me. I think maybe you do not like angels.

MAN: I must confess I find them very tiresome.

ANGEL: You mean you find your own brain very tiresome, with all its convolutions, its water and its pulp. I cannot be tiresome who am lighter even than your own thoughts.

MAN: Excuse me if I yawn *(He yawns.)* I am no longer interested. I shall employ my poor soggy brain in thinking about things I can feel and see.

ANGEL: And will you find in them any real satisfaction?

MAN: A certain satisfaction. That kind at least which you are unable to give me.

ANGEL: Would you like me to go?

MAN: Nobody said "Would you like me to go?" I have just fancied that you said it. I simply supply you with words I think you might say if I were sure you were here.

ANGEL: But you are not sure?

MAN: No.

ANGEL: You are not sure of what God has revealed? Has He not promised to give me charge over you "lest you dash your foot against a stone"?

MAN: I am quite unaware of any influences you have upon my feet.

ANGEL: Just at present I am trying to keep you from dashing your head against a rock.

MAN: What do you mean?

ANGEL: Would you not prefer the impact of a rock upon your head to the soft fusion of your spirit with mine? You have said as much.

MAN: I did not really mean to say you are not here. I meant I do not know whether or not I am talking to you. God did not say that every time I fancy myself talking to you I really am doing so.

ANGEL: I should be a rather poor Guardian Angel if I paid no attention to you precisely at the time when you are paying attention to me, should I not?

MAN: Really, I cannot be bothered with this subject any

longer. It's all too stupid. If you're here, stay here. If you know what I am saying to you, you are welcome to know it. But certainly I have no way of knowing that you know it.

ANGEL: Isn't that rather silly talk?

MAN: Now you can't tell me that anybody said "Isn't that rather silly talk?" Nobody said it. I just made it up in my own mind, and in writing it down I am supposing myself to have supposed what you might possibly have said if you were aware of what I am thinking.

ANGEL: You have to become very involved in order to get rid of me, don't you? You have to take refuge in a muddled, complex sentence. Angels detest complexity.

MAN: What do they like, then?

ANGEL: Simplicity.

MAN: Well then, very simply: Am I thinking about you?

ANGEL: If not, what are you thinking of?

MAN: A possible angel who may or may not be present to me.

ANGEL: But God has said there is a real angel where you suppose the possible one to be.

MAN: But not that the real angel knows that I am thinking about him.

ANGEL: What do you think that I think you are thinking about?

MAN: I do not know.

ANGEL: Oh I see. So we may put it this way: I who am always thinking about you do not know when you are thinking about me.

MAN: No, I admit that you know that I am thinking about you.

ANGEL: But you did not say that before. Or rather, you said it, and then retracted it.

MAN: Well, now I admit it. But this is what I do not admit. I do not admit that we are holding a conversation.

ANGEL: Because I make no sounds in your ears?

MAN: Don't you see what I mean? I grant you that being an angel, you are not supposed to make sounds. But a soundless conversation from my side is quite impossible.

ANGEL: And so you can never hold a conversation with an angel unless he becomes a man?

MAN: We are certainly not holding a conversation!

ANGEL: What are we holding?

MAN: We are holding a monologue.

ANGEL: How can two persons hold a monologue?

MAN: How can one person hold a conversation?

ANGEL: How can WE be ONE person?

MAN: But is there a you?

ANGEL: You have already admitted that.

MAN: But I have not admitted. . . .

ANGEL: What have you not admitted?

MAN: I have not admitted . . . just a minute and I shall tell you what I have not admitted. . . . I have not admitted that the you to whom I am attributing the thoughts I am thinking you are thinking, are really thinking the thoughts I am thinking you are thinking.

ANGEL: Involved again, I see! Worse than before!

MAN: That last sentence of mine may be a bit involved, but it is unanswerable.

ANGEL: Naturally I cannot answer it if you are unwilling to admit that the answer you suppose I am answering is really the answer you suppose I am answering. Now how do you like me in an involved sentence? Let me hear you answer that?

MAN: Who is the one who is talking to me when I suppose you are talking to me?

ANGEL: Who do you think?

MAN: Nobody.

ANGEL: Can nobody talk to somebody?

MAN: But somebody can talk to himself. That's what I am doing, I am talking to myself.

ANGEL: It took you a long time to find that out.

MAN: It wouldn't have, if you hadn't interfered.

ANGEL: I interfered? That's splendid!

MAN: I mean unless I were fool enough to imagine that you were interfering.

ANGEL: Isn't it marvelous what trouble this imaginary angel is causing you?

MAN: Yes, it is.

ANGEL: It's hard to see how a real angel could be more bothersome, isn't it?

MAN: Of course, I'm causing myself all the bother.

ANGEL: Are you both angel and man, to say that you can fight yourself this way?

MAN: No. But I am supplying you a part and trying to imagine what you would say if you were saying anything.

ANGEL: Are you sure I am saying nothing?

MAN: Well for goodness' sake, this is a make-believe story! You certainly are not writing the script for your own part, are you?

ANGEL: Naturally I cannot write.

MAN: Nor are you thinking it.

ANGEL: No?

MAN: You can't be thinking what I am thinking.

ANGEL: You don't say?

MAN: Well you certainly are not my intellect.

ANGEL: Are you thinking your own intellect?

MAN: No, but I am thinking thoughts *with* my own intellect.

ANGEL: About me.

MAN: But you are not those thoughts!

ANGEL: I am the object of them.

MAN: But you don't cause them!

ANGEL: Every object causes the thought of it in some way. But let's not go into that. Can you think of nothing in a thought?

MAN: I can have a sort of a thought about nothing.

ANGEL: And am I that nothing?

MAN: In the way I am thinking about you, you are.

ANGEL: Then why are you so exasperated at me if I am nothing?

MAN: I am exasperated at my own idea of the nothing I conceive you to be.

ANGEL: But conceived as nothing, I am not the angel God sent to guide you.

MAN: No, the angel God sent to guide me is real, but the angel with whom I am holding this conversation is an imaginary angel to whom I am attributing thoughts of my own.

ANGEL: But you began this conversation by wanting an imaginary angel to materialize and make sounds. That's even worse than wanting a real angel to do so.

MAN: I admit there were certain inconsistencies on my part in the beginning of this conversation.

ANGEL: And the imaginary angel cleared them up for you?

MAN: I cleared them up for myself.

ANGEL: Really, you seem to be a better angel, when you play the part of an angel, than I am.

MAN: I think that's true.

ANGEL: My dear man! My dear philosopher!

MAN: Now I know that you are not a real angel. . . .

ANGEL: My dear child!

MAN: Now I know that you are!

THE BLESSED TRINITY EXPLAINED
TO THOMAS BUTLER

You SAID: "Write a treatise on the Blessed Trinity, and explain it just to me!"

You know very well that there are many realizations of the mystery of the Blessed Trinity which you have already arrived at, and which are more valuable than any I can present. Nevertheless, I accept your challenge. 1) Because I have obeyed you in so few things; 2) Because a relish for the mystery of personality—and the contemplation of the Blessed Trinity prompts precisely that—can never be in two persons quite the same, not even in two who were nourished in one womb, suckled at the same breasts. You see I overpower the original mystery by presenting another one. Mystery solves mystery! Do you like it? . . . Diamond cuts diamond!

If I am to go on, I must allow myself some privileges. The first is to omit what I care to omit; the second, to include what I care to include. I shall be a) repetitious, because the mystery is infinitely simple; b) original, because it is infinitely fecund. Our parents produced two boys, and there are resemblances between us which even a passing policeman can notice. But there are differences, and that is why I am explaining to you a subject to which you have given considerable thought of your own. Be humble enough to hear things repeated which you know very well. But also, be independent enough to honor my independence, my originality. Let us

> Not interfere in the least with each other's light,
> No matter how murky the mist, how dismal the night,
> Or whether the clouds conceal or reveal us right.

First, let me rid myself of an annoyance: the statement so often made that because the Blessed Trinity is a mystery, therefore we can know nothing about it. Being, furthermore, the profoundest mystery in God, it is assumed by many preachers and teachers that it is the one phase of God we must dismiss without discussion. All this I deny. God would not have revealed the mystery to us if this were so. The awareness that there is a trinity of personalities in the Deity, all outflowering from a single all-perfect nature, was not dispensed to man to torture him with its intellectual indigestibility. (That last was a horrid phrase, but I meant it to be horrid.) The Blessed

Trinity is not a puzzle. It is not a trick. It is an innocent, profound statement of how life exists in Him who *is* Life. A mystery is not a fact about which we can know nothing. It is a fact about which we can not know everything. But the deeper we plunge, the more we learn. The ultimate veil will be removed from our minds only in the Beatific Vision. But veil by veil we can go tearing and plunging in the direction of that sunlight which is dimly, but surely, seeping through. It is a thicket we are in, not a maze. Not by devious guesses and conjectures, but by a single straight line do we forge out of the forest, crashing down the branches, pushing the leaves out of our eyes. We will not find the open glare of day until we are no more of this world. But we will be nearer the edge of the woods when we finish than when we began. Do you care to follow? If so, stalk in my footsteps; but give me two free hands.

Now here is the second important thing I have to say. We have hidden experience within ourselves of the reality of the Blessed Trinity, for we are the images of God *non tantum Unius sed Trini*. In the intensest region of our souls—that area of us which is always unconsciously cooing around the essence of our Creator, receiving continuation from Him as mysteriously as it received existence—we are being perpetually warmed by the exquisite temperature of the eternal Substance, and continually illuminated by the light from three lovely *I's*: the Father, the Son, and the Holy Spirit. Granted that it is a borrowed light; do we not have what we borrow? Oh, I agree that it all happens down in the mysterious depths of us, at the vanishing point of us, at the verge of our non-existence, where we shriek our pitiful "Keep me, keep me!" to our Creator, as we gaze into the yawning eternal void, anxious again to receive us, from which we came, and to which we can never return . . . not even by the route of Hell! But it is we, it is you, it is I, who are there in that strange basement, clinging to existence by the delicate hinge of God's will. It is a cellar in us too deep from which to call to our upper selves, a chasm too fathomless from which to send up skyrockets to our imaginative and discursive minds. For to be a creature is to be annihilated in an undone nothingness that crawls; it is to be buried in one's own grave—alive! But this life receives, and becomes vibrant with, the sound of three voices encouraging us to go on existing. And the message from these three voices is this: I am Life, I am Truth, I am Love. We are set ablaze with a triple searchlight, streaming from eternity and making concentric circles at our core!

When one of our children in the Sisters' School is told: There is one God in Three Divine Persons, he does about it only what a child should do. He says: *In the Name of the Father, and of the Son, and of the Holy Ghost*, beginning his prayer; and *Glory be to the Father and to the Son and to the Holy Ghost*, ending it. And then he goes about his play. Prayer is the child's little aside; play is his profession. He throws a tiny rosebud of adoration into eternity—not yet blossomed, but a real rosebud, not a false one—and forgets it. He does not know that the Beatific Vision of the Triune God is already in his mind, packed there in the form of Faith, as the flower is packed in the seed. The flower is not another reality from the seed; it is the seed fulfilled. So the child's prayer. It is, in seed form, the adoration of vision which the Blessed bestow upon God in ecstasy everlasting.

THREENESS AND ONENESS

The first simple step towards an appreciation of the Blessed Trinity is to become aware that *threeness* and *oneness* can somehow be reconciled. Of course, if one insists on the fact that *threeness* must have no association whatsoever with *oneness*,—if one forbids that it should, on the score, let us say, that such things do not happen in one's social circle, in one's pantry, on one's dining-room table—naturally we encounter a mind completely closed to an appreciation of the mystery of God. And, as you know very well, an approach to a sublime thought can be effectually outlawed in sophisticated conversation by a yawn, by a "Why bother?" or by a sudden need to hurry and catch a train. I have had, times without number, to surrender the most innocent effort to lift a dinner conversation out of the realm of soup and strawberries and into the region of the immutable and eternal, in the face of such a witticism as: "Oh goody, goody! At last we've found someone who knows all about God!" . . . Heaven immediately clouded before our eyes, and we went back, after an appropriate pause, to a discussion of the unsociabilities of detail in a surrealist's painting.

When St. Patrick picked up the shamrock, as the Irish say he did, and pointed to it as an illustration of the mystery of the Trinity, he chose a most wretched symbol, as we know. For the unity of persons in the Blessed Trinity is not that of three leaves clinging to a stalk. Yet St. Patrick advanced, I declare, by however tiny a trillionth of an inch, nearer to the truth of God's multipleness than one does who points to no symbol at all. For St. Patrick at least opened the minds of his disciples to the startling fact that threeness and oneness can *somehow* be reconciled in a single being. The reconciliation of these opposites in a poor little shamrock is about as pitiful an illustration of God's paradox as I can imagine. But it is better than no illustration at all. And it creates a generosity of mind more salutary than the obstructionist attitude which hangs on the portals of human intelligence a sign: Let no amazement enter here!

St. Patrick used the shamrock as a symbol of the diversity of identity in God. Let me use a better one. I shall take water.

There are three expressions of "self" in a single substance that is now ice, now water, now vapor. And even when the symbol breaks down—and it is part of the Catholic intelligence to know just how far a symbol does serve and how far it does not—for the substance of water has not the per manence, perfection, intelligence, freedom, infinite intensity of the substance of God; and the "selves" of water in solid, liquid and gaseous form are "states" rather than varied supposital expressions of an identical substance—nevertheless, there still remains a vestige of the mystery of God imbedded in water which will never be solved by physics or chemistry. If you have no Blessed Trinity to which to refer in adoration and praise the eternal expression of the mystery you have seen reflected in water, then water will become your God, and your God will very soon vanish like water. I can understand the pagan who worships the elements: fire, sun, water, who wants everything to be a deity, confuses a *state* with a *self*, and who creates a lovely lore of legend for everything which is mistaken to be divine, makes a mythology (the twilight of theology, just as superstition is the twilight of faith) and gives us gods, good and bad, for every phase of our experience and builds up from the unexplained antics of these deities a literature as rich as that of Homer or Omar. But I detest the coarseness of mind of the de-Christianized scientist who pounces upon innocent water as though it were unprecious enough to be a problem, and who blasphemously believes that when he has split the ultimate atom of H_2O, he will have exploded the Nicene Creed.

We must have mysteries in order to keep sane, even the sublime mystery of a single nature in the Blessed Trinity of God, and if you do not accept this truth in its divine pattern and under its divine guarantee, it will keep shrieking at you in the iceberg, torturing you in the torrent, stifling you in steam, and *I am Water, always Water* is all it will tell you. . . . and you won't get much comfort from that; nor much explanation.

THINKER, THOUGHT AND THINKING

The symbol of the shamrock will take the mystery of God only in the most glancing and trivial manner. The symbol of water involves a complexity and coarseness of idea from which the Eternal Innocence shudders. Let me therefore descend (or in this case, ascend) to a simple, abstract statement in which there is concept but no picture, idea with no sensible image. Sensible images get in the way of God when we try to apprehend Him in His spiritual, undimensioned Beauty. Let me say that God the Father is the Thinker in God; God the Son is His Thought; and God the Holy Spirit is the Thinking that proceeds from the Thought and the Thinker. Before we attempt to discover how unfathomably far away we are from the Divine Processions in this statement, let us first observe a few points in which it becomes perilously near to being the truth of Him.

A thinker craves a thought, and a thought craves to be thought of by a thinker. Thinker and thought in severance leave the function of intelligence unfulfilled, whether in Divine or human form. If a thought could survey itself on the brink of existence, it would look about yearningly for the one requisite needed to lift it out of nothingness: a thinker to think it. A thought is in very truth the *child* of the thinker, bursting into being by a genuine act of generation, more generative indeed than a procreation of flesh and blood, more firmly rooted in the status of childhood than an infant is towards father and mother, because an infant achieves in birth the principle of division from, rather than of subsistence with, its parent. Not so thought as a scion of the spirit. For a thought and a thinker in the precise duration of the act of thinking are identified in substance. Each is the one thing in that brief ecstasy in which they commune. I am not I, and my thought something abroad in mid-air. And yet my thought achieves an *otherness* right within me, which, if I do not honor, precisions of statement about what is *I* and what is *mine* become impossible. For I do speak of my thought as somehow distinct from myself. I praise and admire my good thought, disown and belittle my bad one. Who is criticizing whom in this stand-off? Why am I so proud of my infant if it is only myself, why do I scold it if it is not other than I?

The explanation is simple. Our thoughts are other selves, but selves by way of accidental, not substantial nature. In thinking, my intellect submits itself to a form with which it is momentarily identified, and this explains the unity of thinker and thought. But the two made one have in themselves not merely a principle of opposition (which is delightful) but also a principle of abandonment (which is disastrous). All our intellectual children are ghosts of real babies. They do not geyser forth into an I-ness as real and permanent as the thinker who begets them. My thought is a would-be self, not a real one. I speak of it as though it were another, and there is a necessity in that "as though" from which I cannot escape. My thought would be really, truly, everlastingly, blazingly a new self within my nature—would be a second person authentically begot by me—if three requirements were fulfilled: 1) if I were thinking the same thing all the time; 2) if it were the perfect thing to think; 3) if the infinity of its perfection were derived from a survey of my own nature, wholly given yet wholly retained in the act.

But alas, in our vintage of being, such a perfection of performance is impossible. There is in man only one person and one nature. Little pretenders to the dignity of personality constantly arise within him in the form of thoughts: fakers that put on a good show at being somebodys while they last, like pumpkins blinking in a window at Halloween. But no thought I have is perfect or exhaustive of an all-perfect nature, and so it dies. And no love I have is rooted in a substantial wedding of thought and thinker, and so it dies. And I go on forever being, in the total assemblage of what I am, one nature and one person, defeated at every instant from being a Blessed Trinity.

When a thinker can leap at the thought of all truth, as God can, and all truth surrenders itself effortlessly to be thought of by the fortunate thinker, there proceeds from this alliance the function of *thinking**—in an act of infinite goodness, infinite delight. This *Thinking* will go on as long as there is no possibility of distraction, as long as Thinker and Thought are fixed in an ecstasy of mutual affection than which no greater can be conceived. The Thinking, obviously, will be as substantial and immutable as the Thought and the Thinker from whom it proceeds. Its boast is to be all goodness; and its name is Love. There must be two for love; though, speculatively, there need be only one for thought. Love cannot be called a child, because there is no principle of furtherance in it, only of repose and fulfillment. Love languishes in its own leisure. It is a terminal beyond which nothing can reach. It does you no good, simply stares at you in a sacred silliness and asks you "What more do you want, now that I have arrived?" In its temporal pattern it broods strangely in a contingent heart, unworthy to support it, asking of it that thing which it abhors: an explanation. As doled out for our experience, I call it The Oppressor:

* This word is inaccurate if taken to mean that the Holy Spirit proceeds from an act of knowledge in God. The Holy Spirit is rather the term of act of mutual, eternal *love* existing between The Father and The Son. I use it here only because it is expressive of the resultant repose in the Thinker-Thought alliance on which Love thrives; also because it indicates an intimacy of procession from Thinker and Thought. Father Hopkins refers to the Blessed Three as "The Utterer, The Uttered and The Uttering." But he would have trouble with his symbol, just as I have with mine. Such sayings as: "I am thinking of you on your birthday. I am remembering you in my prayers" are expressions of love, are they not? They certainly do not mean "I find you extremely interesting again on your anniversary!" Love has no language of its own, and has to borrow. Its best expression is sometimes abject silence, not the silence of having nothing to say, but of having too much, and of having no medium in which to speak. Thought can be uttered, and *is a word*. The Son is The Word of God. *Love* neither is a word *nor* has a word, and must return to the articulate territories of thought if it is to say anything. And then it always says it strangely, and better by symbol than by language.

The Oppressor

Love makes one weak,
Is hard upon the heart,
Merciless on the meek
If once you let it start;
A pressure is, a pain,
A burning in the brain
From which one would not part;
And though of one's own choosing
And none of one's refusing,
Undoes one day and night,
Is neither wrong nor right,
Nor bloom, nor blight,
In sum:
A dull delirium
And wild delight.

In its eternal pattern, Love is a Comforter, not an Oppressor. In the Blessed Trinity it is called the Paraclete, the Holy Spirit. And we bless ourselves now with new reason:

> In the Name of the Father, and of the Son, and of the Holy Ghost
> In the Name of Life, Truth and Love
> In the Name of the Thinker, the Thought and the Term of Their Repose . . .

or, as you, Thomas Butler, put it in one of your most poignant poems: *In the Name of God the Weaver, God the Wool, and God the Weave.*

Communicability and Incommunicability

Let me now, with the impudence of the moth assailing the flame, attack the mystery of the Blessed Trinity from a new angle. Oh, the Flame will be sure to win, and I be burned.

I shall plunge forth to absorption, not to victory, and the quiet light of the Eternal Candle will burn serenely after I have futilely tried to disentangle its beams. Even so, some spark of me may veer off as I disappear into the conflagration and may lend a momentary lustre to your eye. If so, I shall have been well devoured. A moth is like a mind—and better to die in a dazzle than rot in a decay.

You may well complain that I have not as yet explained to you the difference between a nature and a person, and that there is no dealing with the Blessed Trinity until this has been done.

You know, of course, the impeccable scholastic definition of nature; namely *that which acts,* in an essence (that by which it is what it is), in a substance (the principle of permanence in the agent). You change your wording for this one reality accordingly as you change the focus of your interest in it. . . . And then to Boethius we give a bow for his classic definition of person as: *naturae rationalis individua substantia.* But these definitions are too tight for our purposes. Let me loosen them a little by a few illustrations and considerations that will be more alive and less in formula.

You yourself will do for experiment, and I shall consider two phases of you which can be known and treated, talked about and loved. There is first, your communicability—and that is you *as a nature.* There is second, your incommunicability, and that is you *as a person.*

Your Communicability

Your qualities of body and soul, your stature, height, ability to think, breathe, pray, read, laugh, eat, cry—the things that make you human, sociable, a man, a priest, a poet, a dreamer, one of St. Ignatius's disciples, and one of our mother's children. These aspects of you (and countless others that are similar) touch your *nature.*

Your Incommunicability

There is your uniqueness, your aloneness, your mystery, your private experience of yourself as distinct from others—the phase of you to which you cater when you close your eyes, make a gesture of supplication, a gesture of defense; when you accuse yourself of sin, take responsibility for some good or evil work; when you sign your name, or indelible some revelation of yourself to the outside world with your peculiar flash of eyes or tone of voice, inimitable and un-vicarious. . . . You have undergone those moments of human experience when you have been in the presence of a loved one and could not speak—when the very fullness of your self could not be crushed into words or even expirated in a sigh. You have said, and I recorded, "I am most unhappy when I am with those I love." You did not need to explain this paradox. I understood it. The statement derived from that outlook of yourself upon yourself which we call *personality*.

Communicability and incommunicability are two terms that will serve to set our thoughts gyrating around those mysteries of nature and person that are at one within us. Other terms will also help.

> Our sameness with others is our nature.
> Our difference from others is our person.
> Our likeness to others is our nature.
> Our unlikeness to others is our person.
> Our dependence on others is our nature.
> Our independence of others is our person.

The most dependent creature in all the world is a small child. For food, clothing, shelter, care, cleanliness, protection, it depends constantly on another's charity. And yet it is mar-velous to see what a cast of independence "nature" establishes in a child, even in infancy, to assure it of the ultimate function of an unruled selfhood. For outside of its human necessities, a child is the most independent little moppet that could possibly be. It does what it pleases, laughs and cries when it pleases, runs to whomsoever it pleases, puts on its little antics, smiles, entertains or annoys the company, just as it pleases, and will repose unpredictably on whosoever's lap suits it, whether it be friend or stranger. It is totally devoid of human respect, a little tyrant in the kingdom of tantrums and tendernesses.

When a child grows up, the balance swings entirely the other way, so marvelous are the adjustments of human nature in keeping its dual requirement of person and nature in poise. As a man, a child is now independent of its parents, nurses, teachers, and can feed, clothe and protect itself. But these larger liberties are bridled by an extreme curtailment of personal whim and of the private enjoyments of autonomy. A man is predictable, bound by conventions unknown to the nursery. He will usually go where he is coaxed, and you can be morally sure of what he will do in given situations. He does not go toddling around the parlor, putting his head in various laps, unburdening himself of ceremonies of friendship or disdain that are sometimes disconcerting to the point of being a fright.

Likeness and Unlikeness

Beauty is the likeness of unlike things. So you see, within the essential structure of every human being, because of his likeness-principle (his nature) and his unlikeness-principle (his person), there are justifications for unlimited contemplation, if we would only look innocently into the eyes of our friends, into the unemancipated aloneness of each puzzled human heart, forever needing companionship and sympathy, and forever wanting not to be annoyed by the bothersomeness of others.

Beauty consists in the unlikeness of like things! . . . What must be the unthinkable beauty of a triple, eternal unlikeness in *an identical thing*, **O God! O Adorable Trinity!**

On a trip back from Italy some years ago, I stood one night outside the ballroom window on the boat, and watched a beautiful young boy and girl (in their late teens or early twenties) collaborating in a dance. Their differences before they became partners in the dance were as complete as though a chasm had made them. In size, quality of voice, gender, clothes, strength,—in every bodily and spiritual endowment, they were as divided as only boy and girl can be, in the strange pattern of male and female that sets the human race apart into that twoness that will, in Beauty's name, emphasize the likeness of their differences.

She was dressed in a long, flowing, white robe, with a band of blue in her hair. He was dressed in faultless, black evening-clothes. She was a dressmaker's dream. He was a tailor's job. Her antics preparatory to the dance were light and fluttersome, bristling with a butterfly independence. He was quiet, strong, stolid, with no nervous pre-excitement in a single movement. The off-flash from her, in hair, in hands, in eyes, would seem to be telling us: *I am complex and unconquerable. I am all diffused. In me there is no surrender*. . . . The aura that poured from him would seem to be saying: *I am my own quiet, assured strength. I am rounded, harmonized finished. For me there is nothing left to conquer.*

The orchestra leader struck his baton against the podium. The boy walked languidly across the ballroom-floor and gathered a white parcel of fidgety loveliness in his arms. And the music began.

And then, for ten minutes of faultless co-ordination, encouraged by every shade of sound and note the instruments of the orchestra could supply, the extravagant differences of boy and girl melted into an identity of movement. Every gesture, twirl, advance, approach, glide, hesitation, revolution and recovery were performed, so it seemed, by two human wills fused into one. The separateness of their selves was whelmed in an identity of rhythm, showered and re-showered with melody for a breathless interval in which there was only one-ness between them.

The music stopped. They separated again into black and white, walked to opposite corners of the room. He was once more a boy and she a girl, and they resumed the manners of strangers.

Your awe-struck brother closed the curtain of the ballroom window through which he had been eavesdropping, went over and leaned on the railing of the ship, and looked up blinkingly at the mystery of the stars—each at its appointed post in the Heavens, each shining with the same patient radiance, undifferentiated in kind, yet sundered by unfathomable spaces, millions of light-years apart!

Asceticism and Mysticism

These two phases of the spiritual life are founded on the requirements of nature and person. Asceticism is the law of restraint: it forms us into one nature with others. Mysticism is the law of abandon: it leaves us free in those stratospheres of the spirit that lie above the *rules* of perfection. But there can be no stratosphere until there has been an atmosphere, perfectly blended, upon which it can rest in its fragility, and from which it can draw up its airy independence. As regards our own Religious Order, there can be no mystical Jesuit (left free in the wild liberties of his contemplations, favoritisms and prayers) until there has been first an asceticized Jesuit (one who has obeyed his rules). The ascetical features of our training are those molds of conduct, discipline and restraint that give us the title to be called Jesuits at all (our nature), and which privilege we little deserve at any price. The mystical features of our life are those titles which permit us each to sign a separate name before the S.J. of which we are so proud, and which require the personal government of a living superior to counsel and direct us, rather than a cold formula of rules. For each of us remains unique within the fold, and we require the personal attention a shepherd would give a lamb, rather than the offhand supervision he bestows upon a flock of sheep.

Asceticism establishes a salutary slavery within us (nature) in order to give us a trustworthy independence (personality). At the end of the Spiritual Exercises, that long drill in asceticism, St. Ignatius introduces the marvelous *Contemplatio Ad Amorem*, the Loyolan passport to liberty. St. Ignatius makes us ascetics in order to turn us into lovers, and don't you forget that. He harnesses our nature with suitable restraints and bridles so as to give us the pace of those thoroughbreds of God, each steed with a different canter, clocked in a different time in the race to eternity.

We are in addition an apostolic Order, striving as much for the salvation of souls as we do for personal holiness, and there is no lovelier interchange of chariness and charity than this.

Transcendentalism and Immanentism

You have noticed that even among the professional mystics (which is not our vocation) there are those who emphasize the personal element and those who emphasize the element of nature in the attainment of their spiritual heights. The first group are the Transcendentalists. They stand off from God. God is too much for them. They grovel before the awefulness of His majesty. They approach God, as it were, by repelling Him, by making themselves nothing so that He may prevail. Their overture is a personal realization of the extreme differences between creature and Creator, between themselves and God. The result is, as you can see, a surrender in which personality is almost extinguished, not because it was not sure of itself, but because it was shocked at its own nothingness in relation to the transcendant surety of God's own Being. St. John of the Cross is a Transcendentalist.

The second group are the Immanentists. To them God is altogether too near. They are frightened at the fact that they

cannot get away from Him. The nature of God in its omni-
presence is emphasized rather than the person of God in His
Lordship of the world. Instead of rushing toward nothingness
in order to hide from the greatness of God, they succumb
to the greatness of God in order to lose their own nothingness.
St. Teresa of Avila is an Immanentist. She became so over-
flooded with Grace she floated to the ceiling.

> The Transcendentalists concentrate on the Infinity of
>   God.
> The Immanentists concentrate on the Simplicity of God.
> God is too much for the Transcendentalists (personalists)
>   to take.
> God is too easy for the Immanentists (naturalists) not
>   to take.*

St. John of the Cross, appalled by the person of himself,
ends up by talking about nothing but God.

St. Teresa of Avila, fascinated by the nature of God, ends
up by talking about nothing but herself.

St. John of the Cross is the man, the real man, because in
man's nature the transcendental element, the personal element,
is the stronger. St. Teresa of Avila is the typical woman. Man
is the go-away person in the sexes, the surrendered one in all
farewells, as he departs to sail the seas, discover new lands,
fight a war. Woman is the stay-at-home. The stay-at-home
element in us is *nature*. The go-away element is *person*.

When there is marriage, the stronger personality (man's)
prevails. Woman cancels her own name to write a man's in
place of it. Woman is the loved one, man the lover. When
there is a child from such a union, I always look for the per-
sonality of the father to be reflected, and the nature of the

---

* The divisions in actual practice are, of course, not as clear-cut as these
But the mystics are the loveliest of all folk, and are always amused at our
attempts to classify and understand them.

mother. The little boy has his father's walk and his father's talk; but his nature and all his sensitive endowments are much more from his mother, since he was housed in her for nine months and first fed at her breasts. This complement of the sexes in procreative love is charming, indeed sublime, and would to God it might restore *sex* to some of the dignity the word once possessed when love was a mystery that lent fragrance to a conservatory courtship, not a problem that added an odor to a laboratory experiment.

I might also mention that woman, knowing man's personality is the stronger, is constantly annoying him by telling him what he should do. "Tie your tie! . . . Put a pillow behind your head! . . . Please be on time for supper! . . . You forgot this! You forgot that!" etc.

A man who teases a woman in this way is a scoundrel. A man who cannot bear to be teased in this way is a sissy.

AGREEMENT AND DISAGREEMENT

Nature is the principle of our agreement with others. Personality is the principle of our disagreement. One who agrees with you in everything is either your lover or your liar, incapable, one way or the other, of giving a tang to the relaxed intercourses of friendship. One who disagrees with you in everything is your foe, perhaps terribly truthful, but can never be your friend.

COMMUNISM AND DICTATORSHIP

The paradigms of nature and person could be profitably applied to politics by someone schooled in the latter science. I have no knowledge of politics, and, it may be censurably, no interest. Except that it cannot escape me that in a Communistic system the exaggerated claims of what is common in man's nature obliterates the personalities of all; and in the Totalitarian scheme the exaggerated claims of what is singular in the personality of one despot obliterates the natures of all. Russia's night is a bedlam where all the dogs bark. Germany's night is a graveyard where a lone ass brays.

CHARITY AND CHASTITY

These two moral virtues have deep metaphysical roots. I am convinced there can be no intelligent moral charity and chastity until there has first been intelligent *intellectual* charity and chastity. Charity is the warmth within us we share with others (nature). Chastity is the coldness within us (personality) that keeps us from dissipating into an over-possessed thing. Chastity is not merely the safeguard of physical purity; it is the safeguard of spiritual independence. Charity is the tempering of spiritual pride. The world will never understand the Church's high championship of virginity because the world will not understand the Church's high championship of the rights of personality. In chastity our personality is most established. In charity our nature.

Our Lady was a Virgin-Mother. She has all the mystery, aloofness, independence, inviolateness of a maiden, and all the generosity, warmth and tenderness of a mother. Never in the world's history have the mysteries of person and nature in woman shone so beautifully in one human face. No wonder every artist in Christendom has wanted to go to his canvas and paint our Madonna. She is the matchless mother-maid, virginal and maternal. Among our other women personality and nature are honored in distinct vocations, in separate careers. Nuns emphasize the singular beauty of woman, each unwedded, unpossessed, attached to an eternal mystery, yet living in community so as to give balance to this distortion. Mothers emphasize the beauty of nature in woman, fruitful with child, heavy with milk in the breasts, her separate destiny engulfed in a stranger's name—yet emerging in her own little household, not as a subject, but as a queen.

A nice study of the exploits of woman in the territories

of nature and person can be made by a study of the two parallel phases of her fourfold career. Woman is a daughter, a sister, a bride and a mother. She is complemented in these vocations by man in the rôle of father, brother, husband and son. Father and brother set off the personal dignity of herself as a *self;* husband and son explore the depths of her surrender to others. A woman is most a person in being a daughter and a sister. She is most a woman in being a bride and a mother.

The Hardship of Personality

The hardship of being a person does not derive from the selfhood it bestows on us;—this we would not and could not surrender, not even to God Himself. Our nature can be sacrificed to our Creator in the last detail. But our selfhood can be undone only by annihilation. The hardship of being myself is that my nature has not enough perfection in it to support me in unrestrained delight; and second, because it is a created person that I am, and though a permanent thing now, I can look back with fear and trembling to my non-existent past. An eternal personality, therefore, must be a beautiful thing to behold.

Christ is an eternal person. Since the Incarnation, He has two natures in which to function, the nature of God and the nature of man. Read through the New Testament again with this one point in mind. Watch how the Eternal Word speaks, now out of the sublimity of His Divine nature ("The Father and I are One."); now out of the limitations of His human nature ("The Father is greater than I."). If you do not closely observe this interchange of statement in the paradox of Revelation—that arises out of the twofold nature of Our Lord: the one uncreated, the other created; the one begotten in the bosom of the Father, the other born of the Virgin Mary at Bethlehem; if you do not allow Him to speak, just as it pleases Him, either in time or in eternity—then the whole drama of the God-Man in everything He does and says will be wasted on you. You will find one text of Holy Scripture seeming completely to outlaw another. . . . Yet in the two natures marvelously joined in hypostatic union an eternal and uncreated *I* is forever speaking. How I should love to look into the eyes of an eternal person! Imagine how I should feel if a knock were to come on my door tonight, and in response to my call "Who's there?" the response should be: "*I Am Who Am!*"

STRANGENESS AND INTIMACY

Personality is the principle of strangeness in us: that in us which makes us blush to come too close to another either physically or in conversation or in confidence. It is the part of us which is marvelously disciplined in the Sacrament of Penance when we must undergo the humiliation of owning up to our sins; and the part of us which is marvelously refreshed in Holy Communion in the lovely secrecies of the heart's own citadel. And yet there is in us an urge to intimacy which is constantly defeating our snootiness and our pride. It arises mostly when our strangeness becomes too strange, when we begin to feel uncomfortable and awkward, when left in a lonely room, particularly if there is a mirror present. Solitary confinement—marooned on a desert island . . . there are degrees beyond which such things cannot be borne, and we run shrieking through a wilderness, wanting the clasp of another's hand, thirsting for the sound of another's voice.

SO FAR, SO GOOD

I trust, dear Thomas Butler, there have been in the considerations I have presented to you so far, some intellectual irritant that will at least give you pause when anyone attempt to tell you again that there is no difference in concept between a nature and a person, and that we are talking a contradiction when we speak of one God in three Divine Persons; or that we are embracing an absurdity when we innocently submit our minds to the uplift of Faith which demands such an intellectual assent to the truth of the All-Eternal.

When you say "What" you inquire for nature. When you say "Who" you inquire for person. We are constantly using these pronouns interrogatively, and there must be planted in the depths of our clouded minds some inference as to the difference of their meaning.

There is only one *What* in God.
There are three *Whos*.

FATHERHOOD AND CHILDHOOD

And yet, after all my excursions in the field of theological illustration, apt and inept, I prefer to return to the simple statement of the Blessed Trinity's truth as it was given to us in the Sign of the Cross when we were children.

In God, a Being who is all-perfect, immutable, eternal, absolute and worthy of the last prostration of the mind in adoration, there is a person who corresponds in a consummate and ideal way to every notion we have of Fatherhood. He is *Our Father*. His prerogatives are power, providence, justice, underived dominion over all that is. He is a God of Mercy too, and forgiveness, as behooves a good father. He was generated by no one, proceeds from no one, is the First Person of the Blessed Trinity, and can be dealt with in His own right, and can be called *You* in unique personal intercourse, not directly affecting His Divine associates. He is not less a father than the fathers we know. He is more a father. He feeds the sparrows, clothes the lilies of the fields, arranges the sunsets, regulates the crescendoes of the storms. From Him all paternity is derived in Heaven and on earth. He is the Creator and Conserver of all things.

There is also in the nature of the same, identical God a person who corresponds to everything we can apprehend in the notion of sonship, of childhood, only intensified to an infinite degree. He is begotten of the Father in eternity. He is the exemplar according to which all things visible and invisible were made. He is the *Word of God*, vibrant with a self all His own. Everything the Father possesses in the essential perfections of the Godhead, the Son possesses too, for the nature presented to Him in His eternal birth is not an halved infinity, it is the full infinity of the Parent who gives Him birth. He is begotten in eternity, looks backward to no past, forward to no future. If you went up to Him and asked, as a child might, "When is your birthday?" He would answer "Now!" He appropriates the work of redemption of the Human Race, came to earth, became man, suffered and died for us, is Our Saviour. His name in our midst is Jesus, a name picked by an angel, or at least announced by an angel when it had been chosen in the Councils of Heaven. His temporal generation occurred in the womb of the Virgin Mary, by the power of the Holy Spirit.

There is also another *self* in God, no less real than the Father and the Son, proceeding from them in an eternal spiration of otherness which it is wonderful to think about. He is identical with them in power, majesty and perfection of nature, but different from them when He uses the pronoun of the first person singular. He is called the Holy Spirit. He is the mutual love of the Father and the Son, deriving from the Divine reality so that He may commune with them in an own-ness which is truly His, but for which they are responsible, and He grateful and delighted. He corresponds to all we can conceive in the way of sacredness and holiness, blowing, as it were, like a breath from God's own Being. He appropriates the works of sanctification, organization and comfort towards the created world, broods over it with infinite compassion. Because of some strange prerogative, not fathomed by our minds, it is demanded that we call Him also The Spirit of Truth. Wherever the image of God is implanted in the likeness of the Son, there He rushes to find a temple, and insists on dwelling. He is represented to us in symbol by two beautiful rebuses:

First, a fluttering white dove, suggesting gentleness, peace, repose; second, a flaming tongue of fire, representing Love's raging devouring power.

> *In the Name of the Father, and of the Son, and of the Holy Ghost. Amen.*

A Tie-Up Unexplained

And yet, despite all the distinctions between person and nature which I have been at such pains to point out to you, there is a tie-up between the Persons of God and the Nature of God which it requires a master-hand to express with the proper exactitude. I give you, as such a master-hand, Saint Athanasius, Doctor of the Universal Church, that skilled spokesman of the Divine challenge, ruthless in reconciling what would seem to be opposed in the Blessed Trinity, ruthless in keeping distinct what would seem to have been identified. His exposé you will find under the heading *Symbolum Athanasium,** in Prime of your Breviary, in the most beautiful blend of dogma, poetry and prayer I have ever read. The echoes of the phrases are always with me: . . .

> Fides autem catholica haec est:
>> ut unum Deum in Trinitate, et Trinitatem in unitate veneremur. . . .
> Neque confundentes personas, neque substantiam separantes . . .
> Alia est enim persona Patris, alia Filii, alia Spiritus Sancti . . .
> Sed Patris, et Filii, et Spiritus Sancti una est divinitas, aequalis gloria, coeterna majestas.

* There is a dispute as to the precise author of the Athanasian Creed. But we may give our Saint the same credit at least that Homer would receive for the Iliad, or, according to some, Shakespeare for Hamlet.

Qualis Pater, talis Filius, talis Spiritus Sanctus.

Increatus Pater, increatus Filius, increatus Spiritus Sanctus.

Immensus Pater, immensus Filius, immensus Spiritus Sanctus.

Aeternus Pater, aeternus Filius, aeternus Spiritus Sanctus.

Et tamen non tres aeterni, sed unus aeternus. . . .

And so, on he goes, in forty-one stanzas of such frightening, solemn, confident, incessant exactitude that you would almost know from the very rhythm of the piece that it was stimulated by a beatific beat that always keeps time with it in eternity, whenever and wherever it is spoken on earth.

GOOD NIGHT

It is now well beyond midnight. I have worked hard all day trying to finish these thoughts which can never be finished. I have tried hard to explain the unexplainable. The defect is not in God; it is in the clumsy comprehension of my defective intelligence.

I have wandered a great deal, repeated the same thing over and over again until you have perhaps grown tired of hearing them. Well, one little elusive beam from the Eternal Truth would be worth it, if you can find such in this outline. But I fear you will not find it. Everything slipped through my fingers. But at least I could hold up my fingers tonight and show you that they were poised for the clasping of some beauty beyond this world if God could only be apprehended by any of our human devices of capture.

God is a very blinding light. The experience of gyrating around Him in thought, of sensing Him to be near, yet never finding Him, is a dizzy adventure. And yet the experience is not all dizziness. There is an unexplained delight, an allurement, that draws me back again and again to the same search. God has the human mind trapped. There are only two things worth thinking about: Heaven and Hell. Heaven is ha enough, but a man must go on thinking. Hell is both hard and horrible. One of the hall-marks of the unhallowed in Hell is that they gave up. I shall not give up. Tomorrow I shall give a conference on the Blessed Trinity to the very old men at the home of the Little Sisters of the Poor. You intellectuals are not the easiest people to explain things to.

There are also fruits to be derived even from a fruitless quest. I seem to be a little more aware than ever, at the end of this long day, of the uniqueness of myself, precisely because I have been pondering the uniqueness of the selves of God.

Most of me I can never share with you. So do not expect it. If you love the Blessed Trinity, as I know you do, think and pray for yourself, and forget this "explanation."

I am on the fifth floor of one of our community houses in New York City. I am the last of the wakeful, gone past midnight which is advancing into morning. Window by window I have seen the lights go out in the apartment houses that surround us here. I continue to tap very lightly on my typewriter, for others below me are asleep. At least I imagine they are. But what's Hecuba to me or I to Hecuba?

Sometimes, one takes refuge from the relentlessness of a frightening thought by turning to rhyme. It is the foolish way of the poet. He writes for his own relief much more than he does for the delectation of others. I shall make an ending, therefore, with a little verse, which I shall not attempt to explain, and which you do not need to bother to understand. Let us give the little verse a name. I shall call it:

RESIGNATION AT MIDNIGHT

Sleep has already come to other eyes,
　　Dreams are not driftwood tangled in their thickets;
Nobody else is left without allies
　　To count the clock-ticks and applaud the crickets.

But self is self, assignment without appeal,—

However restlessly one plays the part.
Out of another's slumber my soul would steal
Home to its ache in this accustomed heart.

*Glory be to the Father, and to the Son, and to the Holy
Ghost. As it was in the beginning, is now and ever shall
be, world without end. . . . Amen!*

THE METAPHYSICS OF CHESTERTON

CHESTERTON WAS A MAN of few ideas made expansive by a
gorgeous imagination and a complete and accurate set of
moral sympathies. He said the same things over and over
again, but in so many different ways, and loved the same
things over and over again, but from so many different angles
that he never found it needful to create a brave new world
in order to be either courageous or original.

I

In person Chesterton was a large man who was something
of a strain on his clothes. Tidiness he persistently ignored in
favor of comfort. Everyone who got near him was tempted
to rearrange him, or at least to giving thought as to how it
could be done. Eventually Chesterton gave up the idea of
expecting to be held together in ordinary attire by ordinary
threads and buttons, and went around wearing a cloak. The
simplicity with which one could secure a sort of stylish se-
clusion by the tying of a single knot or the fastening of a
single hook appealed to Chesterton. A cloak was a garment
calculated to reveal not how he was fashioned but where he
was to be found.

In point of kindliness, Chesterton had one of the biggest

hearts that has ever lived. And yet I am told the doctors found it undersized physically when they examined him in one of his illnesses. Nothing daunted, he went right on using what share of heart he had to love the world largely and lavishly until the hour of his death. This is what is known as a paradox.

When Chesterton stood up he was impressive. But it was even more marvelous to watch him sit down. He sat down with an air of supreme humility, as if totally collapsing in the arms of God. In the difficult assignment of being both huge and human he needed lots of support. Once seated, he would doze and dream a great deal, and seemed constantly distracted by the incessant rush of his own thoughts.

As humility was Chesterton's outstanding moral virtue, so what he chose to call "sanity" was what he wanted most for the mind. He was far too humble to suppose that one could appropriate sanity as an assured possession without offering plenty of credentials. And so he undertook to outline what he meant by sanity perhaps more carefully than any man of his generation. One of his contemporaries, George Bernard Shaw, said sanity was the specialty of the superman. This pseudo-preternaturalism annoyed Chesterton, and his reply was devastating. "Shaw criticizes human nature," he said, "as though he himself did not possess it." Another contemporary, H. G. Wells, offered hope that sanity might blossom in some strain of the future. Chesterton was quick to analyze this mixture of biology and guesswork masquerading as prophecy, and he exposed it to relentless ridicule. In the end he made more of a monkey out of Wells than Evolution ever had.

The sanity which interested, and indeed fascinated, Chesterton was the sanity which has already occurred in the world, whose proof is in tradition, whose roots are in the past, whose record is in history. That welter of things which men of all times have accepted as lovable and true he labeled Orthodoxy. Of this Orthodoxy he was prepared to act as Defendant. He did so in one hundred and two books,[1] writing as many as eight in a single year. He felt Orthodoxy to be a cause to which one should be loyal. He called it the Flag of the World. He thought laughter was a good air in which to float the Flag of the World. He conceived laughter as something more than a human roar that went rollicking up to the skies; he believed it to be a divine delight that had descended to earth and was shaking it. He was prepared to trace its tremors everywhere and said its source was in the mirth of God. When criticized on this and other points for not being serious, he made his brilliant and never-to-be-forgotten distinction between the serious and the solemn man.

So much for the "physics" of Chesterton.

II

It will surprise many of my readers to find me associating the notion of metaphysics with the name of Chesterton. One is wont nowadays to associate it more readily with a name like Maritain, perhaps because of the alliteration. But it is my conviction that Chesterton could destroy many of our so-called metaphysicians right in the territory of their own thinking. By way of becoming "pure mentalities" they pretend to have gotten rid of all emotion in thought. They tolerate Chesterton only because of the scintillation of his ideas. They do not approve of him, as is evidenced by the fastidious way in which, kid-gloved with logic, they handle realities which he was prepared to rush at with bare hands, and in the full panoply of his powers. One or other of them will occasionally quote Chesterton, but it is always with a smile—a little, soft, academic smile, as if to say: "Pardon this fantastic

[1] This total is generous enough to include ten items which are more pamphlet-sized than book-sized. But it does not include fourteen books in which he collaborated, three books contracted for but not published, nor the great number of introductions he wrote for other peoples' books.

interruption in my otherwise reliable ratiocination. It will allow us to indulge in the delicate pleasure of depreciation. It may also serve to relieve the tension of the classroom."

By way of defending Chesterton against these intellectual isolationists, I may say that his laughter was not an emotion in the sense in which they take the word unfavorably. It was not a frivolous attitude of mind which prejudiced thought, as in the case of a mere comedian. It was rather the fruit of thought—often of some very grim thought—and it occurred to him by way of a spontaneous explosion which he thought it unwise to resist. When he described himself as "a well-meaning hippopotamus," he did not do so by way of ridiculing the notion of "rational animal," but by way of showing that ideas which get on very well together in the abstract order do so less sociably when outfitted to exist. Logic deals with essences, laughter with existences. Essences may be proved, but existences must be affirmed. Once affirmed, existences can never be identified by definition, only by description, and if description be forbidden to touch them, then something metaphysical gets lost. Laughter is one way of restoring it. When a reality has been reached which is prepared both to define and describe itself with the triumphant affirmation: "I am Who am!" then logic and laughter both subside in an eternal stillness. The mind has at last arrived at the world's most serious secret. There is nothing left to do but blindly deny or boldly adore.

If it be objected against laughter that it is more of an observer than a critic, it must also be said of it that it leaves ideas fully delineated as the mind first found them, completely focused for action. Under such a favorable spotlight what takes place is something in the nature of a prizefight. But whereas logic wants to follow the contestants around in the role of referee shouting rules, laughter is content to sit back as a spectator and cheer for whatever happens. For ideas in action are not only never fully sociable, but there are times when one idea threatens to knock out another so completely as to leave no mystery between them. Laughter enjoys this hugely, for it is utterly a fanatic, known in sports parlance as "a fan." Chesterton was not only willing to admit he was a fanatic, he boasted of it. For a fanatic is merely an enthusiastic witness giving testimony. A fanatic is not a partisan making a perverted report. That Chesterton was never a partisan, I am prepared to show.

It is clear from the early pages of his *Autobiography* that Chesterton's home was not a place notably given to despondency. His parents were kindly, lovable people, and nothing in his early training drove him to despair. Puritanism of a sort was there, but it was not that extreme Puritanism which makes everything pleasurable a sin. Puritanism had done much more harm to houses in Chesterton's neighborhood than it had to his own. Puritanism had, for instance, transferred conviviality from the village tavern to the village bar-room; from a place where a man might sleep off his intoxication to a place where he gets thrown out for being drunk. Puritanism was the cause of Chesterton's "hell-instructed grocer" who ruined the business of innkeepers by making customers of over bibulous duchesses furtively drinking in their dressing-rooms. Nothing of this coarseness had touched Chesterton's own household. It was a household in which he was reasonably contented and to whose inhabitants he was always scrupulously loyal. In this last he differs greatly from those de bunkers of Puritan culture lately derived from Boston, Mass. U. S. A., who air their grudges in melancholy novels that ruin the reputations of their families.

But if Chesterton's home was, on all simple, substantial counts, a happy one, it had not nearly as much happiness as he wanted to put there once he became an adolescent and had begun to read. As soon as he found from his reading what European homes in general, and English homes in particular had been in the past, he sought to improve his own, not in the manner of an interior decorator with a new *motif*, but rather as one who would refurnish it with things that had wrongfully been taken from it by that sad trick of history known as the Protestant Reformation. Within the four walls in which Chesterton proposed to live, he wanted more dining done, more dancing, dreaming and diversion, even more drinking, and particularly more religious devotion. What that devotion was to be in terms of dogma he was not at once ready to say. But that some chill between man and God had occurred right at his own fireside, he was alert and generous enough to see. If this be called partisanship, then the word has no decent meaning.

Later in life, when Chesterton married and made a home of his own, he restored to it much of what he had been deprived of in his youth. But there was one bright item which, by the strange will of God, he was not able to restore. And that was a child. And yet never once, by the slightest petulance or resentment, did he make his own childlessness the measure of a home's true worth. With every talent in his power—by story, by treatise, by poetry, by apostrophe, by prayer, by the writing of nursery rhymes and the drawing of pictures—he sought to please, and pay tribute to, the child. He even went boldly to the defense of the child unborn. He literally blasted Dean Inge of London for his moral stand on the prevention of children. "The trouble with the Dean of St. Paul's," he wrote in words as accurately as I can recall them, "is not that he is merely anti-Catholic, he is anti-Christian. He thinks pride a virtue and humility a vice. This temper of mind governs all he does, and lately when he brought it to bear on the subject of birth-control, it never even remotely occured to him to consider that his own birth might have been prevented."

So certain was Chesterton that partisanship had never influenced his own thought, that he was prepared to criticize it vigorously when he saw it tampering with the thought of others. Arnold Lunn, some time before his conversion to the

Catholic Church, wrote a book called *Roman Converts*. It was a very patronizing book in which Lunn sought to make nice adjustments between the motives which led men like Newman and Ronald Knox into the Church, and those which drove men like Tyrrell out of it. In one unfortunate paragraph Lunn, who boasted otherwise of being a sportsman, so forgot his sense of fair play as to call God's Mother "the patron of a party," remarking that Christ was "never a party leader." Chesterton fairly leapt at this cheap remark and tore it to shreds. In a burst of magnificent indignation he wrote a poem called "A Party Question." "Who made that inn a fortress?" he shouted in defense of Our Blessed Lady. And he ended by calling the phrase Lunn had used, "That little hiss that only comes from Hell." Chesterton could afford to be chivalrous on this particular subject, because twenty-five years before his own conversion to Catholicism, in the days when he was religiously no more than a young agnostic, he paid the "Party Question" this youthful and pathetic tribute:

> Hail, Mary! Thou blest among women; generations shall rise up to greet.
> After ages of wrangle and dogma, I come with a prayer to thy feet.
> Where Gabriel's red plumes are a wind in the lanes of thy lilies at eve,
> We pray, who have done with the churches; we worship, who may not believe.

Chesterton is classified in literature most frequently as controversialist. Some prefer to label him simply: a journalist "Defendant" would be a good name for him, but hardly genre in which to put a writer. "Literary man" is far too loose a term to fit him. True, he excelled in many and varied styles of literature, particularly as an essayist, and very valuably the field of literary criticism. T. S. Eliot, for instance, believed there has never been a better critic of Dickens than Chesterton

But Chesterton was scarcely a literary man in the sense in which Maurice Baring is one, or Max Beerbohm, or the late E. V. Lucas. One archbishop, even during Chesterton's lifetime, was all for calling him a Doctor of the Church. However unofficial, this compliment may be taken as more than a mere pleasantry. For if the requirements of a Doctor of the Church are *eximia scientia et sanctitas*, surely something perilously near to both must be ascribed to a man who could roam without an *imprimatur* through all Catholic theology, hagiology and apologetics and never make a statement which the most meticulous Ultra-montane could suspect of heresy; and who could fill a hundred books with an almost beer-garden joviality and never write a line that would cause a child to blush. It would be nice to have a St. Gilbert taking rank with St. Augustine, St. Bernard and St. Thomas, but the proposal, however exciting, had best be left to the justice and generosity of the Pope.

III

And so, for want of a better rating, Chesterton must fall back into classification either as a poet or a philosopher. By way of escaping this "dilemma" we might make a third choice and say he was a mystic. Indeed, there are in *Orthodoxy* (his most brilliant book) abundant passages that illustrate the mystical quality of his mind. But his was an imaginative rather than an illuminative mysticism. It was not achieved—and it is no criticism of his morals to say so—by that rigid asceticism of the senses which leaves the mind devoutly dark and patiently prepared to receive the pure light of the supernatural. Chesterton's was the colorful approach to mysticism: to mystery by way of magic, to angels by way of fairies, to God the Father by way of Mother Goose. Chesterton saw, and rightly, a serious psychological necessity in Mother Goose; but she is hardly the sacred religious need expressed in the Lord's

Prayer. True, there is, as Chesterton points out, a marvelous asceticism achieved in every simple choice of charity (a man who chooses one woman to be his wife renounces all other women), but this is the choice of charity in the moral order, more properly called charitableness. It is not the infused, supernatural Charity spoken of by St. Paul, which is strictly theological and in which no choice is given: no choice but the pure surrender to the terror and bewilderment of being chosen.

It is also to be noted about the mysticism of Elfland, that it can devise no clear symbol even for what it wants to say in the order of poetry. It is a damnable business to undo a beautiful piece of imaginative writing by pointing out its logical flaw, but that is what we must do with Chesterton precisely at the point where he is trying to show the superiority of imagination over reason. He says in *Orthodoxy* at the end of his well-known chapter on "The Maniac":

> That transcendentalism by which all men live has primarily much of the position of the sun in the sky. We are conscious of it as a kind of splendid confusion; it is something both shining and shapeless, at once a blaze and a blur. But the circle of the moon is as clear and unmistakable, as recurrent and inevitable, as the circle of Euclid on a blackboard. For the moon is utterly reasonable; and the moon is the mother of lunatics and has given to them all her name.

This, however fascinatingly spoken, is arbitrary symbolism of the very worst kind. For it is not the visual clarity of the moon— that soft clarity which is the delight and companionship of lovers—which causes lunatics. It is rather the imperceptible gravity of the moon, that tugs at temperaments as does on tides. But inasmuch as relatively few temperaments are as unstable as water, the weight of the moon may be disregarded while the wonder of the moon remains. True, the moon may not light up the rest of the world as brilliantly the sun does, but in all its shapes, from crescent to full disc, it is the best form in which to look at light itself. The real lunatic is not the moon gazer nor the star gazer but the one who tries to outstare the sun. Furthermore, in Christian mysticism, the moon is Our Lady. "Pulchra ut luna" is God's own phrase for her: a symbol with a divine guarantee.

If one could go through the whole of Chesterton's works and gather together the great number of brilliant and accurate things he has said on the subject of epistemology, psychology, cosmology and ethics, one would have a book full of philosophic wisdom which no philosopher could afford to ignore. But unfortunately the journalist in Chesterton clouded much of what was the true philosopher. In his effort to study the universal within the local—which is the philosopher's task— he frequently became too local, and at times hopelessly insular. Chesterton is in great part untranslatable, which no philosopher can afford to be. His deepest thought is sometimes so bound up with superficial English idiom, or manners, or even politics, that one is often required to know the inside of the mind of some nonentity like J. H. McCabe or F. E. Smith before one can get to what Chesterton himself is saying. The discriminating reader will, of course, make allowances for these provincialisms, especially since they occur within the orbit of such large and valuable thinking. But, alas, philosophy is a science that cannot be safely entrusted to the discriminating mind. It is at once the philosopher's strength and weakness that he must safeguard his most tenuous judgments with a sort of universal language, which at its best can travel instantaneously from mind to mind independently of time and place, and at its worst is a jargon of such words as: *virtualiter*, *potentialiter*, *aequivalenter*, *eminenter*, that capture a minimum of idea and are almost the ruination of speech.

IV

Some criticism similar to that which I have made of Chesterton as a philosopher, must also be made of him as a poet. No poet of the twentieth century (with the exception of Hilaire Belloc) had a better command of the traditional forms and subsidiary styles of verse than had Chesterton. He could write a *ballade* or a *rondeau* as well as any man who ever lived. In satire, burlesque and parody he was superb. Likewise the number of utterly wonderful things he has said *about* poetry (not in any one place, but scattered throughout his work, sometimes in a detective story, sometimes in a treatise on economics) ought to be collected and put in one book. Mr. F. J. Sheed told me he thought of making such a collection some day. I hope he will. It might well begin with the accolade Chesterton gives the poet for being "the only man in the world who knows what he wants to say, and can say it."

But when it came to writing poetry himself, in serious fashion, Chesterton was altogether too committed to a single manner: the grandiose. He was often sublime in his verse, but rarely exquisite. He was constantly the troubadour thumping out a great theme. When the material suited his mood, as it did in *Lepanto* or the *Ballad of the White Horse*, all went well. But all did not go well in his simpler verse, or rather I should say, in his verse that ought to have been simpler.

> When fishes flew and forests walked
>   And figs grew upon thorn,
> Some moment when the moon was blood
>   Then surely I was born

is, I protest, utterance too apocalyptic to suit the plain fact of a donkey, even the humble little beast who carried Our Lord in triumph through the streets of Jerusalem. I myself once wrote a poem on a donkey, so I may be presumed to know hi requirements in verse. At least my donkey is a creature who may be more calmly recognized.

> Hitched by a halter to a rail,
> He twitched his ears and twirled his tail;
> In every lineament and line
> He was completely asinine.

Let my stanza be only the tribute from one donkey to another; at least a donkey remains somewhere in the arrangement, not merely a nightmare on the subject of Palm Sunday.

V

Poor Chesterton! If he be, in the unrestricted sense, neither poet, nor philosopher, nor mystic, then where shall we place him? Must he be the "tattered outlaw" of all categories simply because none could contain him? No. I believe there is one rating he deserves, without any reservation. Chesterton was one of the world's greatest metaphysicians.

If it be objected that metaphysics is, after all, only philosophy (a competence from which I have already removed Chesterton), then I shall object again that metaphysics is not, after all, only philosophy. Metaphysics is what Aristotle—who never used the word metaphysics—called "the first philosophy." It could as readily be called "the first poetry" or "the first mysticism." Briefly, metaphysics is the preoccupation of the mind with *being* as *being*, with *thing* as *thing*. Briefly, metaphysics is what Chesterton called "Aristotle's colossal common sense."

Technically, here is the way the "first philosophy" is handled. The logician discovers in metaphysics the contingency of things, their essential insufficiency to exist by themselves: hence his distinctions between essence and existence, potency and act, imperfection and perfection, accidents and substance. The poet discovers in the same metaphysics the forms by which potencies have been actualized: hence his attention to the integrity, clarity and proportion by which contingent things endeavor to image the *pure act* from which they originate. The mystic derives from metaphysics a loving interest in the undeserved gift which all contingent beings are both to themselves and to those who behold them; hence his tributes of adoration, gratitude and humility. For *being* as *being* has three intrinsic attributes (three transcendental notes) which are inseparable from it: it is *true*, it is *beautiful* and it is *good*. Indeed, it has a fourth inseparable note which is almost the undoing of the other three. It is *one*. Wherefore, no mere logician can be a perfect metaphysician, any more than a mere poet can, or a mere mystic. Each has only a one third interest in the subject of *being;* the logician in *ens qua verum*, the poet in *ens qua pulchrum*, the mystic in *ens qua bonum*. The logician will tell you himself, as he must, that he has no pure ontology. His ontology is necessarily clouded by the analogies in which he words it. The pure *logos* of anything is known to God alone. Likewise does the poet cloud the pure beauty of things with his metaphors, and the mystic the pure goodness of things with his symbols. But the complete metaphysician is the "compleat angler" who fishes for being *qua* being with every bait at his disposal. What cannot be caught with analogy can sometimes be taken by metaphor, or by symbol, or vice versa in any order. How wonderful if all three should work together! In such a metaphysician as Chesterton I believe they did, at least far more strikingly than they do in most men.[2]

[2] In fairness to my reader I think I must say that, as far as I myself am concerned, this is a speculative arrangement, not a practical one. The metaphysical scheme I here outline seems to me sound enough, but, unfortunately, except in the case of geniuses and saints, it is unfeasible for the general run of us. It is thoroughly unfeasible for me. Unlike Chesterton cannot say that I discovered the Doctrine of Original Sin before it was revealed to me. Without my Faith I should certainly be prone to cope with the ignorance, ugliness and iniquity of man by equalizing in him the functions of philosopher, poet and mystic. But, alas, I know from Revelation that Original Sin has lessened the wonder and warmth of the human

In page after page, in book after book, I find examples of this metaphysical harmony in Chesterton's perceptions. As soon as he was able to think, he plunged right into the heart of "the first philosophy." When his tooth ached, along with inquiring "Why have I a toothache?" he also inquired "Why have I a tooth?" and indeed "Why have I anything?" His fondness in early childhood was more than for wood you could whittle, water you could drink, and soap you could wash with; it was for "the toughness of wood, the wetness of water, and the magnificent soapiness of soap." Nothing could be more metaphysical than this.

Almost the very first utterance Chesterton the writer made to the world was the declaration of his own contingency, the confession of his own utter needlessness to anything or anybody. So unnecessary did he consider himself to the universe around him that he immediately rejected Pantheism as a religious creed because it deprived him of a God to whom he could be grateful for his existence. "I want to adore the world," he said, "not as one likes a looking glass, because it is oneself, but as one loves a woman because she is entirely different."

---

mind and left it with little more than a sense of curiosity. At least it is in terms of mere curiosity that nearly all education is now pursued. Curiosity, if thorough enough, will make a fairly good logician (e.g. Mr. Mortimer Adler). The logician wants problems to solve. He regrets the point where problems threaten to become mysteries, where curiosity must cease and let contemplation come in. But, unfortunately again, contemplation can never return to the human race wholesale, and never in the full pristine innocence in which Adam enjoyed it when he surveyed everything with a child's insight and went around calling the animals by name. With our loss of the power of contemplation the simple beauty and goodness of things has disappeared. We are left with nothing but the cold truth on our hands: "the bitter truth," "the hard painful truth," that must be pieced together by the patient study not of things *in themselves*, but of things *in their causes*. Apart from the liturgy of the supernatural, which is safeguarded by the Church, and the special illumination of Grace, which is the free gift of the Holy Spirit, I find no reliable poetry or mysticism in this world. And so I am content to amble along with the philosophers as my best guides, knowing that they have taught me all I know, and hoping that Faith will fulfill in me what their dialectics never can.

The gift of life he defined as "a kind of eccentric privilege" for which we owe an infinite gratitude. He declared he found everywhere "the sense of the preciousness and fragility of the universe, the sense of being in the hollow of a hand." He scorned the pessimist who criticizes this world "as if he were house hunting, as if he were being shown over a new set of apartments." He would not allow any low estimate of our beloved universe to be made. He wrote: "While dull atheists came and explained to me that there was nothing but matter, I listened with a sort of calm detachment, suspecting that there was nothing but mind." The Materialist, he agreed, did explain the cosmos, but "with a sort of insane simplicity" which forced Chesterton to say that "it was not much of a cosmos" when any innocent beholder could suggest a so much better one.

Chesterton was literally entranced with the thingness of things, with facts as facts, not deviously explained, but bravely accepted as they are. He wrote a whole book about things as things, and called it *Tremendous Trifles*. He believed that the very repetition of things was a delightful argument for design. "One elephant with its absurd trunk is a wildly amusing sight," he wrote, "but for all elephants to have trunks suggests a conspiracy." Even in their grotesque form he was anxious to preserve the most fantastic and useless pieces of creation. If someone said: "Camels in various places are totally diverse: some have six legs, some have none, some have scales, some have feathers," Chesterton vowed he would reply: "Then what do you mean by a camel? What makes you call them camels?"

Chesterton brought this simple metaphysical outlook to the deepest experiences of his life. Merely to be in the presence of any human being, however lowly, caused him pleasure. Merely to know that any woman could be his wife astonished him. Here is his charming stanza (from the poem "The Beatific Vision") written, with that detached devotion which is the essence of pure love, to Frances Blogg Chesterton.

But what shall God not ask of him
In the last time when all is told
Who saw her stand beside the hearth,
The firelight garbing her in gold.

"The first philosophy" will not cause a prophet or a super-
man. It will not create a new cosmos, devise a new civilization,
or evolute a new era. Hence, little of our modern thinking is
done in terms of it. But it will give one a healthy, happy,
hilarious outlook upon things as they are, capable of making
every ordinary thing appear as a portent. "It is to the ordinary
man that odd things seem extraordinary," wrote Chesterton,
"to the extraordinary man they are simply ordinary." Ches-
terton preferred to be, and always was, in however extraor-
dinary a way, the ordinary man. "A thing worth doing at all
is worth doing badly" was one of his profundities in the realm
of common sense. He refused to allow the oddness of the
world to be destroyed by familiarity. He felt the short space of
a man's life was not time enough in which to exhaust the
strangeness of the world, or alter his own position in it as a
stranger. Rather than lose a sense of the strangeness of things
(which metaphysics calls "their contingency") he was pre-
pared to look at the universe standing on his head.

I have not read all of Chesterton's books. But I have read
enough to know that his outstanding talent was the one I have
indicated, and that I can expect abundant manifestations of it
wherever I turn in his writings. And so, before I leave him, I
pay him a great compliment, indeed one of the greatest I think
I could possibly pay. I call him "the laughing metaphysician."
He laughed loudly at himself, which is humility; and he made
others laugh, which is charity.

Notes

———◆———

TWO WHO SHOULD BE FRIENDS

THE POET is to the philosopher what the saint is to the theologian. The theologian expounds and proves things, the saint intensifies and lives them. The philosopher uses his discursive mind, and arrives at a much larger and more coherent body of truth than the poet does. But the philosopher uses a much poorer process of thought than does the poet. The poet's way is that of insight, intuition, realization. The philosopher's way is that of ratiocination, which is an inferior form of knowing, for all that it arrives at such extensive conclusions. *Est per imperfectionem intellectus quod abstrahat.* God is neither ratiocinative nor discursive. But He is not imaginative either.

The impatience of the saint with the theologian, or of the poet with the philosopher, is unreasonable. We are constituted in an imperfect state, and logic must correct love and keep it from getting out of hand. The mystic needs the doctor of divinity, and the dreamer the dialectician. A star, however bright, needs the discipline of the celestial organization in order to keep it from veering off alone into space, or of crashing into other stars. Dante needed Saint Thomas Aquinas.

The poet wants truth to be thrilling. The philosopher wants it to be correct, to be truth. One cannot get at truth in any systematic and satisfactory fashion by simply submitting himself to another's thrills. In this comparison the poet suffers dreadfully, becomes almost ridiculous. Still, what is the value of truth to us if it is not made attractive, alluring, alive? In this comparison the philosopher comes off as the dismal one.

Philosophy is a science, not an art, and its findings can be as monotonous as they are exact. Nobody ever comes out of a class in metaphysics shouting: "Oh hurrah, hurrah! Did you know that the primary formal effect of quantity is not to give a material substance local actual extension, but simply to arrange the parts aptitudinally? Isn't it exciting! Doesn't it make you want to cry?" Still, the poet has a right to say to the philosopher when he has executed a faultless syllogism and arrived at an irrefutable conclusion: "Well, what about it! Now that you've got it, what are you going to do with it?" The philosopher, as such, does simply nothing about it. He goes back to his room, lights his pipe, and buries himself in the want ads of the evening newspaper.

The poet has been prepared to unlace his shoes, tear off his stockings and run barefoot through the grass shouting the joy of a discovery. The philosopher discovers lots and lots of things, but, if you will notice, never seems very pleased about it. He knows lots more than the poet does, but he does not know what he knows so richly or so well. Theologian and saint oppose each other with the same differences. It is conceivable that there are some Doctors of Sacred Theology (Licentiates of Sacred Theology, a poet would call them with his usual inexactitude) in Hell. The Curé of Ars seems to have assimilated only one thesis of this sacred science, namely, God is good; and is a Saint, crowned for our altars.

The philosopher goes for a whole, and then endeavors to find the parts. The poet goes for a part, and through it endeavors to find the whole. Think of a philosopher attempting to qualify in examination in only one thesis in psychology: The human soul is immortal! And yet a poet could qualify in this one subject in a single piece of inspired verse. Think of a seminarian expecting to be advanced to the priesthood upon having studied only one treatise in dogmatic theology: The childhood of Jesus! And yet the Little Flower was advanced to sainthood for knowing nothing else.

I repeat that philosophy is a science, and it is best learnt with all imaginative and emotional implications left out. Putting emotion and imagination into a science can be disastrous. Two and two are four, says the mathematician. The poet will, of course, want him to say: Two peacocks and two peacocks are four peacocks. But if you start in to add that way, you may be distracted from the accuracy of the computation by the brilliance of the objects added.

Should the poet and the philosopher fuse together and present us with the perfect man? There is no harm in it, but I think it best to keep them apart; but as friends, not adversaries. Each should have proper sympathies for the other. The poet should not look upon the philosopher as an old fogey. Neither should the philosopher look upon the poet as an old fool. The poet should go to the philosopher for direction. But the philosopher might profitably go to the poet, for relief.

CLEAN LITERATURE

THE PROBLEM is not merely a moral one; it is a psychological and cultural one as well. I should like to offer a few considerations on this subject. There will be no harm in setting them down in thesis form. And some of our young people may be interested in reading them, if only to be provided with topics for discussion.

1. The intellect as such can face any subject without quailing. But none of us is an intellect "as such." Our intellects are united in substantial union to a most delicately exquisite and tenuous instrument of knowledge which is material, the imagination. This imagination is not discriminative, and when it is assailed with foul and brutal pictures it records them with the fidelity of a camera film, and stores them away for future

reference. This imagination can be easily injured. It is the focal point for such disturbances as frights, phobias, nightmares. When it is attacked by a lewd picture or a lewd description in a book, it cannot bear to hold the shock within itself but quickly diffuses it to the sense appetites and desires, thereby destroying the symphony of purity that should exist in a child of Mary. I am not speaking here of "mortal sin, mortal sin." That can come only when the spiritual will enters and freely approves the whole performance. I am simply speaking of the disorder, the disgustingness, the sickness of the whole business.

2. What it is needful for us to know can always come to us under the proper auspices. In such cases we *learn* facts, not merely *luxuriate* in them; the intellect is directly catered to with no effort to inflame the imagination. A class in moral theology or medicine can be as chaste as a lily garden. But it is simply abysmal ignorance for anyone who pretends to be an educator not to know that in the case of the young the imagination always outspeeds the intellect in performance, and that guarded and graded instruction in the matter of adolescent morals is the only intelligent procedure possible.

This does not mean that one must answer the candid questions of a child untruthfully. This need never be done, and God gives to parents, confessors, teachers and doctors who have the child's spiritual welfare sincerely at heart, the Grace to create auspices under which legitimate questions can be legitimately answered. But it is extremely important to remember that a child's problems are those of a child, not of a parent. To force-feed him with sex instruction as to how he shall become a parent before he has well enjoyed the rapturous experience of being a child, is not only a devilish device, not only out of all proportion with the physical capacities of his nature, it is a disastrous spiritual and imaginative experience. That this forced-feeding abounds in our irreligious schools is common knowledge. No wonder our children must pass from the classroom to the psychoanalyst's clinic in order to arrive safely at the tottering maturity of twenty-one. It is tragically ridiculous to read in the newspaper this very day of a psychoanalyst who killed himself with an ice-pick. I thought psychoanalysts were people who teach you how to keep from doing such things.

3. There has always seemed to me something weird, something sinister, something really diabolical about going to a drug store to buy a book. And drug stores, as you know, are going in for literature nowadays in a large way. The innocuous pieces can be displayed on the counter, but the "love literature" is kept under cover with the licorice and the laudanum. One asks for it in a *sotto voce*, sneaks it home without a poison label attached, and then surrenders his precious instruments of thought to the prurient inventions of a writer whose culture would hardly do credit to an object in the zoo.

4. Chastity can be satirized, but this only in the case where it is the only virtue one possesses: the inhibited young girl who is seething with suspicions and jealousies, the refrigerated spinster who gossips about her married neighbors. Chastity is like sunlight; it is meant to light up and embellish the other virtues. No one goes into a room just to see a roomful of sunlight. There must be pretty pictures, agreeable furniture and objects of art. But if there is no sunlight, all the other beauties are lost in a murky haze. And if, in addition, the room is pervaded with coatings of dust and an ill smell, the relish vanishes even from Rembrandt, Michelangelo and Chippendale. Chastity makes the other virtues sparkle, makes them gay. But there must be other virtues. Chastity shining on a vice makes it cruel and cold: a chaste liar, a chaste thief.

5. The edge is positively taken off humor when it is made impure, and that I defy anyone to deny. There is a distinct and appreciable difference between the sound-quality in a laugh that greets an unwholesome and a wholesome funny story. The former is coarse and visceral. The latter is light, airy, in the lungs.

6. It takes no talent to write an unclean story.

7. One should meet a book as one meets a friend. Imagine being invited to meet a friend of whom it is recommended: "Oh, do come to dinner and meet Mr. Pigface. You will find him delightfully frank, brutal and realistic, and he will share with you a rehearsal of all his lewdness, and will now and then give you a companionable kick in the shins."

HOW YOU LOST YOUR FAITH

FOR THE past dozen years I have been noticing that every now and then, with sometimes a six months', never less than a twelve months' regularity, in one of the in-between magazines in this country—and by an "in-between" magazine I mean that sort in which you sense here and there a certain amount of stale Christian sentiment, but never an iota of Christian dogma (the names are too obvious to mention)—there appears an intimate confession-story from the pen of some lapsed Catholic telling how he lost his Faith.

These revealing *Apologias* originate usually from one of two sources: a) from the writer of a recent lubricous novel which has shocked his co-religionists and won him a certain amount of temporary kudos with the devourers of scandal (always finding in the moral defection of a Catholic, who once believed in something as sublime as the Virgin Mary, a little more spice, let us say, than in the loss of faith by a Holy Roller who never believed in considerably more than exercise); and b) an unconscionable nobody, whom nobody has ever heard of before, or ever wants to hear from again, but who serves "the cause" for the moment by making a display in public of the way in which his religious convictions went to the dogs because of the unreasonableness or cruelty of some item of Catholic teaching.

One's first reaction to such an exhibition is always noticeably this: that the magazine which takes and pays for the article is not in the least sympathetic with the author as a person, only as an exhibitionist. The editors have not the slightest charity for or sympathy with what the lapsed Catholic once believed, nor are they in the least concerned about the fact that even in his present petulance and revolt there may still be some point of sensitiveness in which he would not want to be too far pressed. All they look to is the result. "Here is another Catholic," they say, "who in his youth was an angelic little altar boy. See what he has to say for himself now! We loathe the dog. We would not tolerate him for ten minutes as a regular contributor to our columns. The fellow has no style, no competence, no art. But he does serve a purpose. And so we will allow him this one chance to vent his spleen. And it will give us the feeling of having obliquely rebutted the intellectual challenge of the Catholic Church, from which we must veer away by every subterfuge we can. Here is something we picked up in the waste can outside the door of a Catholic sacristy. Can you ask us to believe that it ever smelled sweetly? Or that anything in the place it has been discarded from is more agreeably redolent?" . . . This is invariably the attitude of the in-between magazines who stage once a year a piece of exhibitionism by a lapsed Catholic.

Now in the type of article I am describing you will find, though you may have to wade through a few pages before you come to it (or even through a few installments), that the outstanding grievance against the Catholic Church is persistently, monotonously, always, the doctrine of Hell. There may be other, minor resentments, but these can be waived aside. The sore spot, the inevitable and inescapable sore spot, is our teaching on Eternal Punishment. And there is probably nothing in the world so pitiable as the spectacle of a cashed-in Catholic endeavoring to explain to a public that never believed in anything supernatural the supposed terror aroused in his mind as a child when he had to face the fact of Damnation and Devils as propounded—the example chosen is always grotesque—by some nun who told the boys in her class that if they threw stones at the church they would incur God's eternal displeasure; or of some missionary priest who related in a sermon how a young boy, given to practices of impurity, saw the devil appear at his bedside the night before he died to tell him that forevermore he would be writhing in pitch and blackness, and salted eternally with flame.

Now I am greatly skeptical of statements attributing one's religious and psychological collapse to a mental trauma occasioned by hearing in one's youth of the horrors of Eternal Punishment. I cannot believe that these authors were constituted so vastly different from myself and my best boyhood friends, to say that the Hell-stories they heard drove them out of the Faith, and the Hell-stories we heard kept us in. And did they keep us in? Precisely. I do not say that they were always the ideal form in which to present Hell to a child's imagination, and there may have been on occasion a superstitious excess (an excess which is admirably removed from the excellent Catechism instruction which is imparted to Catholic children in our schools today). But the horror stories we heard about Hell, when they were such, were on the whole eminently salutary. And I will tell you why.

A boy's problem, if I know anything about boys through having been one myself, is *not* the fear of retribution for sin. A boy has a terrible sense of justice. His problem is a fear that there will be *no* retribution at all. Retribution against whom? Against those living nightmares of everyone's childhood: the bullies.

I have seen a bully take hold of the hair of a little girl, twist it, and torture her until she nearly fainted. I have seen a bully on a skating pond hurl a rock with a hockey-stick against the leg of a little girl skater, cut her stocking and draw blood. I have seen a young boy who tried to protect his sister from the foul language of a neighborhood gang, jumped on by a group of them and knocked unconscious in the street. I have myself been chased into an alley and unmercifully beaten for nearly half an hour by five bullies for having done no more than appear in a tough neighborhood with a violin under my arm, on the way to take my lesson. The violin was taken as a symbol that I was a sissie. This is not one tenth of the horrors I have seen.

I remember there was in our town a very nice bake-shop where one could buy a very especial kind of cream-cake. Not the inferior sort, full of milk and corn starch which cost only five cents, but a superior brand, costing ten cents, prepared with a fluffy crust and stuffed full of pure whipped cream.

On a certain Holy Saturday afternoon (Sister had told us that we should fast from sweets during Lent, in honor of Our Lord's Passion; she had also informed us, to our immense delight, that Lent ended precisely at twelve noon on Holy Saturday), another boy and myself, richer because of our penances by thirty cents, entered the bake-shop described above, and purchased three of these luscious cream-cakes. The lady deposited them in a bag. We smiled, thanked her, and walked out of the shop. . . . And right into the arms of the bullies! (It was not that they were so formidable individually. I once had the pleasure in single combat of breaking one of their noses with my fist. But they always travelled in gangs.) The bullies seized us, pinned our arms behind our backs, punched us a great deal, stole our cakes, blew wind into the bag, and exploded it in our faces.

And what was my only comfort, my rampart, my safeguard when, on the nights following such scenes, I lay in bed, tried to put the world's injustice out of my head and get to sleep? Hell! That was my comfort. Hell—and the fact that all bullies, if they went on being bullies, would some day at God's hand pay for the cruelties they had inflicted on the innocent children I loved.

Nor would it have done me any good in those days to have had Hell depicted to me merely as a place where one incurred "the loss of the Beatific Vision." A boy's theology must be imaginative, just as all his stories about any event. Jack must be the Giant Killer if he is to receive any attention at all. So, Hell must be a place in which you suffer in terms of something you know *is* suffering. And fire was a splendid instrument for that. "The bullies will be burned" was infinitely more comforting than "they will not be considered nice little boys by God." And if I had not known that the bullies would be burned, would I have ever got to sleep at all?

I am not in favor of grotesque descriptions of Hell that outstrip sound theology in their extravagance. And I am all too conscious of the danger of injuring the imagination of a child with details of too much horror. But Hell *is* a place of horror, and was described so in no unmistakable terms by Our Lord, Whose great fondness was for little children. And I was always taught that I could expect with completest confidence that One so merciful and forgiving as He would assuredly save me from Hell if I did not desert Him by joining the ranks of the bullies.

Another thing I discovered as a child, all by myself. If you were to suppose that our religious teachers were allowing us to be committed to Hell for minor and pardonable faults, all out of proportion with the enormity of the punishment to be received (let us say, such as "throwing stones at the Church window," or "giving way to desires against holy purity"), was it not strange that the very ones who *did* throw stones at the Church window, and who *did* show by their language and the writings they inflicted on the walls of latrines that their desires were reekingly impure, were the very ones who were also the bullies, trying to tear the hair off the heads of poor little girls?

I must confess that in later years I have wanted to tone down somewhat a few of the descriptions of Hell that I heard or read as a child. Having been on many occasions perilously near being committed there forever, naturally I have wanted to furniture the place with as many comforts as the statements of Revelation might permit. It has always become more important to me of late to view my Eternal Damnation in terms of the loss of the Beatific Vision, which is Hell's essential sanction.

But in childhood it was not quite so. And the reason I did not lose my Faith during childhood is because no one ever does. One loses it later on in life, by wilfulness and sin. Whereupon the temptation is to become retroactive. Never, of course, to ascribe anything to one's own fault; but rather to the conditions of one's childhood. One can be induced to recall, with the aid of a psychiatrist, how one was once frightened by a rat, which accounts for one's emotional instability; and then, of course, the horrible story of Dives and Lazarus related by gruesome little Sister Genevieve, which was the root cause of one's religious collapse.

Then there is left only to doctor up a story about one's spiritual awakening to the absurdities of the Catholic Faith, and sell it to one of the in-between magazines. They will take one about once a year.

THE CATHOLIC AND HIS PRIEST

THE CATHOLIC calls his priest: *Father*. "Good morning, Father!" he will say, or, "Good afternoon, Father!" And, as he says this, he raises his hat.

This combination of respectful greeting and affectionate courtesy is a delightful one, as all must agree. Frankly, our title "Father" is one which ministers of non-Catholic religions sometimes envy us. I know this because they have told me so.

I remember one day walking in New York with a very distinguished and companionable minister of a religion not mine. He was one of those ministers who wear the same kind of turned-about collar I wear, and the same general cut of clerical clothes. His black suit was not quite as black as mine because of the weave of the cloth, and my black suit was not quite as black as it should be for want of a good brushing. But, on the whole, we looked very much like two priests taking a stroll in the avenue together, and I dare say everyone who saw us thought we were two priests. But, of course, we were not two priests, we were only one priest, and one minister.

We were talking about religion, a subject to which, may I say, we clergymen invariably turn when we are together, and a subject we discuss among ourselves a bit more informally than when we are endeavoring to edify the laity with our learning or oratory. And, as we walked and talked, a man passed us, raised his hat ceremoniously, and said "Good afternoon, Fathers!"

The minister was pleased to be called Father by this passerby, and did not hesitate to say so. He said: "I wish I could be called Father all the time; except when I meet a man who is intoxicated. When an intoxicated man addresses me as Father, I am tempted to say to him 'You are no son of mine in that condition!' Don't you feel that way, too?"

"Well, no," I said, "I do not. Naturally I do not enjoy seeing a man intoxicated. But I realize that if I do not take him drunk, I cannot have him sober. If I am to be his true father, I must be his father all the time, no matter in what condition I find him."

And that is why one finds the Fathers of the Catholic Church going up and down the streets of the land, night and day, winter and summer, to minister to their children wherever they are needed. In hospitals, in jails, in pest houses, in burning buildings; on street corners at the scene of an accident. No matter how pitiable or regrettable is the condition of our children, we never abandon them, never disown them, or feel that there is any emergency of their lives to which we are not equal with a Father's compassion, a Father's reverence, and a Father's love.

Nobody could ever deserve the affection and respect we Catholic priests receive from our people. Nobody could ever earn the title we are given by so many thousands of loving hearts. But, as far as we can, we try to deserve it, by never forgetting the preciousness of the immortal souls entrusted to our care, whether they be saint or sinner, old or young, well or ill, whether they be dining sumptuously in a mansion, or lying, bleeding and forsaken, in the gutter.

The first time the Catholic priest becomes acquainted with his spiritual child-to-be, is when the child is an infant, about a week old, and is brought to the parish rectory to be baptized.

Now all babies a week old look pretty much alike. Parents, of course, deny this, and so do fond uncles and doting aunts. A baby's relatives, when they scrutinize him in the incubator, invariably put on some sort of invisible opera glasses that disclose an abundance of good looks, potential intelligence, shapeliness of head, or extraordinary amount of hair, not always visible to the naked eye of a neutral observer. Love always magnifies the value of its own possessions, and it is beautiful that this is so.

But to the general run of eyes, each little infant a week old, looks pretty much like every other week-old infant in the world, so much so, that if you let him out of your arms for a few moments, and allowed him to be mixed with other babies, you would be at your wits' end trying to identify your own child again, for all the supposed superiorities you thought he had before you lost him.

The one who can assess your child at his real value, the value he has in the sight of Almighty God, is Father, the priest. And so to the priest he is brought in the very first stages of infancy. Father does not bother to ask if he be a high-born or low-born baby; if he be a peasant, an aristocrat, or one of the bourgeoisie; if he be a strong, healthy baby destined to live a score of years or a little weakling who may not survive a single season. All Father asks is that he be a baby. And with the sacred waters of Baptism, in the name of the Most Blessed Trinity, Father imparts to that little nobody identification marks which he may never lose: the redemptive Grace of Christ, the inhabitation of God's eternal love in the person of the Holy Spirit, and a title to the Beatific Vision of All Truth, in Heaven, with God and forever. How's that for generosity if generosity is to be taken as one of the credentials of a true father's heart?

Father's next association with his child is when that little boy or girl is about seven years of age, the age at which—as all Catholic children are proud to tell you—they "have reached the use of reason." Now it is Father's business to honor that little mind, which, after its long apprenticeship with the things it could see and hear and touch in the nursery, has at last arrived at the intangible realities of the spirit, and is now possessed of the power of making intelligent judgments, and free choices in the matter of right or wrong.

It is at this stage of his life that Father tells his child in clear, kindly, unmorbid language what his purpose in life is. Father does not hesitate to tell his child that he was not made for this world, and that out of it, sooner or later, every child must go. You may say: "Why tell a child these things at such an early age?" The answer is that a child needs to know these things at an early age, if he is to stand the strain of intelligence and conscience, both of which powers he now possesses. For at the age of seven a young mind has questions to ask about the world outside it, for which there are no answers except those which God Himself has given. And at the age of seven the child has problems to settle in his own heart, for which there are no solutions, unless they be in the acceptance of personal responsibility in the matter of what it is lawful and unlawful to do.

But, side by side with making him aware of his responsi-

bilities at the age of reason, the Catholic priest offers the child
rare privileges as well. Rarest of all these privileges comes on
the morning of his First Holy Communion, when he sees
Father leave the altar of Sacrifice, and come down to the altar-
rail in full vestments, to put the very Holy of Holies, the
Blessed Sacrament, the full Christ under the species of bread,
in the child's mouth, to be eaten, as its food. The mystery of
this sacred privilege no child can fathom, nor is he asked to.
But the intimacy of it, no child ever misses. And the priest,
who is willing to share God with the child in such sacred
intimacy, is looked upon by the child as a Father indeed.

Another lovely day in the child's life, in his happy and holy
association with the priest, is the grand day when Father
proudly presents his young boy or girl to the Bishop, to
receive from the head of the diocese, arrayed in mitre, crozier
and solemn robes, the dedication to a life of Christian courage
in the Sacrament of Confirmation.

And lo, before Father realizes it, on another beautiful morn-
ing, likely to be in June, he may find two of the infants he first
met at the Baptismal font, coming in the full bloom of young
manhood and womanhood, to the altar, to unite romance and
religion in another Sacrament, the Sacrament of Christian Love.
Father dare not be absent on that morning, for it is a morning
for which he has long prayed for his children, and for which
he has tried so hard to make them worthy.

Sunday after Sunday his children see Father at the altar, the
leading visible actor in a great Sacrifice, the Sacrifice of the
Mass, preserved, week after week, year after year, sacrosanct,
integral, perfect, on every Catholic altar in the world. There is
nothing the human spirit craves so much as certitude and
security. There is nothing a Father is asked more to give. The
Catholic priest offers his children both. Father may let his
children down in little things, for he is human, and sometimes
forgets how human he is. But he will never let his children
down in such a big thing as the Sacrifice of the Mass. Father

can be counted on to offer it just as Christ offered it at the Last Supper. His children are sure of this. And that's why they come.

As to Father's sermon at the Mass, it is not always a terribly good one, though it is always founded on a terribly reliable text. But in the matter of mere rhetoric or oratory, Father's sermon is likely to be fairly middling one Sunday, and perhaps not too much better the next. Sometimes when he is fatigued, or worried, or ill, Father may make a verbal mistake as he preaches. He may even split an infinitive. But one thing his children can count on Father never to do. He will never make a mistake in doctrine, or ever split a Christian truth and offer half of it to his children, by way of improving, rationing, or streamlining the Holy Gospel of Our Lord.

Many times in the course of their lives, his children will have met Father in the Confessional, where defects, faults, even willful and serious sins may be, if one is truly repentant, forgiven and forgotten, because the surety of Father's absolving power and the infinite mercy of Christ.

And when a lifetime has passed, as lifetimes will, more rapidly than one could ever suppose, the last time you will see Father and his child together in this world is at the hour of death. If Father has not been warned to come in time to the deathbed of his child, he will never believe he has come too late. When the doctor has given the patient up and says he can do no more for him, and the nurse says he is in a coma and will not regain consciousness, even then will Father come. As long as there is a spark of life in his child's body, it is not too late for Father to arrive; and often through the fogs of fever, the ravings of delirium, or the last wanderings of the human mind at the threshold of eternity, his child will hear Father praying, still trying to reach him with the graces of the Sacraments, never willing to leave him until his soul has departed for another world.

And when the soul of his child has at last gone, for sure

Father will expect that the body be brought to the Church, and Mass said over it, and blessings showered on it, and prayer poured all around it, knowing that it was in life, the sacred temple of an immortal soul.

Father must even go to the grave to see where his child is buried, and bless the very dirt and grass that covers the remains of his loved one.

And, the morning after the funeral, back at the altar, when there is not a shred left on this earth of what was once Father's child, you will find him still praying: praying to a saint in Heaven, or at least for—a soul in Purgatory.

Father will never admit that any soul to whom he has ministered is lost—never—until he hears Christ say so on the day of Last Judgment—a judgment which will be more merciful to Father's child than any of the cruel judgments made about him in this world.

And so, as we go along the streets of the land, "Good morning Father! Good afternoon, Father!" a nice lady will say as he nods her head reverently; a little girl will say as she makes curtsey; a poor old beggar will mutter as he raises his hat.

This is the Catholic and his priest.

THE MENACE OF PUNS

"You LIKE CHIPS, don't you?" said the little girl, as I kept reaching my hand into the dish and extracting another and another flaky fried-potato and began crackling it with my teeth. "Yes," I replied, "I'm a regular chip monk."

Now how funny are such things? How good is a pun? Even at its best I claim it is never very good. In fact, I think it is somewhat harmful to the mind.

The other day it was reported in the newspaper that a Maine

hen had won a prize for having hatched nearly two hundred pullets in the course of a single year. Now what ought the faithful punster to remark on hearing that? He ought to remark that the hen deserved the Pulletser Prize. I see.

Obviously the mental level of a pun is not deep. For a pun is only surface humor. Real humor lies in seeing an incongruity between a fact and an imitation of a fact, between a truth and an almost truth. The incongruity observed is not complete, but only partial; because a likeness as well as an unlikeness must exist in the bogus that pretends to be real before it becomes funny. When both are presented to the mind in contrast, we laugh. Why we laugh is a mystery. It seems that the intellect is submitted to some sort of hot and cold douche in one shower. The mind half accepts, half rejects what is being offered to it for recognition. At one and the same moment it sees a darkness and a light, a nothingness and a somethingness; it becomes simultaneously aware of its own madness and its own sanity.

This experience makes it rush to the exercise of knowledge with a new freshness and delight. It leaps, jumps at truth, snares it out of the trappings that try to conceal it, and fairly hugs it with joy, beholding it, as it were, like sunlight seeping through a cloud, like bright water bubbling out of the parched earth. The mind becomes tremendously excited over the fact that it cannot be fooled, over the surprising accuracy of its own function in the face of a plausible mistake. This causes surplus activity to take place in the spirit, which reverts inward, and, finding no place to go, turns outward, quickly overflows into the body, and results in that beautiful explosion called laughter, which is not only analogically divine, but also specifically human. Animals do not laugh; neither do angels. The former cannot see the point of what is laughable; the latter have nothing to laugh with.

It will be well to make here a most important observation. One cannot laugh at the false which imitates the true, unless one knows clearly that there *is* a true, and that the false, though approximating it, is not achieving it. A toy frog is funny both because it is a frog, and because it isn't; also because there is a real frog which it isn't. A monkey is amusing, first, because he is not a man; second, because he certainly looks and acts very much like a man; and, third, because there is such a being as man.

Other things being equal, our ability to laugh depends on the number of our certitudes, because the more certitudes we possess the more counterfeits of them can occur. People who believe in little laugh at little. The world of the skeptic is an utterly humorless one. If, when I go to the zoo and am confronted with an almost human-featured chimpanzee who amuses me with his antics and the expression he assumes while munching peanuts—if I am suddenly persuaded that this tailed, hairy, smelly creature is in reality a sleeping Shakespeare, a dormant Goethe, an undeveloped Milton, on the verge of breaking into speech, asserting his intelligence, and announcing his rage at the injustice of being confined in a cage, then the chimpanzee not only ceases to be amusing to me, he becomes positively and shriekingly tragic. I know of a college professor, a psychologist, who keeps a statue of a gorilla on his desk. For his own amusement? No. For his own contemplation. The professor's bronze gorilla is not a toy; it is a terror: a horrible picture of what he believes he himself would be if his ancestors had not mated correctly.

Some years ago we had not lost our enthusiasm for the circus, that delightful world of topsy-turvy where all the men behaved like animals, and all the animals like men. While attending the circus we enjoyed our sanity all the more from having it rubbed the wrong way. We admired the intelligent elephant, we chuckled at the unintelligent clown. But only because it was all a few hours of make-believe. Nobody went to the circus laboratory-minded, or imagined for a moment that after the show the elephant went out and bought a copy

of the evening newspaper; or that the clown trotted off to a
cage and began drinking water through his nose. How long
the circus, a world-old institution, will endure depends on how
long a still large number of normal minds can withstand, let us
say, the influence of university psychologists, who observe in
rat mazes those pedagogical principles which they supply gen-
erously to school teachers for the training and edification of
our children. . . . Animals, by the way, never go to the cir-
cus. They have to be forced there, and forcibly kept there
too.

I think I am now able to say exactly what a pun is. It consists
in seeing the incongruity between the true and the false in the
matter of *words*. The reason why a pun is never unequivocally
funny is because words are only arbitrary symbols of thought;
their truth is due entirely to custom, not to essence or idea.
Humor consists in seeing incongruity in idea. Puns are only
pseudo-humorous.

The French have the right name for a pun when they call it
un jeu de mots. It is true that a pun besides being a mere *jeu
de mots* can sometimes carry a humorous overtone in idea, as
for instance, calling Mr. Chesterton "a tank of paradoxygen."
But the pun-ness of this statement might be taken away with-
out destroying the humor. Mr. Chesterton would be funny as
a tank of anything, having once described himself as "a well-
meaning hippopotamus." But in the strict pun it is required
that there be only an incongruity of words without letting in
any incongruity of idea. When Voltaire remarked to a lady
seated next to him at dinner, who insisted on dropping tobacco
ashes in his tea-cup: *J'aimerais mieux mon thé que des cendres*
(*J'aimerais mieux monter que descendre*), he uttered a perfect
pun, in which there is clearly no vestige of humor, though
there is much of wit. But a witty man is admired for his mental
adroitness rather than for his mental hilarity. He can often be
as Voltaire was (Alfred Noyes to the contrary notwithstand-
ing), the most cruel and cynical of men. He can even be

atheist. A humorist cannot be primarily a cynic, nor ever an atheist.

Sometimes, because of its extreme appositeness to a situation, a pun can acquire an elegance that makes it relatively delightful. As good a pun as was ever spoken, to my memory, was made by a young English Jesuit, now teaching at Wimbledon College. He met in a railway train a young man who said he was constructing a philosophy of his own. The young man declared that he set the foundation of his private philosophical system in the following epistemological principle: "I am, therefore I think!" "Oh," replied the young Jesuit, "isn't that putting Descartes before the horse?"

The trouble with the inveterate punster is that he does not wait for puns to occur, nor even for one to be needed; he goes about seeking them, forcibly making them up. And this requires almost no talent, because word resemblances (which can be easily turned into word absurdities) are uncountable.

Likewise, a pun requires no art whatsoever in the telling. A genuine joke often demands some dramatic ability in putting it across. But a pun is equally good in anybody's mouth, with anybody's voice, with anybody's gestures. And once heard, one wants nothing more than never to hear it again. Our tendency on hearing a pun is almost as much to jeer as to cheer, not because it is bogus, but because it is bogus-bogus. That most withering of all depreciations, "He thinks he's funny," is applied most frequently to whom? To the punster. American radio comedians, with a plethora of puns on every program, have long since ceased to be entertaining. They have become positive nuisances.

The English are incorrigible punsters, but their puns are better than ours because they take more care with them, and, being conservative by nature, they do not try to make too many. Americans must always over-produce, and over-production in the matter of puns is disastrous. We would do better to leave all puns to the English and turn our minds to that field of humor where extravagance is no handicap, and where nobody in the world is able to compete with us: the field of metaphors. The metaphors in Cole Porter's remarkable ditty, "You're the Top," are not only the most inventive imaginable, but their very extravagance enhances their charm. The head-line-writer on a New York newspaper, who, when John Mase-field visited America a few years ago, captioned the story of the poet-laureate's refusal to give an interview to the news-paper reporters with the title *King's Canary Refuses to Chirp* produced a specimen of what we can expect any moment in our daily journals. And no English low-brow would be capable, as Ring Lardner's baseball player was, of giving his sweetheart a look "that you could pour on a waffle."

I said in the beginning of this paper that puns can be harm-ful to the mind. They can, because they teach the mind to become flaccid and lazy, lazy in a sublime activity where it should be most alert: in laughter, that delightful paroxysm of soul and body together, in which human nature rejoices in its own sanity in a way no ape has since the world began, nor will until the world ends.

NOTES ON NAMES

THE MOST frightening name I have heard is *Edmund Blunden* and the most friendly, *Laura Benét*. For a clumsy name I give a choice among *Negley Farson*, *Avery Brundage*, *Aldous Huxley*, and *Westbrook Pegler*. The most musical name I know is *Cyril Martindale*, and the most imaginative, *Helen Twelvetrees*. Also, here is one of my favorite sentences: "Helen Twelvetrees drives an Oldsmobile and lives in Wellesley Hills."

Winnie the Pooh's *Milne* deserves an award for being the most beautiful monosyllable. And in the English cinema there is an actress with a name like a curious jewel: *Nova Pillbeam*. This readily suggests *Eva Lightwafer*, *Ada Moontablet*, *Ida Sunlozenge*, delightful double-exposures in the imagination.

I think it is a pity to have wasted such excellent names on articles of food. Forget your mental associations in taste and in smell for the moment, and see what graceful girls these would be: *Mayonnaise*, *Oleomargarine*, *Angostura Bitters*. *Diphtheria*, a very pretty name with a little curtsey in the middle of it, should have been attached to a damsel, not a disease.

In a choice of good names three things should be considered: sound, number of syllables, and accent. Accent is very important. Rossetti's "five handmaidens whose names are five sweet symphonies, Cecily, Gertrude, Magdalen, Margaret, and Rosalys" are placed so sensitively in point of accent that if the order of one of them is changed the symphonic effect is destroyed.

Sing-song in names, especially when both first and last names are dissylables, can be avoided by counterpoint, *Fanny Burney*, *Leonard Feeney*, *Percy Bysshe Shelley*, *Eugene O'Neill*, are sing-song. But *Aubrey De Vere* and *Louise Guiney* are not, by reason of the counterpoint.

When naming a child at a christening, or a character in a novel, a good general rule is to have an unequal number of syllables in the family and Christian names. This is especially true in the case where one of the names has to be a monosyllable. *James Joyce*, *John Keats*, *Sol Blum*, are not good names. When a monosyllable occurs in either name it should be buttressed with a polysyllable in the other: *Alexander Pope*, *Christopher Wren*, *Nathalia Crane*, *Rose Macaulay*, *John Galsworthy*, *Jacques Maritain*. This combination of one-three or three-one is almost invariably successful. If a monosyllable must be in first and last names, then a polysyllablic middle name is required to relieve the staccato: *George Bernard Shaw*, *John Bannister Tabb*, *James Montgomery Flagg*. Never *George Shaw*, *John Tabb*, *James Flagg*.

Beauty of vowel sounds can never be successful in a name if accent is neglected. For all its music it is impossible to take a name like *Amelita Galli-Curci* seriously. And *Edna St. Vincent Millay* (who is the first half of a dactyllic hexameter) was lucky she escaped being *Edna St. Vincent McGonigle*. Rising accents make a name distinctive. How majestical: *Rabindranath Tagore*! And a flourishful name can be kept dignified if a change of pace occurs in the accents. For instance, this: *Sister Marcela de Carpio de San Felis* (sixteenth century poet and mystic).

Where three names are used let them be of one, two and three syllables in any order: *Ralph Waldo Emerson, Gilbert Keith Chesterton, May Lamberton Becker, Harriet Beecher Stowe*.

In view of the fact that Americans, unlike the Italians, are not precise with their consonants, avoid clashes in these or you will become *Kathlee Norris, Bernar De Voto* or *Jame Stephens*.

WATER AT WORK

THERE ARE seven sacraments, and each effects an alliance between the spiritual and material world so as to give us visibl contact with the divine. But let me speak of just one of thes sacraments, the first, the simplest and most fundamental, th child's sacrament: the sacrament of Baptism. Through Chris tian Baptism, right here on this earth we are adopted into divine childhood by the power of God wedded to one of ou noblest and simplest substances, water.

When on the head of a little child we pour water and say, we were told to by our Lord, "I baptize thee in the name the Father and of the Son and of the Holy Ghost," we will some be praised for having performed a worth-while religio act; we will be ridiculed by others. Those who ridicule do so for a more subtle reason than appears on the surface of what they say. It is not that they want to ridicule God (because, generally, they believe in no God at all); it is because water has never meant anything more to them than a few drops of moisture that drip into a sink when you turn the faucet. The unreligious have never once looked on water for what it is, that marvelous raiment of wonder and refreshment with which God has clothed the world.

The pagans respect water because they have religions. Among them, libation is a sacred ritual and every pool has been adopted as a deity. But sentimental Christians, or rather people in whom Christianity survives not as a set of truths and facts but as some sort of take-it-or-leave-it emotion indefinitely identified with Christ, despise water when used for any purpose higher than the wash basin.

Water does look very prosaic and uninteresting if you hold a little of it in a glass, or dry a little of it from your hand with a towel. Water has neither taste, odor, color, nor even shape, for it takes the shape of that into which you pour it. It would be impossible to describe water to one who had never seen it. Water follows a most freakish physical law when it cools, for at 32°, on its way to becoming solid, instead of continuing to contract as other substances do, it starts to expand, so that ice may be lighter than water, and float. Instead of sinking and freezing the world to death, it may rest on the surface and be mercifully melted by the sun.

Water is the one thing without which it is impossible for us to live for any length of time. When men lie on the hot sands of the desert, parched and feverish, they do not cry out for money or gold or diamonds or any fantastic forms of food. They cry for water, for we are mostly made of water, and death is nothing more than a drying up of our resources.

Water has a noble history: in the Flood, in the passage of the chosen people through the Red Sea; and in all journeys, discoveries and explorations. It is impossible to spoil water, for no matter how much filth you pour into it, you need only drop it on the earth and let it sink into the ground, and it will purify itself and return to you in the spring and fountain, as pure and virginal as it was originally created.

Indescribable as this essentially colorless, odorless, tasteless, and unshaped substance is, God lets it roam through our world in all manners and varieties so as to give interest and color and light to our thoughts. A dehydrated human mind cannot function physically, cannot think imaginatively. Water supplies us with a whole reservoir of thoughts and words.

Water is the brook and the well and the spring and the fountain and the pond and the lake and the river and the gulf and the strait and the bay and the sea and the ocean. Yes, and water is the whirlpool and the eddy and the falls and the torrent and the geyser. It is surf, foam, breaker, wave, roller, brine, mist, dew. It is hail, snow, frost, slush, and sleet. It is ice, icicle, and iceberg; rainbow, cloud, and steam. The swimmer dives and splashes in it. The sailor travels on it. Water is what makes things damp, wet, and soggy; and it sprinkles the world, laves it, and rinses it, for there is never an end to what it can do. Water is one of the world's greatest natural mysteries. And when God's only begotten Son, Jesus Christ, entered our world to talk our language and take us on our own terms, He used as the first instrument of our sanctification that which was most natural for us to know and understand. He saw water all around us and did not despise it. He turned it into the child's sacrament. He took water and sanctified it with spiritual power. He transformed it into the sacrament of Baptism, by the union of water and the Holy Ghost.

You may say, all this is poetry. But, poetry is not its own preservative. Poetry is never religion, but it is the illustration of religion, and without religion it ceases to be even poetry. If we cannot do something more with water than give it to poets to wash with after they have written a lot of unintelligible verse, then let us give it back to the pagans. The pagan poets are religious. They respect water.

But most of us are not going to give it back to the pagans, for Christ has given it to us, to do with it what no pagan ever dreamed of. Most of us are going to remember that water has nineteen hundred years of sacred Christian history, and that spiritual wonders are wrought with it when we use it as Christ wants it used. Most of us are not going to let Christian Baptism be dried up by a couple of wars and a few despairs. As in the material world, so in the spiritual; with water we are going to refresh the world.

Oh, God is very versatile, I know, and on those who have not yet heard of the covenant that has been set up by Christ between the water we see and use, and the living water that imparts to our souls the adoption of a divine childhood, God will be able to bestow the fruits of redemption in other and special ways. But the honest, simple, clear, affirmative way of the sacrament is the best way, the way of God's own institution and choice, which we are free to reject, at our peril.

FORTITUDO ET LAETITIA

No ARMY could be more fortunate than the one that enlists in its ranks the Catholic soldier.

The Catholic soldier not only fights for the right cause, he knows how to fight for it in the right way.

The Catholic makes a good soldier. Every general will tell you that; every captain and corporal. So will every draft board when the eligibles for service are being recruited. So will every war citation when the heroes in battle are being counted.

The call to be a soldier comes to the Catholic boy with less surprise, less shock, less need for psychological adjustment than it does to most. For even in the days of peace, he has always been a soldier, always at war. The Bishop made him a soldier when he was a little boy. The Bishop anointed him with oil, signed him with the Sign of the Cross, even gave him a slight blow on the cheek, to remind him firmly in Sacrament that he must be—and had the Grace to be—a strong and perfect Christian and a soldier of Jesus Christ.

If anyone thinks this warfare of the spirit, waged to preserve the Christian certitudes and moralities in the face of a hostile opposition, is not a soldier's task, let him have tried it from childhood and see.

Nobody bothers very much with your Christianity if you confine it to a few pleasant, aesthetic opinions about Christ. But once you dare to phrase it in the adamantine truths of the Apostles' Creed, you find yourself under siege, a soldier, and at war.

Even the simple certitudes of a prayer as innocently and essentially Christian as the Hail Mary, will expose your theology to attack, turn you into Our Lady's defender, and surround you with foes. I do not refer to our small foes either: the sceptics, the sophisticates, and the snobs. I refer to our large enemy: Lucifer and the Powers of Darkness.

You may say: are not all men—and not merely Catholics— at war with the Powers of Darkness? And the answer is: all men are. But what will you say of making a strong fight against an enemy you do not believe exists? Suppose the generals of the United Nations, deceived by the effectiveness with which Hitler sticks to his hideouts, should persuade themselves that no Hitler exists. How would they go on from there?

"Holy Archangel Michael, defend us in the battle!" is the prayer every Catholic boy says, on his knees, with his priest at the end of the Holy Sacrifice of the Mass. He always knows he is at war, and with whom.

And even when the Catholic soldier falters—even when his sins are grievous—he takes both the shame for them and the blame for them. He believes that Heaven—God's beautiful home "where the forgiven meet"—is a city to be taken by storm. He does not believe it is a refuge for irresponsibles who are allowed no share in their own victory.

When he turns his energies from a spiritual to a material war, the Catholic soldier completely disavows in his heart those two well-exploited, but thoroughly unmilitary sentiments: hatred and fear. Hatred and fear are weaknesses. Hatred and fear are oratorical emotions. But wars are not won on the radio.

Let us put the matter in its simplest terms. Suppose you *do* make the enemy "bleed and burn." Suppose you even boil him in oil! Do you thereby unbleed, unburn and unboil the millions of innocent lives he has already destroyed?

Vengeances of such a kind were best left to God, Who alone is equal to the task of vengeance with dignity.

Hatred and fear are for the unconfident. The soldier's task is not a butcher's job. It requires a mind, and nerves, and a technique as clear, cool and collected as those of a surgeon. The soldier's assignment is not to avenge his enemy, but to outsmart him by completely destroying his opportunities.

And when victory comes—as it is sure to come, eventually, to those who are without hatred and without fear—the soldier retires from his triumph as gloriously and gracefully as he entered it. He goes back to a civilian's life still civilized. His mother, his sweetheart, his wife, his little daughter, find him undegenerated by the sentiments of a savage: hatred and fear.

Bad nerves, hysterics, high blood-pressure—these may be the symptoms of epilepsy, but they are not the signs of patriotism. How many victories do they achieve, even when provoked by propaganda? A mouthful of expletives to hurl at your foe! Are these as fine—or effective—as a good gun in your hands and a good song in your heart?

Fortitudo et laetitia. Courage and gaiety. These are the soldierly emotions. Who tells us so? David, the royal psalmist does, constantly, in his one hundred and fifty Psalms, those divinely inspired songs written to motivate a soldier for any kind of war life has to offer.

Fortitudo et laetitia. I started to count, the other day, the number of times these two words, or their equivalents, go together in the Book of Psalms. And the number was so great, I stopped counting.

Courage and gaiety. The soul must have its resources in time of war, just as the body must have its food and drink. Courage and gaiety are the soul's best resources. They are—among the realities of the spirit—like brother and sister, full of striking resemblances. They are more. Courage and gaiety are like bridegroom and bride.

Fortitudo et laetitia. When they wed and become one, in the holy citadel of a soldier's soul, they bear fruits, not the least of which is to give war—all war—a meaning and a memory. A meaning of what it is for. And a memory of—for whom.

THE OLD MAN

NOT LONG AGO I saw a picture of an old man who was a hundred years old. I saw it in the newspaper. Everyone knows that old man who keeps cropping up year after year in the newspaper. He always seems to be the same old man. But of course he isn't.

Well, anyhow, I saw him again this year, wrinkled and toothless and a hundred years old, sitting on the front doorstep and having his picture taken on his one hundredth birthday, by way of showing how old one of us can occasionally become when he tries to overdo it.

Well, I looked at the picture of this old man of a hundred

years, and I admired it. I always admire it. There was a short account in the newspaper to go with the picture.

He never seems to come from the city, this one-hundred-year-old man; always from the country; usually from "up state." We are told that he smoked a pipe all his life, or he didn't; he drank, or he didn't; he was a vegetarian, or he wasn't; and one way or the other, tobacco, or alcohol, or vegetables were, or were not, responsible for his good (or bad) health at the age of one hundred years.

There never seems to be any real birthday celebration for this man who has survived for a century. No mention is made of a birthday cake. Perhaps the thought of a hundred candles has created such an extraordinary problem in the matter of a cake as to discourage the idea of it altogether.

And so our poor old man spends his one hundredth birthday pretty much the same as he spent his ninety-eighth and his ninety-ninth, without any fuss or bother. He sits on the front doorstep and has a few words to say about the weather. He says "O Pshaw!" when the newspaper photographer arrives to take his picture. But finally he lets it be taken. And then, the next day, we see him in the paper, the old man of a hundred years, with that quizzical look in his eye, that seems to say —at least it always does to me—"I am not a hundred years old. Nobody ever is. For by the mercy of God I moved, a few decades ago, into my second childhood, a childhood so like the first, that all its innocence and helplessness have returned to me. I don't *do* anything any more. I just *am*—am what God has made me, in all its stark simplicity: a child, waiting to become in a few months more as ageless as eternity."

Survival Till Seventeen
SOME PORTRAITS OF EARLY IDEAS

———◆———

THE VOICE

DURING the first year of my life, I lay in the cradle and mumbled innumerable sounds into which it was impossible to read any meanings.

At the age of one, I began experimenting with the syllables of the English language, and six months later spoke my first sentence. My parents were startled to discover that one of the words contained in it was "Damn!"—an expletive picked up—so my parents hasten to assure me—from a tramp who came begging at our door and was invited in for coffee.

Although such a precocious display of profanity might well have induced my parents to believe that I was destined to become a desperado, they had the unique consolation of remembering that I had been born into this world free from the guilt of original sin. This extraordinary privilege came as a result of my having been baptized some hours before birth at a moment when it seemed certain that the price of my life was to have been my mother's death.

Among the very few papers in my possession which might be honored with the dignity of being called "notes" is the certificate of my birth, a copy of which I secured some years ago from the Registry of Births in my native city. It is such a decisive, laconic, frightening document, that I have often stared at it with something of the feeling one might have if he could tip-toe into his own nursery and find himself asleep in his own crib. The document remarks, concerning an existence which is indubitably mine:

NAME OF CHILD: Leonard Edward Feeney
DATE OF BIRTH: Feb. 15, 1897
SEX: Male
COLOR: White
PLACE OF BIRTH: 118 Adams Street, Lynn, Mass.
FATHER'S NAME: Thomas Butler Feeney
MOTHER'S MAIDEN NAME: Delia Agnes Leonard

It was the original intention of my parents to give me no middle name, but by a combination of my father's and my mother's family names, to make my own a happy union of the two. The Edward was thrown in at Baptism in honor of my Uncle Edward, who was my sponsor, but was thrown out later after we had satisfied him with this courtesy.

When I went to school I came to believe that Leonard derived from the Latin words: *leonis ardor,* meaning "fierceness of a lion," and I was wont to boast of this signification. Some years later, however, I met an Italian priest in Florence named Leonardo, and he told me that our name is taken straightforwardly from the Latin: *leo* and *nardus,* meaning "lion and spikenard," and rendered freely as "strength and fragrance" or "strength and healing." However gracefully he put it, I was not pleased with the new translation. I preferred being "a wild lion" to being a "sweet lion," and wish I had been left under my original illusion.

This same queer feeling of an identity retroactively experienced by looking at a birth certificate, was also mine a few years ago when I was examining an old family album, and came upon a picture of a small boy named Leonard, snapped at the age of ten, on his front lawn, by way of exhibiting how dressed-up he looked in a new Easter suit and hat. I felt impelled at the time to commemorate my emotion (one of the

oddest human experience has to offer) by pencilling a few
lines under the picture which ran as follows:

> So that's me, taken on the lawn,
> At ten,
> In my new Sunday hat!
> Good Lord, have I been going on
> Since then,
> And was I that?

But let us go back again to my infancy for a few more
hurried observations.

My mother was eighteen when she married, and I am her
oldest child. She is now in her sixties, and by way of describ-
ing her—if now, *a fortiori* then—I can only repeat what an
astute observer said of her in my hearing not long ago: "She
is like a little doll!"

My mother claims that my father was her first and only
beau, and I believe her. My father disavows this, maintaining
with great emphasis that when he married my mother, she
had in her keeping a letter written her by another suitor and
inscribed to her "in his own blood." My mother says it was not
"in his own blood" but "in red ink." My father insists it was
not "in red ink" but "in his own blood." And thus they argue
back and forth, and have been doing so since I first met them.
My father seems inordinately proud of the fact that he was
able to wrest the hand of my mother from the clutches of such
a gory rival. My mother, on the other hand, grows indignant
at the accusation of having been associated in any way with
such a Bluebeard. At all events, whatever pigment stained the
precious paper, it has since been either destroyed or lost
("destroyed" says my father, "lost" says my mother), and so
historians will be left forever in the dark concerning this
sanguinary phase of my parental past.

One romantic experience of my mother's before marriage,
he herself will admit. One would need to know first hand

my mother's radiant innocence—an innocence uniquely pos-
sessed by immigrant girls who are at once Catholic and Irish
—to appreciate both the charm of the following story, and
the guilelessness which induces my mother to tell it.

"One day," says my mother, "when I was seventeen, I was
riding in the train from Boston to Lynn. A young man came
in and sat beside me. He was quite handsome, and handsomely
dressed. He had the most elegant manners. He was a travel-
ling salesman. We talked all the way from Boston to Lynn.
When we were about to leave the train, he invited me to take
dinner with him at one of the hotels. I was tempted to accept
the invitation, because he was the soul of courtesy. But some-
thing inside me grew frightened, and something my mother
once told me as a child kept saying 'Don't!' So I said 'No!'
and I didn't." . . . Then there is a pause, and my mother looks
at you sharply with her challenging grey eyes and says, half
reflectively, half in interrogation, "Wasn't I the coward?"

This is my mother, pro and con.

Genealogy is a fascinating pursuit, and I have often wanted
to investigate mine for the sake of studying certain unexplain-
able traits in my nature. On my mother's side our roots are
easily retraceable. We are, through her, of the O'Briens of
County Clare, Irish pure and undefiled, possessed of the quiet
gentleness of the West Coast folk, and with as reasonable a
claim as any to have descended from Brian Boru, County
Clare's great warrior and king. On my father's side our
ancestry is more difficult to review.

My father, who is often mistaken for an Italian, is a mix-
ture of Irish ingrained with Spanish. This latter strain would
account for his swarthy complexion and terribly dark eyes,
eyes that scrutinize you as though you dwelt in a dungeon.
He has been fairly copied in looks by each of his four children,
since none of us resembles my mother. But it has often struck
me that there is little of the authentic Latin in my father's
temperament, or in ours. We possess the Latin excitability, but

not the Latin repose. We gesticulate precisely and close to the body, never in the expansive full-flung fashion of Southern Europe. We are sensitive without being quarrelsome, and our impetuosity, which is unpredictable, is interspersed with sudden bursts of caution. It is one of the strongest hunches of my life that what passes in us for Spanish blood is really something too fantastic to mention. Our modal quality of thought is different from all our kindred, and our Celtic lightheartedness is chastened, and sometimes completely shut off, by bursts of mysterious and exotic loneliness, occasionally verging on despair.

A mathematician standing in the Garden of Eden when Adam and Eve were being banished, and endeavoring at the time to quote the odds against our chances for existence, would be driven into a problem in differential calculus containing so many numerical symbols and such a vast procession of zeros, that all the forests of the world would scarcely supply him with paper sufficient on which to make the estimate. He would give us up as a bad job and say that it was mathematically certain that none of us should ever be.

And yet, we are! We are by reason of a million romances that came out correctly. In each generation there were the necessary infants who invariably survived the wars, the plagues, the famines and the pestilences of history, matured to the age of courtship, were mellowed with the enticements of love, and became the acceptable bridegrooms and consenting brides requisite for prolonging the pattern of the human race to the point where we took on. Some years ago I attempted to express this profundity in a verse, which ran as follows:

> When I said Mass at Christmas
>   And candles were aglow,
> I saw a white old woman,
>   Two thousand years ago:

My very great grandmother,
    Who spun me flesh and bone,
Who felt my fingers aching
    In the atoms of her own,

In whom my eyes were shining,
    However far away,
When Christ was in His cradle
    And it was Christmas Day!

This verse, executed, as I supposed, in a moment of high seriousness, was accepted by most of my critics as a piece of whimsy; for I have suffered under the curse of being considered a whimsical poet, and have been laughed at when I thought to make others cry.

Be that as it may, it is with extreme seriousness that I contemplate a certain summer evening years ago, in a little cottage by the sea, overlooking the rocks on the North Shore of Massachusetts, just at the point where King's Beach in Lynn is separated from Fisherman's Beach in Swampscott, where my mother in a light blue dress and a summer hat disporting a streamer, was invited to "spend the evening" with some friends. By a lightning-like stroke of *timing* on the part of the Providence of God, it happened that my father was there too, airing his Irish idiom, flashing his Spanish eyes. It need not be said that my existence hung by a thread on every item of that meeting: on the fact that my mother chose to be there instead of elsewhere; on the fact that the conveyance brought her early and not late; on the detail of her seeming more attractively dressed for the summer evening than any of the other young ladies. My existence likewise depended on the avoidance of anything that might have kept my father away, such as a rash from poison ivy, or the throbbing of a sore tooth.

It was a pleasant gathering, so I am told, and everybody enjoyed everybody else's company, particularly my father my mother's. There was the gaiety and song appropriate to a group of merry exiles dwelling in a Puritan stronghold by the beaches of the North Shore. There was ginger ale for the girls, which makes them giggle, and beer for the young men, which makes them bothersome. My mother in her light blue dress and delicate manners easily prevailed, and my father was taken captive by the little steamer dangling from her hat.

There was a short courtship, a sudden proposal, and a very simple marriage. Everything happened precisely at the right time, just as it had been accurately happening all through the ages A. D. and B. C., back through the eras of the dripping hourglass, back through the clockless centuries of the caveman, back to the early pages of Genesis and the first meeting of a maid and a man. Even my conception occurred exactly at the time when God had planned it. The child arriving in our home at any other season or year which was not the winter of 1897 would have been my brother or my sister, not myself. And what chronicle he or she would care to write concerning the same parents, or what tribute pay them for an existence not mine, must be left in the realm of the sheerly metaphysical.

I am not a child psychologist, nor indeed a psychologist of any kind, but I should like to offer some of the experiences of my early childhood for clinical examination by those capable of appraising such things scientifically.

It is my belief that in those years of a child's life which antecede the use of reason, when his mind is slumbering in a world of sensations and playthings, there are definite moments when the intellect leaps forward, so to speak, ahead of its cue, takes in some situation by swift intuition or insight, makes a judgment—and then returns to dawdle on in its haze of simple apprehensions. I can recall three such experiences happening to me before the age of six.

The first occurred when I was four, and was brought into the parlor to see my grandmother lying in her coffin. Frankly, I did not know I had a grandmother at all until I found her dead. Then, for one brief instant of reasoned consciousness, which I can recapture now as vividly as when it first occurred, I looked at the lifeless form of my grandmother and said to myself, if not in the maturity of these words, at least with the absolute clarity of this idea: "Oh! So there is death attached to this business of life! And this is the way we all end!" . . . An hour later, my grandmother, living or dead, had infinitely less interest for me than a shadow dancing on the wall of my playroom, or a rubber ball rolling elusively across the floor.

My second experience with the use of reason in an embryo stage (my mother declares I was five at the time) was when I heard a woman say to my mother concerning another woman who was suffering from asthma, that she was *drinking kerosene oil for a cure!* Upon hearing this, I paused long enough to wrinkle my brow and soliloquize: "This is a queer world I have gotten into!"; and then went back to the logger-headedness of my normal development, paying no further attention to what my mother and the other woman had to say to each other.

The last incident of this kind, in which I executed a premature judgment with a definite awareness of mind, occurred, according to my best calculations, in the summer of the year in which I was six years old, and brings back to me my mother's voice calling through the kitchen window . . . calling across the fields, over the hedges, through the trees . . . calling desperately to whatever place I was lost in and could not be found . . . calling in the poignancy of a beautiful tone over-pitched in its anxiety . . . calling with the uncertain tremor that is attached to the airing of one's private shame to the other open windows of the neighborhood, behind which halting housewives listen suspiciously and are anxious, in their jungle maternity, to gather little trickles of evidence that will establish flaws in their neighbors' children and magnify virtues in their own . . . calling once, twice, a half a dozen times, into the indefinite spaces of the hot noon hours . . . calling plaintively with a combined crescendo of fatigue and alarm which the light vocal powers of a slender girl are not strong enough to support in an appropriate key:

"Len . . . errrrrrd! If you don't come in now for dinner, you won't get any pudding!"

The voice—or its echo—at last reached me. I stood where I was and listened. And something in my mind snapped, and awoke. And for the first time, standing in a field at the age of six, in one, wild, rapturous act of reasoned reflection, I knew that I had a mother! I knew that she was young, and was beautiful, and was my own. I knew that it was her business—and had been hitherto, though I had not consciously noticed it—to feed me, clothe me, and spend her life in my service. I knew that she worked too hard. I knew that she hated to call through the open window in this fashion and to make herself conspicuous for the open gossip of the street, for she had great pride. I also knew with a startling realization, hitherto unappreciated, that we were poor. Pudding was only a piece of stale cake with sauce on it, yet this was to be my reward or punishment. Pudding for the poor!

These were the apocalypses of my early childhood.

GENTLEMAN WITH A GRUDGE

Upon attaining the use of reason in a positive and permanent form, I found that among seasons, summer was most to my liking. During my favorite months—the hot ones—I used to don a pair of overalls and a farm-boy's hat, and plucking a blade of grass on which to chew, would go wandering in our neighborhood so as to explore its houses and inhabitants by way of discovering what sort of world it was I had come to live in.

A favorite rendezvous of mine was a nearby shop whic[h] aspired to be a general store in a very small way. This sho[p] had only one window and a little side entrance, and exteriorl[y] it gave the impression of being a fruit store, for there wer[e] always oranges and bananas exposed for sale at the door. Bu[t] inside, it proved to be a bit of everything. It was a grocer[y] shop if you had forgotten to order a can of peas; it was [a] bakeshop if you needed a sudden loaf of bread; it had a play[-]thing department selling tops and marbles for boys' games; an[d] it would do for a drug store if you needed liniment or iodin[e] in an emergency. It always seemed to me to be a brave littl[e] shop, trying to be all these things at once. It was open days an[d] nights, and even Sunday mornings.

The full-fledged fruit shops of our town were exclusivel[y] in the hands of the Italians, but this amateur fruit shop wa[s] owned by a Yankee. He was a tall man, with loose-fittin[g] clothes, a walrus moustache, and spectacles, and his name wa[s] one of those odd Yankee names that so amuse the Irish, [a] name in which the syllables are words and give you a strang[e] association of ideas, like Frothingham, Saltonstall, Winterbot[-]tom. The proprietor's name was Wigglesworth.

Though I had read no Dickens at the time I first met Mr[.] Wigglesworth, once I had gone through David Copperfiel[d] and Nicholas Nickleby, I knew that he was definitely [a] Dickens character. For he had that odd quality which [a] Dickens character can display, of being sufficiently crazy t[o] amuse you, without being sufficiently dangerous to do you an[y] harm. Mr. Wigglesworth's mild dementia was revealed in hi[s] fondness for making speeches to an audience of one. If th[e] audience happened to be only one small boy, but lately pos[-]sessed of the use of reason, it made no difference to Mr. Wig[-]glesworth. He went right on orating in adult language a[s] though addressing the Senate or the House of Representatives[.] He would discourse on war, on politics, on marriage, on litera[-]ture, on anything that supplied him with enthusiasm. He like[d] especially to air his grudges, his grudges against life in general and particular, to tell what was wrong with men and their affairs, and how it could be corrected. One of his chief grudges was the bad fruit Americans are given to eat.

"The United States," Mr. Wigglesworth once said to me as I sat on one of his onion crates, chewing a straw, "the United States, my boy, is a nation of unripe bananas!"

While saying this, he made a most contemptuous gesture toward the front door of his establishment, by way of indicating that his own bananas, hanging on a stalk there, were included in the censure.

"Yes, sir!" Mr. Wigglesworth repeated, because he always repeated anything that seemed to him like a weighty pronouncement, "this is a nation of unripe bananas!"

"Is it?" I said.

"Is it!" Mr. Wigglesworth replied, because he always repeated you as well as himself, "Good God, did you ever see the things the way they ship them to us from South America?"

"No, sir."

"No, sir? Well, you ought to! They're absolutely green, my boy, so green and hard you couldn't crack one with a rock. Imagine a banana taken off the tree in that condition!"

I at once closed my eyes, and endeavored to visualize the fruit interiorly, and to appreciate its horrible state.

"Bananas, my boy," Mr. Wigglesworth then went on, having sensed that he had begun to impress me, "should be left on the tree until they are *ripe*!"—and he would rip off the word as though snapping a whip—"not torn off the tree while they are *green*! put in a cellar till they become *yellow*! and hung up for sale until they become *rotten*! Do you see what I mean?" and he made an odd gesture of futility, like a scarecrow gyrating in a storm.

I assured him that I was *trying* to see what he meant, and then sat quietly and awaited further developments of a theme upon which I knew he would be glad to expatiate.

Having refreshed his mouth, inside with a bite of tobacco, and outside with a rub from a red handkerchief, and having adjusted his collar so as to give more comfort to the throat, Mr. Wigglesworth continued.

"There isn't a single person in the forty-eight States of this Union, my boy—excepting someone who has travelled to South America, like myself—who has ever tasted the flavor of a real ripe banana, a golden banana that has been left on the tree for the sun to work on, to mellow it and bring it to maturity, with a full rich flavor, and a firm brown skin. No, sir, there's not a person in this country that knows what a banana like that tastes like. They either eat green bananas, and that gives them appendicitis; or else they eat rotten bananas, and that gives them dysentery. Now which will you take?"

I said I thought I should take the second, if forced to a choice.

"What!" Mr. Wigglesworth shrieked out, "You would?" And then a sudden reserve which all adults arrive at eventually when they are dealing with children, restrained him. He looked at me with a hesitant regard, and knew immediately two things: first, that I did not know what the disease he had mentioned was; and second, that it was well for me not to know. Children catch these flashes of caution in the conversation of their elders with unerring accuracy. That is why it is foolish for a grown-up to answer all the questions of a child.

One could not fail, however, to admire Mr. Wigglesworth's consistency and sincerity when dealing with his customers. If, in the course of one of his banana harangues, a lady customer should enter the shop to buy bananas, Mr. Wigglesworth's strong aversions concerning the unsuitability of that fruit for human consumption would not in the least diminish.

"Which do you want?" he would say to the woman, "that yellow bunch, which is unripe, or that spotted bunch, which is rotten?"

This disarming frankness on the part of her tradesman would seem to give the woman only more confidence in Mr. Wigglesworth and his wares. She would order the unripe ones, or the rotten ones, as the case might be, then pay him the price, and depart cheerfully. Mr. Wigglesworth would then clink a cash drawer with a bell attached to it, deposit the dishonest money therein, slam the drawer until it closed again, and continue to be thoroughly disgusted with his profession.

"What can I do, my boy?" Mr. Wigglesworth would muse, as he surveyed the woman he had cheated, while she went waddling down the street, "I give them advice, but they won't take it! But I repeat, the United States is a nation of unripe bananas!"

"Or else rotten ones, Mr. Wigglesworth!" I would add.

"You're right, son!" Mr. Wigglesworth would say, as he patted me on the head, for he loved one who would agree with him, "Or else rotten ones!" And there the subject might end for the moment.

I have said that Mr. Wigglesworth liked you when you agreed with him. But with all the good will in the world, it was difficult to do this consistently. For he had the habit of planting false leads in his conversation which made the trend of his thought difficult to follow, and threw his listener completely off the track. I shall give an example of what I mean.

"I see," Mr. Wigglesworth said one day, while misting and drying his spectacles, "that young Slocum's gone and got himself engaged to be married. The darn fool! That kid ain't set for marriage yet, not by a long shot. Furthermore, he ain't got any money. Furthermore, I understand the girl he's going to marry has a perfectly impossible disposition. Cranky as a rattlesnake, so I hear. That ain't no kind of a girl to marry. I fell in love with a cranky girl myself when I was young. I even went so far as to become engaged to her, before I discovered how disagreeable she was. And then do you know what I did?"

"You threw her over, Mr. Wigglesworth?"

"Nope! I married her, went right ahead and married he
Shows what a darn fool I was. Not only was she cranky, m
boy, but do you know what she was? She was a hypocrite. Sh
told me she had a thousand dollars in the bank, all her owi
That's what she told me."

"And was that a lie, Mr. Wigglesworth?"

"Bless your heart, no! She had one thousand, one hundre
and three dollars in the bank, all in her own name, certified t
by a bank book. That's what she had. But do you know wha
she promised me? She promised that when we were marrie
she would turn the whole sum of money over to me; said sh
would sign it all over to me just as soon as we were marriec
That's what she promised."

"But she didn't do it, Mr. Wigglesworth?"

"Didn't do it? I'll tell you she did. Every darn cent of it. Sh
signed on the dotted line the day after the minister hitche
us. But that ain't what I'm comin' to. What I'm comin' to, sor
is this. Do you know what that woman, that woman with th
cranky disposition, whom I married through sheer pity, do yo
know what she went around sayin' about me after we wer
married? She went around sayin' that I married her for he
money! That's what she said. Good God, what can you d
with a woman like that?"

I was not able to answer this last question. But it echoed
thought that was already simmering in my own mind. I ha
already heard of a lady who drank "kerosene oil" for asthma
Now I had met a man who hated bananas and was being falsel
accused by his wife. It set me believing at an early age tha
human existence was bound to be full of such alarms and dis
appointments.

Mr. Wigglesworth passed out of my life as casually as h
had entered it. I can go back to my native city and locate th
shop where I first met him, but it is no longer the shop of Mi
Wigglesworth's day and mine. It is now a large establishmen
with two windows instead of one, and with a door for en

trance at the center, and is owned by a chain-store grocery company.

One feature of Mr. Wigglesworth's companionship I shall always be grateful for. He never spoke to me as though it were necessary for me to be stupid by way of being young. He spoke to me always as though I had intelligence, intelligence which needed to be guided in many points, and supplied with a vocabulary in others, but intelligence none the less. This is the greatest compliment a child can receive. As a child I always hated to be talked down to. I hated all nursery nonsense directed towards my ears. I hated in every way to be babied. I particularly hated to have things over-explained to me. Mr. Wigglesworth never treated me as though I were a dunce. He treated me as though I were a man, and that's what I liked, and was the reason why I visited him wearing a laborer's overalls, and chewing a conversational straw.

Whether or not Mr. Wigglesworth died with his antipathy for bananas still unabated, I do not know. I thought of him particularly after the first World War when the popular song was being sung: "Yes, we have no bananas!" I thought how much Mr. Wigglesworth, if he lived, would have rejoiced in that song.

DESIGN FOR A GRECIAN URN

To give my father credit, when he found he had some children on his hands, he decided to go out and do something about it in the matter of finances. Having carefully analyzed the likes and dislikes of his children (we were ultimately three boys and one girl), partially by listening to their prattle, partially by receiving reports thereon from the neighbors, he made up his mind that we needed luxuries to go with our fantastic imaginations, and he was determined to supply them.

Perhaps one of the reasons why I could never rouse myself to a Communist's rage against what has been lately called the Capitalistic System, or the Republican Rule, is because it was possible under such a system or rule for a poor boy with energy and ability to rise from a state of poverty to one of practical comfort bordering on wealth.

My father gave up working in a shoe factory and joined the forces of a life insurance company. In no time he was raised from the status of agent to that of assistant manager, and thence to the post of manager and given the running of a large office with five or six stenographers and more than forty men under him. In a single season he produced more business for his company than any other manager in the United States and Canada. He was invited to New York to attend a great banquet, and sat next to the President of the Company.

I always feel very proud of my father on that occasion, sitting next to the President, wearing the light blue tie my mother had given him, instead of the stiff black one of formal dress, and letting the officers of the largest life insurance company in the world know that it isn't decoration that makes the hero. I learned from other sources that my father impressed all present on that occasion, for he had youth and considerable charm.

My father had great shrewdness in business. Life insurance, at the time when my father was making his company famous, was suspect in many quarters. It seemed to many like a silly investment of money in case you didn't die quickly and cash in on the investment. I once heard my father say to a man who was abusing the notion of life insurance in general: "What are you talking about? You couldn't get any life insurance, anyhow!"

"Why not?" said the man.

"Because you have cirrhosis of the liver. No company would take you."

This worried the man, and he called on my father a few days later to see if my father had meant what he said.

"Well, let us go over to our medical examiner and have him look you over and see," said my father, and they both went.

The medical examiner found the man's liver in excellent condition, and this so pleased the man that he let my father write him up for a ten thousand dollar policy. The man insisted that the joke was on my father. He slapped my father on the back and shouted: "You see! You were wrong!" And, of course, my father had to admit that he was.

My father, when addressing his agents in their weekly meeting, told of this incident, and reminded them that it was a good idea at times to give people the impression that they can't get a thing, so as to make them want it all the more.

At the next meeting of the office force, one of my father's agents came in with a black eye.

"Where did you get that eye?" my father asked him.

"From putting your business principles into practice," said the agent; "I told a man who said he didn't believe in insurance that he couldn't get any because he was sick. And he said: 'Oh, I am, am I?'"

When my father's income reached the stage where it supplied him with a satisfactory bank account, he undertook to supply his children (a) with the best of educations, and that in a Sisters' school where each of us was exposed for nine years to the lovely radiance and elegant manners of Catholic nuns; (b) with a training in music; I was apprenticed to the violin which twisted my neck and gave me astigmatism; my second brother was assigned to the clarinet, which nearly blew out his ears; my sister took up singing, and sings beautifully to this day; while my youngest brother espoused the piano, and has since forgotten all he learned; (c) with the best of vacations in the summer time.

Being sea urchins, practically born on the beach, my father

thought it nice for us to spend our vacations in the country. He secured a boarding house for us, which was almost a hotel, in the New Hampshire hills, not far from the foot of Mt. Kearsage, and equidistant from the shores of Lake Sunapee. Thither we excursioned for at least three weeks each summer so as to see how good it was to be away from the ocean, and so as to appreciate it better on our return.

Our host and hostess were twangy New Hampshire farmers who specialized in home-like courtesy and good food. Their conversation was full of that rustic wisdom and native wit which needs to be savored in actual experience to know how delicious it can be. We enjoyed these vacations, but I remember them particularly by reason of a little girl who stayed one summer at our inn, a little girl whose name I never learned and never shall, but who enchanted me while listening to her half hour of practice on the piano every morning at nine. She began with fifteen minutes of scales, and ended with fifteen minutes of attempted Chopin. Maybe it was Madame Chaminade who was the composer, but I think it was Chopin, in one of the Preludes. I was as faithful in attending these practice sessions as the little girl was. I knew exactly when she was to begin. There was a circular staircase descending from the second floor to the music room. And every morning found me seated on the stairs, listening to her while she played.

There is a moment in Art (and in Life too, where it approximates the ideal state of Art) which may be variously described as the inchoative moment, the moment of poise or suspense, the moment of the sustained instant. It is the artist's brave, hopeless attempt to fix the present, by denying it a future, so as to refuse it a past. Lessing speaks in his Laocoön of "the extended stationary object" required for a painting, that supreme moment of magic when all the figures are poised for action. Picasso said to Gertrude Stein after he had painted her portrait "It doesn't look like you, Gertrude, but it will!" The peasants in Millet's Angelus are always *on the point of making* the Sign of the Cross. Cellini's Head of Perseus is always *about to drip* blood. Leonardo da Vinci's Mona Lisa is forever *on the verge* of smiling. Were La Gioconda ever once to open her lips and laugh, that, my dears, would be the end of art! . . . What I speak of is also the theme of a poem, Keats' "Ode on a Grecian Urn," where the heifers and the maids with garlands are always *going to the fair*.

I once read a story about a rich family who had erected on their estate a beautiful sunken garden and filled it with objects of art. There was a stone hound, about to run in the chase. There was a stone archer, about to shoot a bow. There was a stone lady, about to eat a bunch of grapes. The rich family exhibited the garden once—that, in a large week-end party to their friends—and then went off to Europe and left it. In their absence they made no provision for the care of the garden. The fountain dried up. The flowers in the urns decayed. The benches were overgrown with weeds. And the statuaries became covered with cobwebs. These granite beauties, angered at being so disregarded, held a conspiracy one moonlight night. They resolved to undo themselves as objects of art. The lady ate the grapes. The archer shot the bow. The dog ran away. Thus did they avenge themselves on the unappreciative rich family who owned them.

It was such a moment of sustained suspense that existed between me and the little girl who played the piano in the summer boarding-house near Lake Sunapee. Precisely at nine o'clock each morning I would come and sit on the stairs (the seventh step from the top, if I remember) and resting my elbows on my knees and my chin in my hands, would listen for the half hour of her practice. Precisely at nine o'clock she would enter the guests' parlor, and twirling the piano stool till she could both sit on it and touch her toes to the floor, and suitably arranging herself in other ways, would begin her scales, to be followed by the incipient phrases of the Chopin

Prelude. Not for all the kingdoms of the world would she turn her head to look at me. Not for all the kingdoms of the world would I descend one further step on the stairs. She knew that I was listening to her, and I knew that she knew it. And she knew that I knew that she knew. It was a perfect collaboration in a perfect ruse between two strange children, too shy to be playmates, too immature to be lovers, too young to be disillusioned, too old to be deceived.

We both knew that it was part of the requirement for preserving this haunting half hour that we should be inconspicuous to each other for the rest of the day. I never knew where she went when her lesson was over. She never saw me except at mealtimes. I never spoke to her. Neither learned the other's name. At the end of a fortnight she departed with her parents to mix with the maelstrom of common life and be carried on in its relentless tide. We never met again.

But she has lingered with me always in the manner of a dream and often returns to me as a symbol. Whenever I have been seated in a theatre and the house lights were lowered and the curtain about to rise; whenever I have watched a symphony conductor raise his baton for the first down-beat that will release a great splurge of music; when I have stood on the threshold of the Pitti Palace about to gaze at the wonders, or shaded my eyes to enter the cathedrals of Milan and Cologne or peered for the first time from the balcony of the Hôte des Invalides, to catch a glimpse of the little casket of Napoleon; at every pent-up moment of my life when I have waited for some artistic surprise to flash before my senses, there has come back to me the vision of a little girl in the hills of New Hampshire about to strike her first chord on the piano during that fortnight of magical summer mornings, at the precise hour of nine, when she was contemplatively mine.

What became of her, I do not know. I doubt not that life has dealt roughly with her, as it does with all precious things. But I like to think that I am unforgotten in her memories a he is in mine, and that amidst the stale platitudes that serve her or comfort in the fatigues and yawns of middle age, one right picture lingers with her still: that of a boy who was content to admire her for her music, and sat like a sculpture nd listened like a painting, at a point on the staircase that was half way down the stairs.

SUNDAY EVENINGS

OUR HOUSE was always ablaze on Sunday evenings. We invariably had at least three roomsful of visitors, and what with music, laughter and oratory, I do not know what the neighbors thought of us. It must have seemed as if the Feeneys were putting on a perpetual bazaar. As far as I can remember we never visited anybody. People always visited us.

If we are bankrupt today—and we nearly are—it was my father's gargantuan sense of hospitality that is responsible. The first thing my father asked you when he met you in our home was to stay all night. My mother needed continually to keep extra food on hand against the sudden overnight invitations issued by my father to guests who had merely dropped in to say Hello. If you came from out of town, it was absolutely impossible to get away from us. I have often got up in the morning, and peeking into our spare rooms on the way down to breakfast, found sleeping in our beds people I never knew existed. Our borrowed-pajama bill was enormous.

We domesticated at different periods at least a dozen of our relatives, and they lived with us until they either (a) died, (b) married, or (c) entered religion.

My father was an incorrigible cenobite. He detested solitude and had a positive horror of silence. He delighted in noise in any form. He particularly liked to hear others sing. The worse you sang the more my father applauded, and the more he urged you to an encore. He had an extreme fondness for the noises made by musical instruments. There was McCarthy who came with his clarinets, and would squeal on them till two in the morning, but never too long for my father. There was Clancy who played marathons on the violin.

Clancy was an ex-tinker from Ireland. His family was a troupe of musicians and Clancy was born out of doors at one of the crossroad fairs. He claimed to have ten thousand tunes in his head, and it seemed to be my father's greatest ambition to hear every one of them before Clancy's nimble fingers succumbed to arthritis. I have known Clancy to play continuously for a stretch of six hours in our parlor, and to be fed by my father while he played. However, I must say that Clancy was worth listening to. He had the most delicate sense of cadenza I have ever heard on a stringed instrument, and could pizzicato like nobody's business.

Yet for all his virtuosity, Clancy was shy in his art, and needed to be coaxed into a performance. I have seen him sulk through a whole Sunday evening, refusing to play a note. This would invariably happen if there were a single person in our parlor whom Clancy disliked. Hostility of any kind petrified him, for he was sensitive in the manner of great genius. My father hit upon a nearly infallible device for getting Clancy to play when he was disinclined to. It was to take up the violin himself and saw a few notes on it badly. Then my father would give a feeble imitation of Clancy himself, playing one of his favorite hornpipes. This would amuse Clancy enormously, but after one bad round of the hornpipe by my father, Clancy would begin to fidget, and commence lighting and relighting his pipe. He would twist nervously in his chair and wince at every note misplayed by my father. Finally, unable to stand it any longer, he would shout: "Give me that thing, Tom!" He would then wrest the fiddle out of my father's hands, retune it to his own desires, limber his fingers with a few scales and flourishes, and then he was away on his own. And he might never stop until the milkman arrived in the morning.

When there were no musicians or orators around, my father would read—by which I mean to say, he would read out loud. Nothing suited my father better than a spell of quiet among the company while he recited "Robert Emmet's Speech from the Dock," or one of the political orations of Senator Jim Reed. If a crowd were lacking, one person would do, provided he would let my father read to him. The auditor need not necessarily listen, as long as he kept quiet and did not interrupt my father. I have known my father to read the whole of Enoch Arden to Guy Pelosi, an Italian tailor, to whom every line of the poem was unintelligible. Pelosi had merely sauntered in to gather some pants to be pressed, but my father took the afternoon off to treat him to Tennyson and the extensive art of narrative poetry. Pelosi was very fond of my father, secretly believing him to be an Italian in disguise, and patiently listened to yards and yards of English literature dramatically delivered to him by my father's voice. "Your father has a darn gooda voice" was Pelosi's invariable comment when my father had polished him off with an epic or two. This poetic influence of my father on his friend, Pelosi, was bound to be felt, and my father keeps in his scrap book one of the cards Pelosi issued in advertisement of his trade. It is written entirely in verse, and runs as follows:

> Read this from beginning to end,
> And you'll find out I'm your good friend.
> If you wish to know my nationality
> I came from Italy.
> From the time I left Naples City,
> After twelve days I reached New York Liberty
> I began to get acquainted in this country,
> And I found the people in the shade of the apple tree.

Everybody treated me kind
Now, don't leave me behind,
Don't be sorry to come and see me,
I'll give you first-class fit and good quality,
If I make you a suit
Among your friends
You will look like a beautiful posy
And I am Yours Truly, Guy Pelosi

I have a suspicion that my father helped Pelosi in the composi-
tion of this poem, but my father says "No," and Pelosi refuses
to answer.

The number and range and quality of our callers on Sunday
evenings was prodigious. We have had guests from Nova
Scotia, Central America and the Aleutian Islands. We knew a
heavyweight wrestler, a symphony conductor, a roller-skating
champion, and an ex-end man in Lew Dockstader's minstrels.
I have counted in our parlor at a single sitting, a ventriloquist,
a magician, an impersonator of animals, and a lady who told
fortunes with the assistance of tea leaves.

My father's chief office as host was to get everyone to per-
form, whether by way of musical instrument, in song, or in
telling a story. My father believed solemnly in the Parable of
the Talents. If you had only One Talent my father would find
it, though you buried it in a napkin and hid it in the ground.
My father was a splendid interlocutor, and few could resist
him. My father had contempt for only one vice, and that was
timidity. "Oh, what's the matter with you!" he would say if
you positively refused to contribute anything to the general
amusement by way of song or recitation. My father, who is the
most charitable man I have ever known, had one supreme
condemnation: "He's got no gumption!" It was the worst and
only thing I ever heard my father say in dispraise of anyone.

So if you hadn't any gumption, Feeneys' on Sunday nights
was the wrong place for you to go to. The fact that practically

nobody we knew ever stayed away, is probably a proof that gumption had been rather largely distributed among our friends. Of course my father's interpretation of the Parable of the Talents was, in the strict sense, open to criticism. You might have talent for other things besides songs and stories, and yet not fall under the censure of Our Saviour. But "talent" to my father, meant talent for entertaining. It meant that and nothing more.

How my father could be wrong, I propose to show in the case of one of our best loved friends.

The same was Mary's Joe. Mary was the wife, and Joe the husband. There were many Marys and many Joes among our callers and acquaintances, but there was only one "Mary and Joe." "Joe's Mary" or "Mary's Joe" would serve to identify either of them in complete contradistinction to any others who had poached on the same names. And if you were referring to an incident that happened in their home, you would say that it happened "up at Mary and Joe's."

Mary and Joe were as opposite in disposition, temperament, taste, as any two persons could possibly be. She was all feminine, he was all man. It was their hardship that they were childless.

Joe was a plumber. Mary, who was given to euphemisms in his regard, used to call him "an expert mechanic." But we knew he was a plain plumber, and loved him none the less for it. At any rate, among our incorrigible visitors, among those who were practically fixtures at every Sunday evening party —so much so that if they didn't come, we called them on the telephone to ask what was wrong—were Mary and Joe.

Mary had talent, in my father's sense. She could sing, she could clown, she could tell a joke. But Joe had none. Histrionically he was a complete flop. All he could do at our gatherings was sit and listen. My father tried to prod him into action for the first two or three years of our acquaintanceship, but finally gave him up as hopeless. "Joe has absolutely no gumption!" my father decided, and even Mary was forced to agree.

So there he sat, Sunday evening after Sunday evening, the strong, silent Joe, always taking the most uncomfortable chair, always getting up to give his seat to another, always carrying in furniture to supply repose where it was needed, always getting out of somebody else's way. "I know I have no gumption!" I once heard him say; "Your father's right! But what can I do about it?"

Yet there were many things Joe could do in other fields besides that of entertainment. He was the spare godfather for everybody's baby, the spare pallbearer at everybody's funeral. That is to say, if the godfather or pallbearer you had chosen didn't show up at christening or wake, then, as the saying amongst us went, "You could always get Joe."

Joe was a particular favorite of my mother's. My mother was always saying that Joe had depths in him that nobody had sounded, qualities that nobody had appreciated. Joe, in turn, fairly worshipped my mother, and said boldly in the presence of his wife that my mother was the most beautiful woman he had ever seen. In one of my mother's illnesses Joe used to come to her sickroom, and just sit there and look at her for hours, never saying a word. He was always at my mother's beck and call on Sunday nights. If something were lacking in the collation my mother was preparing, and someone were needed to run out to the store, Joe was invariably the messenger for that. There was hardly a Sunday night when we did not hear him say "Here's your change, Mrs. Feeney!" as he returned from an errand, and then deposited himself in silence in some distant chair, to gaze in wonderment at the general entertainment.

Joe was also a great favorite with us children. He was always quietly listening to things we had to tell him, always quietly approving of what we had to say. It was not possible for us to read his eyes then as we could read them now, and perhaps fortunate as well. For there is a hunger in the eyes of a childless husband—a bewilderment, a sense of defeat with no explanation—that would wreck the heart of every child he looks at, were it other than the heart of a child.

Mary went out of her way, so to speak, to compensate for Joe. Whereas he told no stories, she told an extra one in his stead. Whereas he laughed little, and that always undemonstratively, she roared to the point of slapping others on the back. Whereas he used bad English when he spoke at all, she polished up hers to suit the queen's taste, and dealt it out in interminable chatter.

There was one point in which Mary and Joe perfectly complemented each other. He was healthy, and she was unwell. It was not until a number of years had passed that her illness became tragic, but when it did, it became tragic indeed. She contracted the various diseases a woman, as woman, can be heir to. She was confined to her bed for years. Her fundamental ailment was put down in that most exasperating of all diagnoses: *nervousness!* And what can you do about that?

Joe waited on Mary hand and foot. He cooked the meals, washed the linen, scrubbed the floor. He paid countless doctor's bills. He sat by her bedside endeavoring by every device he could employ to calm her excitement, to quiet her hysterical fears. She drooped one night, and died in his arms.

But I like to think of them most in the years before this catastrophe, when they were younger, more hopeful, when it was Sunday evening and they were ours; when almost the very first ring of the front door bell was a signal for one of us to say "Ah! I'll bet that's Mary and Joe." And it very nearly always was!

I should like particularly to tell of the one night of triumph Joe enjoyed at our home, a night that was his so manifestly that not even Mary could enhance it by crowing about it or exaggerating its importance.

We were all gathered together one memorable Sunday evening. Our parlor and dining room were full. Andrew Philip

Pumford Dunk, from Glasgow, was giving us Scotch jokes and imitations of Harry Lauder. Tom Murray, a tenor, built like a bass, was rendering the pitiable strains of "Mona" a lady who, it seems, died and left somebody lonely after her. John Z. Kelley, chief soloist in our parish choir, had just finished one of his beautiful Ave Marias. He alternated between Gounod's and Schubert's with a slight preference for the latter. My mother had served an excellent collation, and in the periods of respite for eating and conversation, my father was winding the victrola. When suddenly we heard the sound of a big wind, blowing in the distance.

"Phew!" said somebody, while munching a sandwich, "sounds like a storm beginning!"

Louder and louder the wind blew, a torrential lot of it, bound to take off our roof if it kept on that way.

Finally the voice of our maid, who had gone to the attic to close all the windows, was heard screaming at the top of the stairs.

"Mrs. Feeney! Mrs. Feeney! The pipe has burst in the bath-room, and it's flooding the place with water! It's running down through the floor, Mrs. Feeney, and it's ruining the ceiling in the kitchen!"

The fun stopped suddenly, and there was a great hush, while we listened to the falling water. Each of us looked at the other in consternation. Then all eyes turned to Joe. This was no moment for a nit-wit entertainer. This was the time we needed a plumber, and a plumber, thank God, we had!

Joe arose quietly and took off his coat. He was masterful in the way he assumed command. All decisions must be made like lightning, and like lightning his were made. Where did he rush to? To the bathroom, to see what was going on? Not Joe. But to the cellar, where never a Feeney would have ever thought of going.

"Have you got a candle?"

My mother had one.

"Do you know where the main line comes in?"

My mother didn't know.

"Doesn't Mr. Feeney?"

"Oh, Heavens, no!"

"Well, we've got to find it!"

And candle ahead, we all went traipsing down to the cellar, with Joe leading us.

Quietly he surveyed the pipes, made a conjecture, and found it correct. Then down on all fours, disregardful of Sunday clothes, crawling amidst the coal, the cobwebs, the footprints of the cats, he found the necessary valve. It was rusty and would not turn. Not for one of us. But it would for Joe. He would *make* it turn! . . . Ugh! Ugh! Ugh! . . . Twist! Twist! Twist! . . . Turn! Turn! Turn! . . . Ugh! Ugh! Ugh! "One more'll get it! There! . . . That'll hold the water for awhile! Now let us go up stairs for the repair."

We were absolutely wide-eyed in admiration. Every action was a masterpiece. Even to the way he plugged the broken pipe with cork and rags until it could be soldered with lead in the morning.

A half an hour later found Joe seated placidly in the kitchen, being served hot tea by my mother, and wearing one of my father's shirts.

About once a year my mother refers to my father as "Mr. Feeney," by way of re-surveying the man she married.

"Mr. Feeney couldn't have fixed that thing in a million years," was my mother's summary of our bathroom explosion. And we all knew it was a just one.

The guests departed a little earlier than usual that Sunday night, in respect for our upset nerves. You can be sure there was no further attempt at any kind of entertainment.

There was nothing to talk about while our friends were leaving except Joe, and how wonderful he was.

Mary epitomized our praise with a triumphant twinkle in her eye. "No gumption, eh?" was what the twinkle kept saying. And she led her husband by the arm to the door.

My father watched them descending the front steps.

And then Mr. Feeney went back and turned off the victrola.

LESSON FROM THE LITTLE MOSQUITO

MY FAVORITE word is "little." At least I use it more than I do other words. It occurs so frequently in my earlier work that I have been tempted to go back and delete it here and there. It occurs in the title of one of my books: "In Towns and Little Towns"; in the titles of many of my poems, such as "The Little Kingdom of Thingdom"; and in the titles of several of my sketches: "My Little Minister" and "This Little Thing." In the writing of my biography of Mother Seton, called "An American Woman," I resort to the word "little" so often that it is practically an impediment in my speech. One of my critics was quick to notice this and sent me a devastating parody of my own style, which ran as follows:

"Dear little Leonard Feeney. I read your little book on America's first little sisters-school nun, little Mother Seton. I think she is the nicest little nun I have ever read about, and you do say the most charming little things in her praise. Won't you please write us other little books on kindred little subjects, so as to make our little hearts a little more happy?"

A man can survive such ridicule only with the aid of prayer.

Another of my critics, a married lady, writing in one of the weekly reviews, scores not only the frequency of the word "little" in my vocabulary but its essential inappropriateness to some of my ideas. "The author," she says of me, "refers to a nun as 'a little lady all consecrated to God,' whereas we all know that many nuns are large, impressive persons, born to command."

I did not answer this enormous matron, for I believe in free criticism; but had I, I could have defended myself to some extent.

I think that "little" is definitely a Catholic epithet, used not in a dimensional, but in an appropriative sense. We call anything little that we like so much we want to make it small enough to consider it our own. There is an order of nuns in the Church known, one and all, as The Little Sisters of the Poor. But they do not weigh their postulants before receiving, nor send them reducing exercises so as to establish vocations. Our Lord speaks of the whole Church as His "little flock." Saint Francis of Assisi is known as "The Little Poor Man," and Saint Thérèse of Lisieux as "The Little Flower." Even Saint Ignatius, perhaps given to diminutives least of all the Saints, refers to the regiment of his spiritual soldiers as "this little Society of Jesus."

I have a further propensity for the word "little," because it is mostly in small things that I am largely interested. Had I become a scientist, I should have been an astronomer among the biologists, with microscope for telescope, peering into worlds beneath me, studying my heavens upside down.

At any rate, I think that not even the most captious of my critics will object to the word "little" as applied to a mosquito.

Of all the world of little things a mosquito makes the loudest noise. If you, proportionate to your weight, could make as loud a noise singing, as he does, proportionate to his when he whines, you would sound like all the factory whistles of Bethlehem Steel going off in a simultaneous blast. You would literally blow the roof off.

I first became acquainted with the little mosquito (he always seems to be the *same* mosquito) when I was a little boy lying in bed. First I shall tell you what he did to me harmfully, and then what he did to me by way of help.

By way of harm, he cost my father hundreds of dollars. It was the summer I contracted malaria and was quarantined for three months. This malaria was the work of one mosquito. He * raised my temperature five degrees, and sent me into such a series of fevers and chills that our neighbors, alarmed at my plight, and fearing contagion, would not let their children admit to ever having known me.

This same mosquito caused my mother to invest in innumerable hot water bottles and in at least a thousand pounds of ice. I wore out two ice men in the course of the summer.

My parents went scurrying to neighboring stores to purchase soups and broths of such exotic kinds and flavors that the grocers advised my mother to buy her canned goods wholesale.

Still the work of one mosquito.

And what he did to me by way of upsetting my environment was nothing to what he did to me inside my head.

Have you ever seen an elephant uproot Bunker Hill Monument and hurl it like a javelin across East Boston Harbor? . . . Well, I did, thanks to one little mosquito.

Were you ever lost for a thousand years in a dark, lonely forest, and did you eat lobsters with a giant who had streetlamps for eyes? . . . Then you never met the mosquito I met.

Were you ever, in a delirium, the only being in existence, without father or mother or friend or any one to know you or love you; with your whole body seething like a furnace, your head a conflagration of distorted ideas, your soul cindered down to the last ash, your will clinging to the last remnants of religion . . . calling to God, to Mary, to Jesus, to come and either deliver or destroy you, asking where everyone was but yourself, promising never again to be naughty . . . if only, if only, if only, if only, you could have ice on your forehead, ice on your feet, ice to hold, ice to listen to, ice to eat . . . ?

* The scientists tell me it is the female mosquito, not the male, that carries disease germs. But I prefer, chivalrously, to blame it on the male.

Do you wonder that the subject of the mosquito impresses me, and that I dedicate to it a chapter from the pages of my youth?

The little mosquito is hatched in the afternoon, in the warmth of a pleasant swamp.

Ten minutes later he is a finished aviator, ready for flight.

He is merely a bit of gauze informed with animation, and so delicate you could not weigh him on a pharmacist's scale. Yet he knows to a nicety all the currents of air and can balance himself skillfully in the most formidable breeze.

After less than an hour of personal tuning, he begins a flight more remarkable than Lindbergh's. He sails to the nearest dwellinghouse to await the retirement of the sleeper. Disregarding the basement and the bedless lower floors, he finds the sleeping-chamber and the slumbering little boy.

Daintily he alights on some susceptible part of the body, and studies carefully the mechanics of the operation. He braces himself solidly, summons all his strength, and inserts his dagger accurately in a narrow little pore.

He deposits his poison, and extracts his toll of blood.

He makes another take-off, whining contentedly, and is wafted by the wind to his sources in the swamp.

By midnight he is the father of a hundred little mosquitoes, who will follow on the morrow the example of their sire.

It is an astounding performance.

It is one of the most remarkable feats in the history of the world.

WING LEE, HAND LAUNDRY

OUR STREET was intended to be purely a residential one. But the owner of a vacant lot directly opposite our house grew tired of paying taxes on property that yielded him no revenue.

And so he erected two small shops on his land and rented them for business. A baker hired one of these shops, and Wing Lee, Hand Laundry, the other.

A rumble of resentment went up in our neighborhood when Wing Lee, Hand Laundry, moved in. Our neighbors were mostly Whigs, but they became Torys when ruffled in the matter of prestige. Appeals were sent to the City Ordinance Department, and even to the Mayor, to prevent Wing Lee from joining us. But the Mayflower legislators, when writing our local rules, had, by some miraculous oversight, failed to proscribe a Chinaman. The reason was simply that they had not foreseen him. And so Wing Lee, Hand Laundry, remained in our midst, by way of a yellow blunder in the Blue Laws of Massachusetts.

One can easily be mistaken in interpreting data reported by the senses, but hardly in the case of a Chinese laundry. And so it was no time until our noses knew that Wing Lee, Hand Laundry, had not only set up in our street, but was going full steam. And what is more, the bakeshop adjacent to his had an electric fan to blow off the foul air, with the result that the odors from the two establishments became so confused in the general let-off, that there were times when you did not know whether you were smelling a mince pie being scrubbed with ammonia, or a winged collar being fried in lard.

Wing Lee may have been an annoyance to our elders, but he was a revelation and a delight to us children. He was one of a wave of Chinamen who came to our shores in the early nineteen hundreds, a type highly tenacious of the exalted customs and ancient culture from which they sprang. For, unlike the Japanese—who are of a decidedly inferior civilization—the early Chinese were slow in adopting the Western manners and dress. The Japanese have always wanted to ape us. Not so the Chinese. A Japanese will be smuggled into New York one day, and the next go marching down Riverside Drive dressed like a Wall Street broker. But a Chinaman has always clung to his ancestral garments, observances, food, as long as it was humanly possible to preserve them. The later-day Chinaman has, alas, succumbed to the hammering imposed on him by life in our crowded cities, and his pig-tail, chop-sticks, baggy blouse and decorative slippers have largely gone. He has even become Joe Lee and John Lee in place of Wing Lee and Lung Foo. But a greatness has been sacrificed in these surrenders. Nothing survives in the Americanized Chinaman but his jaundiced complexion and his almond eyes.

Our Wing Lee, thank God, was an authentic Chinaman, primitive, unspoiled, dressed and mannered exactly as he would be in his ancient country. He fascinated me beyond anyone I have known in my youth. Make no mistake, I was reluctant to believe he was not an animal, for his skin was a perpetual yellow and he smiled like a chimpanzee. If he *must* be taken as human and I saw eventually that he must—then he seemed a composite of both sexes and all ages. He had a face as smooth and fresh as a boy's; he had long braided hair like a girl's; he had eyes like a doll's; but he wore a lady's blouse like your mother's and ornamental shoes like your fashionable aunt's; yet he smoked a pipe like your father, and made a noise when he talked like your grandfather being recorded on a gramophone.

I have never seen anyone so dissociated from human consolation as Wing Lee was—so inarticulate, so sad-eyed, so alone. He slept in the rear of his shop, and seemed to have no wife, no children, no relatives, not even any friends. There were times when I was prepared to believe that he even escaped having parents, though there seemed to be something logically wrong with that theory. At any rate, I asked few questions about him of those capable of instructing me. Wing Lee was my discovery, and I was determined to figure him out by myself.

Our family was one of the first to patronize Wing Lee. We sent him some collars to do. He was conveniently located just across the street, and you could bring the collars any time; you did not have to be prompt with them as you did with our Yankee laundryman, who would penalize you an extra week if your wash was not ready when he arrived. Wing Lee's work on our collars satisfied us, and we proceeded to let him do some of our shirts. But there the matter stopped. We had a superstition, partly religious, partly hygienic, about giving Wing Lee any of our more personal clothing. So he saw only the externals of our wardrobe. The rest of our things were sent to a wash factory to be torn apart by wringers and mangled by machines.

Oh the patience of the East! Was it not this lesson Wing Lee was sent to teach us? Night and day he toiled, washed, ironed, smoked, without the solace of a single friend. He had no companions, only customers. He strengthened his morale by humming little curious tunes, making little curious marks on sheets of red and yellow paper, identifying merchandise with his own private signals, keeping ledgers secret to himself and his gods. What an assignment for a man with whom not one of us could compete in ancestry, who had heirlooms in his family that had descended through the ages!

Bereft of his relics, his rice fields, his tinkling temples, his open-air pagodas, Wing Lee braved the sloppy springs, sweltering summers, and icy winters of New England. He piled up his pennies against a slow return to his homeland and a burst of riches and surprises for those he loved. He endured a decade as though it were a day. He spoke seldom and saw all things. Nothing interested him less than a clock. He listened without a murmur to the angry landlord, scolding him for something he did not understand. He bore the complaints and rebukes of his clients, and sought always to appease them with Oriental courtesies. He hated the mechanical contrivances employed in the laundry trade. He washed every single item of your clothing with his own bare hands. He would have done even better if you had put him out of doors, given him some good strong suds and supplied him with a river. His was not the artificial cleanliness of the Occident, but the essential cleanliness of the East, where libation is a religious ritual and every pool has been adopted by a deity.

One day, suddenly, with no warning, the sign "Wing Lee, Hand Laundry" was taken down. He vanished as silently as he came. No one knew why, or where. Was it that this great lover of silence could no longer stand our noise?

I do not know. It may be that he went to New York and drugged himself with opium in an effort to forget us. It may be that he was killed in one of the tong wars in San Francisco, still trying to put us out of his mind. But I have a suspicion that Wing Lee sailed home to China, and that he remembered us very well. I have a notion that you might find him even now in the suburbs of some metropolis, in the hills above Canton or the valleys below Peiping, chuckling to his grandchildren, patting their heads, and telling them of his days in distant Massachusetts when he laundered the dirty linen of the low-brows of Lynn.

HEAVEN IN A POND

IT WAS STRANGE being told in school by our Sisters that we were not made for this world. My grandmother's death had given me a suspicion on this point, but the nuns turned it into a certitude and made it part of our program. We were to plan for death just as much as we planned for life, and were to expect it at any moment, perhaps before we were promoted to the next grade in school. I found the predicament rather exciting: that of anticipating another world before you had quite got on to the hang of this one.

I used often to count the children in my class in the morning, and if any one was absent with a cold or a sore throat, I felt sure he had died during the night, until reassured to the contrary. If I remember correctly, only one of my classmates died in the first nine years of my attendance at school, and this did not seem to be a very good record in the face of such a universal threat. Nevertheless, in other quarters of our town, I had seen with my own eyes the undertaker arrive and pin a crêpe on the doorposts of many comparatively young people; and then, there was always the graveyard, where two easy dates and a simple problem in subtraction would give you an integer as small as four, three, two, even as small as one. So what the Sisters were prophesying for all of us, old and young, had better be taken seriously.

It might be thought that this waiting-room attitude toward the life to come would have induced us to take little interest in terrestrial surroundings so precariously ours. Quite the contrary. The psychology of the waiting-room, as those who have visited the dentist's will testify, is one of fervid interest—interest in the furniture, the wall-paper, the pictures, the magazines on the desk, even begetting in the patient an impulse to translate the Latin of the dentist's diploma. You make a minute study in a waiting-room of details you would never even notice in your own home.

But did not this thought of death persistently proposed by the Catholic ethic and philosophy have a tendency to make us morbid? This was not so either. Morbid thoughts are all too frequently the result of a morbid physical condition of the thinker. Children, with healthy appetites and good digestions, unlike their melancholy elders in the throes of liver ailments, have the happy habit of turning tremendous truths to their own gay purposes. "Take a good look around, for you won't be here long!" was death's fundamental message to me as a child. Life, when surveyed thus, became like an idea you get while whirling on a merry-go-round, waiting for the thing to stop. The thought might be dizzy, but it was certainly not drab.

Nevertheless, I was intrigued with the notion of the here-
after, once it had been suggested by my religious teachers, and
I was anxious to gather as many descriptions of the celestial
state as it was possible to find. Needless to say, it was not pos-
sible to find much. The hereafter proposed to us by the Sisters
was in the form of Heaven. It was also, of course, proposed to
us in the form of Hell. But, in the manner of perfect ladies,
the Sisters supposed that their precious charges would never
be so rash as to want to take any decided steps in the latter
direction. Wherefore, Heaven—so the nuns graciously assumed
—was to be our lot when we died; that is, if we were good, or
reasonably good, or, at least, not unreasonably bad. But by way
of describing Heaven, the Sisters had only this to say, relying
on a quotation: "Eye hath not seen, nor ear heard, nor hath it
entered into the mind of man to conceive what God hath pre-
pared for those who love Him!" This text, it has to be ad-
mitted, was more effective as an exhortation to a good life than
as a description of the reward that awaits it. Intellectually, it
might rouse us to hope; but there was little or nothing in it on
which to pin the imagination. I was one who liked pictures to
go with my pleasant thoughts, and was loath to be stumped by
a Scriptural challenge refusing me a view of Paradise until the
clouds of Faith are cleared.

Any absolute picture of Heaven I knew was impossible. But
were there not relative ones, glimpses, approximations one
could acquire, aided with clues from the Cathechism, and the
help—so it happened in my case—of a little fish pond?

There was in our town, not far from my home, a beautiful
little heart-shaped basin of water known as Gold Fish Pond.
It was one of the minor bounties bestowed on us by the Com-
missioner of Parks as a reward for giving him a good substan-
tial vote for office in the annual Fall elections. In winter this
pretty watering spot was used for skating. In summer it was
used for fish; not fish to fish, but fish to contemplate, with
alert attention and a roving eye.

Gold Fish Pond was the scene of innumerable summer pic-
nics, and served as the place of regatta for the paper boats of
small children. The fish with which it was stocked ranged in
color from violent purple to screaming gold, and these little
beauties, when tired of their orgies in the mud, would swim
to the surface and leap in the air, or else nibble idly the floating
crumbs and wafers distributed for their sustenance by youthful
admirers.

Gold Fish Pond was a place to which one could bring
fancies of all sorts, and find them reflected in patterns and de-
signs beyond belief. It was a veritable cauldron of liquid and
light, bursting with bubbles and glinting with gold. It always
seemed to me like the picture of the brain of a fairy-tale maker,
such as Grimm, Aesop, or Hans Andersen; or, better, the heart
of one of these poets exposed for view.

At any rate, it was on the banks of Gold Fish Pond, while
prostrate on hands and knees, with my nose almost touching
the surface of the water, that I came to learn by analogy what
Heaven was like.

Heaven, so the Catechism of Christian Doctrine declared,
was a place of supernatural happiness. That meant to say, that
the happiness which will be ours in eternity has no points of
comparison with the happiness of this earth. For Heaven is a
state of beatitude beyond the expectations, beyond the needs,
beyond the normal capacities of our nature. Heaven is the sub-
stance of the great feast of existence, not a dessert added on by
way of ice cream. One must not try to apprehend Heaven as a
place of super-sunsets in the west, super-breezes on the lake,
super-flowers in the garden. Heaven is utterly different from
earth's panorama of aural and visual delights. The beauties we
behold here below are only a promise of Heaven, not a por-
trayal: in some sense a symbol, and surely a hint, but infinitely
inadequate as an illustration.

Armed with these premises, and restrained with these cau-
tions, it was possible to make some estimate of our present con-

dition of life in comparison with the life to come, by looking at the fish in Gold Fish Pond.

Suppose, I mused to myself, these little fish were put in this pond by way of probation. Suppose they were told by God a number of things they must do, in reward for doing which well, a heaven would be allotted to them. What would a heaven for fish be? First, naturally; that is to say, in terms of "wetter water and slimier slime."

A natural heaven for fish would be easy to construct. As a reward for serving God faithfully in a foul pond, God would put them in a fresh pond, and there let them abide. Theirs would be a "promised water" serving them in the guise of a 'promised land." It would be fed with rivulets from luscious springs, sanded with clean, bright sand, foliaged with rich coral blooms, abounding in plentiful grub worms to eat. It would be inviolated by unsuitable muck, tin cans and rubbish; perpetually preserved as a museum, never utilized as a dump. There would be no hooks to molest the fish in summer, no ice to freeze them out in winter. They would never grow old, and might never die. . . . This would be a natural heaven for fish, a heaven fish could imagine, one that a mother fish might propose to her minnow, by way, let us say, of religious instruction.

But now let us suppose that the destiny of fish was to be a supernatural heaven instead of a natural one. Let us suppose that their ultimate beatitude was to surpass the barriers of a pond, and be extended to the comfortable enjoyment of the earth and air. Let us suppose that fish were destined ultimately to know the open sky in full glory, the majesty of mountains in clear view; to borrow the delights of human laughter and learning and intelligence, and to begin to romp and play like children. This would be a supernatural heaven for fish; but a heaven impossible to describe to them while they were still below the surface of the pond. For how can you describe a child in terms of a grub worm, laughter in terms of a soggy gurgle, or starlight in terms of mud?

It is the same way with us, I said to myself. We are like fish
in a pond. Heaven cannot be described to us because it is "life
beyond the top of the pond!" But it is as much more beautiful
than this life, as ours is above the life of these poor little
creatures diving in the waters.

There were many who came to Gold Fish Pond in the days
of my childhood. The young came for recreation, the youths
and maidens for courtship, the old for reflection. I liked often
to be found among the old, and to sit with them in their
silences, and undisturbed by noisy play, to make a submarine
meditation and think the thoughts I was thinking.

ALICIA

SOME of my readers will feel that in the last chapter the philos
opher (or shall we say the poet) got ahead of the child. This
do not admit.

In an autobiography, it is not the adult analysis of childhood
impressions that counts; it is the quality and receptivity of
mind existing in the child when the impressions were first
received; else, how explain what a child remembers from an
age when he needed to be reminded of nearly everything?

I know no childhood except my own, and can take stock of
no other. I did not go around in childhood like a freak reporter
interviewing other children, by way of ascertaining what it
was like to be one of them.

Knowledge at all stages depends to no small degree on char
acter. In life, early or late, we come to know what we want
to know. There is an intimate connection between growth of
mind and generosity of will. We remain perpetually ignorant
of truths we are not disposed to receive. Wisdom is a virtue
deserving high merit in Heaven, not merely a semester-repo

deserving high marks in school. Grace, likewise, is the signature of self on one's surroundings. No one can be taught how to be charming, nor made original by environment.

The rough draught of character is completely drawn, I believe, at ten. Hence, it is important that the child be taken seriously, even by his older self. Personality after the first decade is a matter of adding the proper details to a finished blueprint. Virtue will inevitably follow the strokes of an original moral design, and vice will be a matter for suitable erasure of inharmonious lines.

One gets few, if any, new ideas after ten, only fuller information. Likewise, one acquires no radically new habits after ten, only new motives and further example. Habits acquired after ten (the age is arbitrary, but I use it to indicate roughly the period of the parent and the primary school) superimpose themselves on the old like spirals of new wood around the central oak. If the pattern is not kept, if there is too much of a quarrel between the layers of development, the oak cracks, and the person explodes in a psychosis.

Expression is only a by-product of thought, and maturity of vocabulary does not re-originate an idea, only re-phrases it. I was able to say at ten with a gesture what I cannot express at forty, though armed with the arsenal of the dictionary. Shall I be accused of telling a false tale now, simply because I express it worse than I did thirty years ago?

There are thoughts that lie too deep for tears. There must indeed be thoughts that lie too deep for ink. Ink will do as a makeshift when one can no longer weep; but a writer of his early reminiscences is only trying to plumb depths in himself already established by first impressions when the initial soundings were made. He is not putting on a false face and pretending to be young.

A child who never wept till he was ten years old, would likely never weep at all. And a child of ten who had not already thought of most of the things worth writing, would never write a thing worth reading, though he lived to be a hundred.

I believe that everything centers around the philosopher in us. Yet no one can walk the narrow line of metaphysics and be happy, or even sensible. The scientist is the philosopher minus; the poet is the philosopher plus. On which side of the line will you place the child? On the side of curiosity, or the side of wonder? I am emboldened to make a brief for the poet in the child.

In my schooldays, the professions were summarized in a two-line poem:

> Rich man, poor man, beggarman, thief,
> Doctor, lawyer, Indian chief!

What a marvelous epitome for vocational guidance! Could you substitute "refrigerator salesman" in the above couplet and ever expect a boy to want to grow up?

We were educated in the hard school of wonder. We were not taught to be observant, it being assumed that we were nothing else. We were drilled with dogmas that might serve to make our observations valuable. Whatever talents appeared in us did so by reason of an inner impulse. A boy who could draw was considered an artist; a boy who could act was considered an actor; a boy who could sing was looked upon as a singer; and so on. Certain subjects were considered for most of us largely a waste of time. We had a classroom rascal, but we would have been positively frightened, not to say disappointed, to see him reform. We met in school a cross-section of what we might meet anywhere in life. You did not know whether you were sitting next to a future gangster or a future archbishop. Frankly, Sister did not know either, and that is why she was so solicitous for all of us in her prayers. I am not saying ours was the best education in all points. I am simply saying what it was.

We disliked school on the whole, and were not expected

prefer it to our homes and holidays. Our lessons were tasks, not recreations. We did, of course, take recreation, by engaging in games in the yard during the recess periods, but we never got any marks for that. Our classrooms were not museums, playrooms, menageries. Toys were not brought in to teach us mechanics, flowers to teach us botany, nor fossils to enable us to visualize our grandparents in the jig-saw puzzle stage. Marvel and moron, we were all herded together; the bright learned lots from the stupid, and were kept by them from the nervous strain of being always in competition. Amusing incidents occurred always of their own accord; our teacher was no vaudevillian, and never told jokes. Spontaneous drama arose out of the dullness of the environment and the versatility of our own invention. Such was the incident of Alicia and the inkwell, for the telling of which it will be necessary to know that children of my day were scolded when they were bad.

Alicia was the belle of our class. I do not remember that she was pretty, for the young are no connoisseurs of physical beauty, but I do remember that she was unusual and had ingratiating airs. Alicia was fragrant, fastidious, reserved. She was always striking a posture, preserving a pose. Her parents were wealthy, and her mother dressed her with impeccable taste. She had the most radiant assortment of hair-ribbons in Essex County.

Alicia was haughty. She condescended. She even condescended to the teacher, making it seem the latter's privilege to ask her a question; and if she muffed the question, which she not infrequently did, she did it with the air of seeming superior to knowledge.

Alicia was vain, but vanity is the lightest of all venial sins, and Alicia's innocence kept it from being willful. It is probably not till twenty or thereabouts that a girl's vanity descends to deliberate tactics, making her dangerous as a débutante, wicked as a wife, pathetic as a widow. Vanity was not a fault with Alicia, it was rather an aura with which she found herself possessed at birth, causing in herself, as in others, the surprise and delight a peacock experiences when it spreads its fan.

The discipline of our classroom was very severe. There was never a spot allowed on the desk, a speck of paper on the floor. What was our consternation, therefore, one day when Alicia, in the act of making a Cleopatrine gesture, struck a bottle of ink with her wrist, and sent it crashing in the aisle. What! Ink on Sister's floor!

"Who knocked that bottle of ink on the floor!" said Sister whose angers were known to be righteous.

There was a dead silence. Alicia stared in horror at the remnants of her recklessness: the rolling stopper, the broken glass, the large black smudge of ink, the queer odor tincturing the air.

Sister eyed us row by row, hoping to trap the culprit by a stare.

Alicia's prestige, meanwhile, was in positive peril. She straightened herself stiffly, and prepared herself in the grand manner for a public humiliation.

"Who knocked that bottle of ink on the floor?"

"I did!" said a brave boy in the back row, raising his hand so as to be recognized.

"Come up here!"

He went up in Alicia's stead, stood by Sister's desk, and was given a scolding which it took Sister an unconscionably long time to administer. To this was added a punishment lesson which it took him hours to do at home. And finally a commission to remain after class and scrub every inch of the inked floor with soap and water.

I sat at my desk and writhed in agony while Alicia's hero was being court-martialed. "Oh, why didn't I think to say what he said?" I kept repeating to myself. "Oh, why didn't I think to say that?"

I asked my mother that night when I went home why

didn't think to say it, seeking her aid in analyzing the lack of chivalry in my character.

"Maybe you will think to say it next time," said my mother.

But there was no next time. Though I secretly placed ink-bottle after ink-bottle in perilous positions on Alicia's desk, not from then till the day we graduated could I get her to go near one with a ten-foot pole.

ART

IT WILL BE largely among those people called philosophers that a child's thoughts will be developed. Therefore a child should admire the philosophers. Theirs may not be an adventurous voyage, but theirs is indeed a safe harbor, and one a child will never want to be out of reach of as he bobs around in his little boat. Whenever he is beyond his depths and in danger, these faithful lifeguards of logic will rush out to rescue him. And a child in the arms of a lifeguard is surely one of the most beautiful sights in the world.

It will be largely apart from those people called mystics that a child's devotions will be pursued. But he will come to learn that it is because of their prayers that he is what little he is. Therefore a child should love the mystics. Theirs is a perilous experience, but a child will no more want to uncrown a mystic of a halo than he will want to quench a lighthouse, faithful and constant, beckoning ships with treasures to come to him, winking to himself to stay where he is.

> The time has come, the walrus said,
>   To talk of many things:
> Of ships and shoes and sealing wax
>   And cabbages and kings.

Somewhere between the lifeguard and the lighthouse you will find the child at his best, without ship or shoe under him running barefooted in the wind. It will be just at that point where the sea and land meet each other on those terms we call the shore. There the child is at once safest and most adventuresome. There he is most himself. He will imprint his footsteps on the wax of the soft beach and watch them being washed away by the wave. He will furrow with his motions the foamy ruffles of surf and watch them being absorbed by the sand. In point of importance he will think himself to be no more than a rolling pebble or a drifting seaweed. But in point of independence he will be king of all creation.

The wind on the seashore comes at you in widths and depths. It has no length. So you trap it and send it streaming through the smallest aperture you can find—your own lips pursed—and release it in the form of pure line. You whistle. And lo, you have music!

Later on when this pure line begins to surface (to paint) itself in your music lessons, you will have harmony. Still later when it begins to shape (to sculpture) itself, you will have symphony, as you discover the afternoon your mother and father bring you to hear the Boston Symphony Orchestra, just twelve miles away from Lynn. There in a large hall, with lowered lights and hundreds of people listening ever so intently you will find that music is still music, able to triumph over an instrument that can make it. Being music it will never be able to define itself, for art cannot define anything, least of all itself. It does not know what anything is or what it is for, but simply that it is, and points to that. Its only credential is beauty (the *splendor formae* of St. Thomas). Its only excuse is delight (the *id quod visum placet*). What music is or why it is, we do not know. But *that* it is we do, because we have heard it giving such a magnificent account of itself in symphony, pitched half way between sheer silence and sheer noise—sculptured with noise by the mallet of the kettledrummer, sculptured with silence by the baton of the conductor. And yet, brought indoors and put on expensive display, music will never be more or less than the same little free whistle you made on the beach when you were running barefooted in the wind.

However, I have no intention of experimenting with childhood so as to discover the meaning of art. There are some child psychologists who enjoy doing this. They put a child in a nursery, surround him with tunes, pictures and blocks so that grown-ups may learn from his unerring reactions what are music, painting and sculpture. The compliment is enormous, but the procedure is vicious, and one that is violently protested by the child's Guardian Angel.

> Art is for childhood, not childhood for art,
>   The lesser for the greater;
> Neither is the other and they must be pried apart,
>   Sooner or later.

Fortunately the job of prying them apart was nicely done for me by the Providence of God.

In the year 1907, when I was ten years old, my father and I went to New York for a business trip. My father went for the business, and I for the trip. We had relatives there—"distant relatives" my father called them—and with them we stayed. At least I stayed while my father went—about his business.

These relatives could not get over the fact that I was their relative, for they had never seen me before. I could not get on to the fact that they were my relatives, for I had never seen them before either. They seemed afraid that at any moment I might stop being their relative, so they tried to talk me into it, even saying I looked like them. I was afraid that at any moment they might begin to be my relatives, so I tried to stare them out of the notion, inwardly denying that I looked like anyone. They spent most of the time talking, and I staring.

There is nothing so dangerous as an epidemic of cousins. Once you get infected with the idea it will begin to spread. You will end up by being related to practically everybody. Grown-ups are great ones for claiming relationship. Children are great ones for protesting it. I thought these cousins of mine were called "distant cousins" because New York was so far away from Lynn.

Across the hall from my cousins lived a young lady who was in love. She was the great subject of interest and discussion among my cousins while I was visiting them. The young lady across the hall was in love with an artist. Thinking love to be art, she went in for it all day long, and gave up all leisure. He, thinking art to be love, went in for it all day long too, and gave up all work. Mornings, noons, nights made no difference, for they had both lost all sense of time. They broke up later with a big bang, as my cousins predicted, and as was bound to be, for she expected marriage to be a perpetual court-ship and he wanted it to be an unperpetual vow.

By the very worst of luck I unstabilized this romance. My cousins had to go one morning to a funeral, and they left me in charge of the young lady across the hall. I was, for the space of a morning, on the young lady's hands and in her artist's way. So we compromised in terms of a triangle—love art and childhood—and went out for a walk.

With my left hand in hers and my right in his, you might have met us promenading on Fifth Avenue one morning back in 1907. We looked just like a husband, a wife and a child, and were greatly admired by all who passed us. The young lady enjoyed the experience because it seemed so real. The artist was pleased because it was so make-believe. I was totally disinterested either way, had serious distractions when passing store windows, and at times had to be forcibly dragged along.

Where did we go? To the Metropolitan Museum of Art sent there undoubtedly by the devil. The devil can never touch love, nor art, nor childhood, but he can raise the devil with them when they enter the Metropolitan Museum of Art in the form of a triangle.

The artist was continually paying the lady compliments born of his trade. She was a picture, a song, a poem. I believe he even mentioned Helen of Troy, Venus of Milo, and Jeanie with the Light Brown Hair. The lady kept returning him tokens born less of judgment than of sheer affection. He was the equal of Rubens, Rembrandt, Raphael—in fact, on the point of surpassing them. But here was the devil to pay. She came off badly as a masterpiece and he as one of the masters, the moment we entered . . . the Metropolitan Museum of Art.

Sensing this clearly, they immediately made frantic efforts to keep up the pretense when genius and the fruits thereof threatened to destroy it. They proceeded to become totally oblivious of all the Metropolitan Museum of Art contained except themselves. I was the very first item included in this sweet forgetfulness, and I went around the place for a solid hour, totally lost.

When I found myself alone, I first made sure there was nothing there to frighten me, and found nothing. So I kept on walking and looking. None of the things I saw either surprised or interested me. I knew too little about art to be surprised at anything, and art knew too little about me to keep me interested. I simply wandered, and wondered.

> Private faces in public places
> Are wiser and nicer
> Than public faces in private places

says the poet, W. H. Auden, and he is right. But he is describing surprise and fright, not wonder. Private faces in public places are surprising: for instance, meeting your next-door neighbor in London. You say: "Why my goodness me! My

goodness gracious! Mrs. Jones! You? And of all places!"
Public faces in private places are frightening: for instance,
meeting Mahatma Gandhi in your bath. You scream!!

But when you wonder, you neither talk nor scream. You
take out of the store-house of silence one of those little soft
exclamatory syllables which are words pared down to a point,
to show you have seen the point of something. Surprise is a
love disturbed. Fright is a *thought* disturbed. But wonder is a
silence disturbed. You say: Oh! . . . Ah! . . . Say! . . .
My! . . . Gee! . . . Gosh! . . . Wow! . . . These are the
wonder words.

What did I wonder at, when I was lost in the Metropolitan
Museum of Art? Well, I wondered at a number of things in
a simple sort of way. I did not know what the pictures and
statues were about, or who had painted or carved them. I was
absorbed merely in the fact that they were there, and kept
noticing what wonderful things they did to a room simply by
being in it. For instance, the paintings made the small rooms
seem large. And the sculptures made the large rooms seem
small. This rather primitive discovery delighted me, and I
began to whistle softly to myself. The setting was now com-
plete. For one of the three r's of aesthetics is missing in the
Metropolitan, but the music of my whistle added Rubenstein
to Rembrandt and Rodin. And my little whistle, though
smaller than any of the paintings or sculptures, easily filled
every room I entered. Music is the only art that leaves rooms
at their proper sizes.

I think it was the half-truth lurking in this absurdity that
caused me to burst into laughter (a series of silly syllables
totally uncontrolled, the result of almost seeing too many
points at once). At any rate, the only thing that surprised and
interested me in the Metropolitan Museum of Art was what
myself had contributed. So I laughed all the more.

But I stopped suddenly when I saw the artist and the lad
returning.

The artist came up to me angrily, seized me by the arm, and was prepared to scold me.

"Where have you been?" he said.

"Here!"

"What were you laughing at?" and his eyes filled with suspicions.

"Nothing!"

But beware of the dissyllable in direct reply. It is hesitating around the truth. The truthful answer was:

"You!"

THE POETS AND THE MYSTICS

I THINK it was good of our teachers to foster the poet in the child, rather than make a practitioner of him. Nor do I feel, as I succumb to middle age, that poetry was a bad thing, simply because it was not the best God has to offer. I know it was so much better than the lesser things children are now given in laboratories of learning, that I am not afraid to put it in its proper place in relation to that better form of knowing which the pure contemplatives enjoy.

But I will need the full maturity of my powers to show where poetry falls short of mysticism, and I need to do so precisely here in order to make a sort of celestial preparation for some further things to come. If the reader does not find this chapter very childlike in content, at least he will find it childlike in arrangement.

Poetry is another world, absolutely. When you are in it—in the throes of composition—you do not know what you eat, what you wear, what time it is, what day of the week. Some are prepared to say you are not responsible for what you do, but this cannot be admitted. Conscience is ultimately stronger than concentration.

Francis Carlin calls the poet's state one of "fixed imagination." And when the imagination gets into the habit of fixing itself to beauty, it begins to fix itself to other things, worries for instance. Poets are born worriers.

I prefer a deeper explanation of the poet's misery than that offered by Francis Carlin. I think poetry is a case wherein that phase of us which was not destroyed by original sin tries to get back to its Paradisal state, and to see by simple insight in place of round-about logic. But alas, the escape is never complete because of the wound of original sin. The heavy fetters of iniquity hang on the wings of the mind trying to soar. And sooner or later the strain tells, and down we tumble to earth, wounded and depressed. It is an awful price to pay, as only those know who have paid it.

The reaction to the writing of poetry is terrific, and history is strewn with the wrecks of those who could not stand the pace. But the real poets have got to stand it, and that is why, next to the mystics, they are the greatest heroes in the world.

The experience of the poets and the mystics is totally different. The poets go back to Paradise. The mystics go forward to the Beatific Vision. The hardship of falling forward from Paradise is not as great as that of falling backward from the Beatific Vision. Hence, the dark night of the mystics is even worse than that of the poets.

The poets admire the mystics and praise them. The mystics do not understand the poets, but in weaker moments they envy them.

The devil hates the mystics, but he also hates the poets. He is determined that human nature shall go neither forward to the Beatific Vision nor backward to Paradise.

The mystics want the pure white light of the Divinity. The poets want it diffracted among creatures. Poets make wretched mystics, but mystics make even worse poets. Saint John of the Cross was a great mystic, but a poor poet. John Keats was a great poet, no mystic whatsoever.

Poetry is an infinitely lesser thing than mysticism, but it is greater than ordinary thought. It is also, to some extent, a vocation. No one ever asked to be a poet, nor could he wholly escape the assignment once given. The writing of poetry is not its own reward. The poets suffer, and either Heaven awaits them or they shall have had hell on both sides of the grave.

The poets work in perishable material, endeavoring to give permanent form to words, sequences and sounds. But all these babblings will be drowned one day in the music of a celestial noise. The poets know this in their deepest hearts, and yet they go on pretending not to know it. *Sunt lacrimae rerum, et mentem mortalia tangunt,* Virgil wrote; and another poet supposed he was convincing himself of a truth when he began:

> No voice is ever drowned;
> Nothing becomes a stillness that once was a sound.

What nonsense! Even a physicist could explode it. And yet what a haunting nonsense to indulge in! The poets deal in dangerous values. They are constantly trying to eternalize the temporal and make the hereafter seem like now. And they can fool us from time to time with their pleasant tricks. But the mystics refuse to be fooled. They know we have been banished from Paradise by an angel with a flaming sword.

The mystics work in the field of imperishable material, their own immortal souls. They give forms, perpetual and harmonious, to hidden masterpieces within. They are inarticulate, mostly, in this life. But when they do burst into song, their poetry will be found to be an integral part of the hosannas of The Blessed which will vibrate forever and ever.

The poets are dreadfully insincere, but they are never deceitful. "But she is in her grave, and oh, the difference to me!" sang Wordsworth of little Lucy. But after a time it did not make *much* difference. A mystic, bereaved of Lucy, would keep her as a perpetual part of his prayer, his suffering, his very life. It would *always* make a difference to him.

Yet the mystics, unlike the poets, are deceitful. I do not mean this by way of moral, but of supernatural inconsistency. If you ask the mystics how they feel, they will reply: "Excellently, thank God!" though they may be referring only to an excellent ache in the head or an excellent pain in the stomach. They appraise such things in the light of their direct relationship to God, and talk accordingly. The poet does not understand such subterfuge. If you ask him how he feels, he will answer "Rotten!" if such be the case. He knows nothing of the brave evasions of the mystics, just as he knows nothing of their unswerving loyalties.

What purpose does the poet serve in the frightening supernatural scheme of things to which we are consigned? Well, even at his worst, the poet is at least a document, illustrating, in its positive phase, the truth of original sin, proving that there was in the primal childhood of our nature a cognoscitive directness in the mind's approach to truth never wholly destroyed by the transgression of our First Parents. The poet is one of the apples left over from Paradise, which, remaining unbitten, perished by blight.

I know there are those who want to pamper the poets and send them all to Heaven as a reward for mere aesthetic skills; but these persons are chiefly those who have never known by direct experience the emptiness of poetic achievement. To the honor of the poets be it said that very few of them have surveyed themselves with such a beatific stare. The best poets know well their own limitations, and are not ashamed to be saved by humility, as Chaucer was not, who, at the hour of death, begged Our Lord to be mindful, not of the excellence of the Canterbury Tales, but of the heinousness of his own sins and to blot these out in the gentle Christian mercies.

If there is any point in which poetry is a good preparation for mysticism, I insist that it is neither in the object sough for as such, nor in the method of seeking it. The poet is seeking for created beauty, the mystic for uncreated. The poet is perfectly helpless without the instruments of the senses and the imagination. To the mystic the senses and the imagination ultimately become hindrances, obfuscating the clear vision of God's essence.

But this much the poet and the mystic do have in common. Both look upon the object of their quest as an absolute, for which they are willing to make any and all sacrifices. The poet for the sake of his poem will starve, go sleepless, penniless, friendless, consign himself to solitude, and bravely endure the badgering, suspicion, misunderstanding which is the lot of all those who have a precious secret to hide. In brief, he practises asceticism of the extremest kind. The logic of asceticism he can see, and, conscious of its necessity in the realm of art, he is easily persuaded to admit its reasonableness in the realm of sanctification. He is sensitive also to the value of "form," and is often led into the Church by his admiration for the liturgy. And as regards the full-time contemplatives in Religious Orders, the poet may be indifferent toward them, but he is rarely if ever intolerant of them, and that is more than you can say of the common garden-variety of men, even among Catholics. Mary seated at the feet of Christ is as thoroughly convincing to the poet as Martha cooking the dinner, though there is probably nobody in the world more desperately in need of a dinner.

Fortunately for the sake of poetry, the mystical state is one to which many are called but few are chosen, and so there is no particular danger of the poets surrendering their trade in favor of a higher urge. And once God the Father gets hold of a good poet, He seems intent on keeping him, in preference to giving him the added lift that is needed for mysticism. Furthermore, the poet is one of God's best credentials, too valuable to dispense with. For if there are poets, there must be God. If there are those who can make words that fall so beautifully on our ears in time, there must be One Whose Word will reach us even more exquisitely in eternity. Therefore, God does not banish the poets, as Plato would. For God's Republic is more generous than Plato's. Others, besides the few, can enter the Kingdom of Heaven. And, short of seeing God face to face, it is something to have trapped His vestige in a rainbow or His image in the eyes of a child.

Likewise, the poet offers most stubborn resistance to the efforts of the materialists to break down the dignity of our nature and formulate it in terms of the guinea-pig. The mystic, since his is a celestial secret locked in the heart, suffers an easy dismissal by the materialist, on the score of being frustrated, inhibited, and so on. Not so the poet, who sings an open and free song for all to read. The delicacy of the spirit's tones is in it, and the materialist has no recipes for explaining this away. And so the poet, precisely because there is something in him that is of this world and something in him that is not, is one of the best defenses civilization has to protect itself against those whose education is pursued in terms of two epistemological criteria: suspicion and surmise.

Therefore, let the poets be kept, and let the mystics be kept, too, but with their differences properly noted in time, since they will be even more conspicuous in eternity.

In the pursuit of his eternity the poet has need, just as the mystic has, to go to the theology of the Church for counsel and direction. The mystics are constantly complaining that they have difficulty in finding suitable directors. They do not ask that these directors be mystics, but that they be those who have extended theology to the point where it can exercise its domain over them with understanding, rather than ridicule.

Likewise, I know of no poet who wants a poetical confessor. But he would like a confessor who at least knows of the existence of poetry, and this by way of appreciation, not condescension.

It would be well if the theologians would realize their importance as the last refuge of all of us, and with sure knowledge and generous sympathies save both mystic and poet from the horrors of private revelation.

POETRY

Now THAT POETRY has served us so patiently in unriddling the mystery of mysticism and art, it would be ungrateful of me not to pay it a few compliments for itself. I cannot do this by defining it, as I have already stated. Nor by telling how much I admire it, which I have been doing all along. I can only point it out and present it. It is sufficiently capable of introducing itself.

Poetry stands midway between philosophy and mysticism, and is at the service of both, but in itself is neither the one nor the other. Poetry is the field in which philosophy tries to become lovable. Poetry is the field in which mysticism tries to become intelligible. Truth expresses itself in poetry by way of illustration. Love expresses itself in poetry by way of symbol. Illustration is the art of the singular in universal things. Symbol is the art of the universal in singular things. Poetry is the art of illustration and symbol: the illustration of truth and the symbolization of love.

Truth lends itself to illustration reluctantly, because it thrives on exactness and is tolerant of nothing short of a perfect illustration. Love lends itself to symbol freely, because it thrives on excess, and is lenient toward any symbol that will serve it. Somewhere, ideally, there is a perfect illustration of truth. Nowhere, save arbitrarily, is there a perfect symbol of love.

The philosopher is concerned with the universal in things, and that is why he seeks the singular in illustration. The mystic is concerned with the singular in things, and that is why he seeks the universal in symbol. The philosopher is the guardian of the chastity of being, the mystic the fosterer of its charity. When being "stays at home" it is truth, and it is the philosopher's purpose to keep it at home as much as possible. When being "goes abroad" it is love, and it is the mystic's purpose to send it abroad as much as possible. The philosopher follows being when it goes abroad in the rôle of chaperone, so as to make abroad seem at home. The mystic joins being at home in the rôle of governess, so as to make at home seem abroad.

The philosophic error against God is pantheism; against the world, monism; against origin, evolution. The mystic error against God is polytheism; against the world, manichaeism; against origin, myth. The fruit of the philosophical error is scepticism. The fruit of the mystical error is superstition. The psychological escape in scepticism is stoicism. The psychological escape in superstition is neuroticism. It not infrequently happens that the evils of both sides are dumped into the field of art, and you find the poet in the form of the pantheistic polytheist, the superstitious sceptic, the stoical neurotic, in a word: the madman. Fortunately in our day he never comes much closer to literature than the "psychological novel," in which it is impossible for poetry to understand him, much less be harmed by him. Fortunately also in our day he is coming no closer to art than some form of "dadaism" or "surrealism" in which states poetry can wither him without raising an eyebrow. Let us do so.

> Though art be on vacation,
>   The studio remains;
> The well of inspiration
>   Is backing out of drains.
>
> Come, let us daub, my crazys,
>   Surrealize the thrill
> Of soapsuds on the daisies
>   And skylarks in the swill.

Ours not to reason whether
Surprise surpasseth wonder,
When man hath joined together
What God hath rent asunder.

In states worse than this, poetry must leave the artist to the alienist.

Humor is the poetry of ideas that do not match. But madness is the *philosophy* and *mysticism* of ideas that do not match, which are neither true nor good nor can even pretend to be, not even in fun.

The philosophic approach to art (the illustration of truth) is what we call Classicism. The mystical approach to art (the symbolization of love) is what we call Romanticism. Classicism is ultimately from the Greeks. Romanticism is remotely from the Romans. The hallmark of Classicism is reticence and restraint. The hallmark of Romanticism is exuberance and abandon. Classicism is suspicious of beauty; Romanticism is over-trustful of it. The danger of Classicism is prudishness. The danger of Romanticism is promiscuity. Classicism begets false virgins in the form of vestals. Romanticism begets false wives in the form of mistresses. The art of Greece perished because it starved illustration of truth. The art of Rome passed because it over-fed symbols with love. Classicism cast aside its cloak and posed in the nude. It was trying to show the body in the soul of things, and ran out of soul. Romanticism donned all raiments and went roaming in rags. It was trying to show the soul in the body of things, and ran out of body. The Age of Pericles stiffened into stone. The Middle Ages melted into paint. Art was the innocent victim in both catastrophes.

Greece gave us the athlete, bounded by a circle, with a discus frozen in his hand. Rome gave us the troubadour, divagating in the byways, with a mandolin trembling in his fingers. Greece gave us Narcissus, casual and conceited, admiring his image in a pool. Rome gave us Romeo, importunate and impetuous, adoring his idol in a balcony. Truth looks down, for it is vain. Love looks up, for it is proud. Narcissus found his image, which was really only sunlight, but he admired it and called it himself. Romeo found his idol, which was unmistakably Juliet, but he adored her and called her the moon. Illustration is truth in shadow. Symbol is love in silhouette.

> The sun begets the shadow,
>   The moon the silhouette;
> The noon is for Narcissus,
>   The night for Juliet.
>
> The image in the water,
>   The idol in the sky,
> Are opposites that alter
>   The angle of the eye.
>
> The love behind the window,
>   The truth within the wave,
> Will keep the heart unhappy
>   And make the head behave.
>
> The bridge is set for vanity,
>   The balcony for pride:—
> Beneath a man his body
>   And above a man his bride.

I have paused to compose the above lines, partly for the respite and pleasure of my reader, partly to clarify and summarize my own thought, and partly to make an ending to this chapter, which otherwise might never have an end.

By way of one last word, I should like to call attention to the subtle relationship that exists between poetry and verse.

Verse is not poetry. Verse is merely a suitable filament of words strong enough to resist, yet delicate enough to take the poetic charge. If the resultant incandescence in language is blending of warmth and light, then poetry has made a verse poem. Truth wired to the language of all illustration would fall short of poetry as does the Apologia. Love wired to the language of all symbol would fall wide of poetry as does the Apocalypse. Neither of these masterpieces requires, nor could it use, the precision of verse. Poetry is neither rhetoric nor revelation.

Poetry is truth going lovewards and love going truthwards: truth with a positive and love with a negative charge. These are the repulsions and attractions in a poet's soul which start whirling the dynamo of inspiration that generates poetry. A poet must think with the intensity of the lover and love with the accuracy of the thinker. This counter-rotation of spiritual forces when it touches language will transmute it. The only theme capable of attracting a poet is one which contains a contrariness and a compromise. It is his to see the failure in all successes and the glory in all defeats.

God is very kind to the poet at Bethlehem, letting him kneel like a listening ass and a staring ox in the presence of that complete resolution of all poetic values: a Virgin-Mother and a God-Man.

God to poets: "Unless you become as little children, you shall not enter The Kingdom of Heaven!"

Poets to God: "And unless You become a little child, You shall not get out!"

CHILDHOOD

BEGAN this book with my first sound. I shall end it with my first silence. Now that I am nearly through with my story, let me tell its secret. It is really time for a nap anyhow, if you have been reading me continuously, so do not mind if this chapter lulls you into silence. Do not even mind if it rocks you to sleep.

When you are really asleep but think you are awake, you are in a nightmare. When you are really awake but think you are asleep, you are in a dream. Sleep may be said to define itself in terms of a nightmare. Sleep may be said to desire itself in terms of a dream. But true sleep is neither a nightmare nor a dream. It simply is, and is sleep.

When you are always asleep but think you are awake, you are a simpleton. When you are always awake but think you are asleep, you are a loon. But a child is neither a simpleton nor a loon. I learned the first lesson from a noisy adult in the city. I learned the second lesson from a quiet adolescent in the country. Poetry was my preservative in the one case, silence my preservative in the other.

When the simpleton and the loon are united in one person, you have the childhood of the madhouse, the most monstrous example of happiness in the world. If you are undergoing this double experience in terms of genius, you are some people's definition of a poet. You are William Blake, unravelling the metaphysics of a nightmare, revelling in the mysticism of a dream. If you are enjoying the experience in terms of innocence, you are Little Boy Blue. If you possess it in the form of ingenuity, you are The Wild Man of Borneo. This is the best distinction I can make among Little Boy Blue, William Blake and The Wild Man of Borneo, for those who conceive childhood, poetry and madness to be merely different phases of the same reality.

Thought was made for the head. Love was made for the heart. A sentimentalist is one who tries to love with his head. An emotionalist is one who tries to think with his heart.

> Pease porridge hot,
>   Pease porridge cold,
> Pease porridge in the pot,
>   Nine days old.

Sentiment and emotion are really pease porridge in the wrong pots, and a child is a stickler for getting games right, especially when the rules are put rhythmically. Hence you will find the child to be neither a sentimentalist nor an emotionalist. Sentiment fires his head with fever, as it did mine in the case of a little winged mosquito on vacation. Emotion chills his heart to ice, as it did mine in the case of a little hair-ribboned girl at school. The thinker must be cautious, but a child is the boldest of all thinkers. The lover must be bold, but a child is the shyest of all lovers. Can it be that hair-ribbons are the wings of a girl, and wings the hair-ribbons of a gnat? No one would think so, really. No one would want them to be, really. But a poet would say they were, to the single applause of the child.

I have balanced the child with the philosopher and found him to be the poet who soared into Heaven. I have balanced the poet with the mystic and found him to be the child who fell back to earth. I have balanced the child with the artist and found him to be lost in the labyrinth of his own ubiquity. What is this earthliness of heavenly things and heavenliness of earthly things, which is constantly being lost and found, and in which poetry and childhood unite? We all know what childhood and poetry are in terms of performance. But what are they in terms of essence and idea? The answer is: "Nobody knows, and nobody cares," least of all poetry and childhood. Neither knows *what* it is nor *why* it is, but simply *that* it is, and it is enough.

The perfect recollection of self in remembrance is silence. The perfect recollection of self in forgetfulness is sleep. In this sense poetry is silence. And in this sense childhood is sleep.

You never have childhood completely, even when you hold it in your arms. You never lose it completely, even when you send it abroad to play. The same is true of poetry. Poetry will come to you when you least expect it, and will go from you when you want it most. The same is true of childhood. Both are impervious to analysis and synthesis, the analysis of ratiocination and the synthesis of rapture.

> They draw no conclusions,
> And make no resolutions.

How then can you get them to behave—I mean in the sphere of their clear and especial duties. It cannot be done by petting them. Parents try petting their children and patrons try petting their poets, but there is in both childhood and poetry an essential chastity that resists all excess in affection. Neither can it be done by scolding them, as preceptors do with children and critics with poets. For both childhood and poetry have a charity that forgives and disregards all excess in correction. Frankly, childhood and poetry are both imps, amenable to no motives except reward and punishment. Frankly, you must either bribe or scare them. Ultimately you will need both Heaven and Hell to be effective. For Heaven is the poetry of bribe, and Hell the childhood of scare.

Are poetry and childhood the same thing? I do not know, neither does anyone. If they are one, then they will never know how to divide, for their essence is in simplicity. If they are two, then they will never know how to unite, for their uniqueness is in distinction. But this much I do know: there are no two things about which it is possible to say so many same things as about poetry and childhood—unless they be silence and sleep. And the importance of silence to sleep is the importance of poetry to childhood.

Every little boy is enough of a poet to imagine he is the general of his soldiers. Every little girl is enough of a poet to fancy she is the mother of her dolls. Now a shortage of soldiers and a shortage of babies might be responsible for a world collapse. And wouldn't it be awful if the soldiers started killing off the babies in an effort to put things right again?

Humpty Dumpty sat on a wall.
Humpty Dumpty had a great fall.
All the king's horses and all the king's men
Couldn't put Humpty Dumpty together again.

And who is Humpty Dumpty? He is an egg on a wall: poetry's symbol for all things unborn.

A child turns his playthings into thoughts. It is the only way he can learn. A poet turns his thoughts into playthings. It is the only way he can teach. The education of the child is in the playthings of the world, and the instruction of the world is in the playthings of the poets. So, the nursery never ceases and life is forever a game.

Armed with such wisdom one might conquer the world. Armed with such wisdom one does. All things fall swiftly into place when you are playing a game.

Rockaby baby, on the tree top—
When the wind blows the cradle will rock,
When the bough breaks the cradle will fall,
And down will come baby, cradle and all!

Incidentally, I might mention that the "all" in the impending catastrophe of the last line in the above ditty includes not only childhood, but also poetry, silence and sleep.

Now as far as there can be a definition, Rockaby Baby is a perfect definition of both poetry and childhood. Of course no philosopher will accept it, for he wants it in terms of a syllogism which he can share with others. Of course no mystic will accept it, for he wants it in terms of a hieroglyphic which only he can decipher. M. Maritain in his *Art et Scolastique* tries to turn poetry into prudence, so it can be passed around among the metaphysicians. Abbé Bremond in his *Prière et Poésie* attempts to turn poetry into prayer, so it can be whispered to a few mystics. But poetry will not be laicized or clericalized by these easy snares. I cannot think of a more imprudent place to put Rockaby Baby than on a tree top, yet that is where poetry puts him and the child likes it. I cannot think of a more unprayerful thing to say to Rockaby Baby than to remind him of the pleasures of infanticide. Yet poetry does and the child thinks it is grand. Prudence is an excellent thing, and so is prayer. But whatever else poets and children are, they are not *pious prudes*.

I am willing to sway with Rockaby Baby on the tree top in a perfect statement of what poetry is. If the bough breaks and the cradle falls, then down will come baby, cradle, and the author of this book. But they will not, and I shall show why.

The to and fro of sound is a lullaby. The to and fro of motion is a rockaby. The to and fro of music is a melody. The to and fro of words is a poem. The to and fro of thought is beauty. The to and fro of expression is art. The to and fro of silence is sleep.

> The vanity of water is a fountain,
> The vanity of land is a mountain;
> The modesty of wet is a well,
> The modesty of dry is a dell.

And what are vanity and modesty but the to and fro of some lovely thing that deserves to be admired? But let us go back to Rockaby Baby.

The to and fro of water is a wave. The to and fro of air is a breeze. The to and fro of sky is a cloud. The to and fro of light is a star. Look out! We are rocking too hard! The bough is about to break and the cradle fall, not downwards, but upwards, into the infinite spaces! . . . *The to and fro of God is a Child!*

Far beyond the tree top . . . far beyond the stars, those occasional clarities of the philosophers . . . far beyond the background of the sky into which the mystics perpetually stare . . . tucked in the nursery of The Divinity—in the great silence of God, in an eternal sleep which is neither a nightmare nor a dream, but the living ecstasy of The Blessed Trinity—there is a *Filius Unigenitus*: an Only Begotten Child, who is the to and fro of The Father and The Holy Ghost, everlastingly rockabied and lullabied in the sacred processions of The Godhead.

THE EXILE

ON ANY DAY but Saturday—and for our sakes not on Sunday —but with haunting regularity on five days of the week you could hear his call in our street. He was whiskered and hunchbacked and wore a long-tailed coat and an over-sized hat that slid over his ears. He drove a loose-wheeled wagon that seemed to be rolling all ways at once and was drawn by a horse that had not been currycombed for months. The horse looked more stuffed than real, and there were times when so did the driver. Taken together they seemed an epitome of lazy motion, yet they were models of persistence in faithfully returning for the errand which brought them to our street. The boys pelted the man with bad fruit and called him vile names. He never answered them, except to go on shouting in a monosyllable the purpose for which he had come.

I was eleven years old when there suddenly dawned on me the tragedy of this poor vagabond's existence. True, I had never joined with the hoodlums in stoning or abusing him, but I had failed to appreciate the extent to which he was a victim rather than an enemy. When this realization came to me, I decided to let him know how I felt toward him by offering a few cheery words of sympathy. These he disdained as something suspicious. He merely rubbed his long beard and drove on. His refusal to be pitied made me all the more interested in his desolation, so I determined to follow him, discover his origins, find out where he lived. This I did during one of the summer holidays. I shadowed him for a whole day, even going without lunch at noon. I trailed him to the waterfront, and under the bridge, and down several side streets, and into a slum of sorts. I saw him unhitch his wagon and leave it standing in a yard. I saw him put his horse to feed in a shed, and then mop his brow wearily, and enter his house for supper. It was just at the hour of sunset. The insults of the day were over. He had a wife, so I discovered, and she was preparing his evening meal. And he had a daughter.

There she sat on the door-step, in the midst of her own, a dark Madonna of seventeen, waiting for the waters of Baptism to fulfil in her eyes the New Testament promised by the Old, and to which she had far more title than any of us Irish and Italian interlopers who mingle the Faith with fun.

She was reading a book when I first saw her. Eyes are never so lovely as when they are avoiding your own. Later I saw her rise and carry a basket on her head, and move among her kind as one destined for election and sacrifice. Her tribe sensed this in her, and that is why she dared not, save in ambush, talk to a Christian, even to a Christian child.

The incident left me speechless, and it was not until years later that I knew what I had wanted to say—not on my own account, for such loves are purely literary—but as hostage for someone who would be songless in her bereavement. Here is what I wrote, finally:

> In your dark eyes I see is so,
> Something I needed lots to know.

> Something Isaiah said I find
> Now makes a meaning in my mind.

> What Judith, Ruth and Esther were,
> For the first time I now infer.

Our Lady's voice unto my ear
Becomes more definite and dear.

Rarest, the world is all awry,
But father, mother, you and I

Will quadrilaterally allied
Defeat the death we shall have died

When . . .

and I dared not add the last line, which would be prophetic
of her destiny.

"But where shall I go?" she said after her Christening, which
was undertaken at peril of her life, even over attempts to
poison her food.

"For contemplation, warm countries are best," she was told.

"Will South America do?"

"It will do."

"Is it far enough?"

"Not quite far enough, but it will do."

"And there can be no attachments?"

"In your case, none. For you the price of God is everything
else. You must make a supernatural equivalent of what is native
in you: 'an eye for an eye, and a tooth for a tooth.' "

"What about my prayers?"

"It were better to be free even in your prayers. Let Christ
choose your favorites. Remember, you are of His blood, even
before it was poured on the Cross. There are cheap attach-
ments one can make to creatures under guise of offering
novenas in their behalf. Yours must be a sword renouncement,
like Abraham's with Isaac!"

"Can't you put it more gently than that?"

"There is no way of putting it more gently than that."

But there was, and I was determined to find it, even though
it might take me years. For it is the business of the poets to be

the servants of the mystics, to catch their cast-off thoughts, and to phrase their farewells. Even a martyrdom is softened when it is set forth in song. That a strong song was needed, I could clearly see, one equal to the mettle of the maid.

Because of the girl in the Gospel who lost her groat,
Because of the little boy by the fountain who lost his boat,
Because of the nervous piccolo player who lost his note—

Because there are partings on earth too hard to be had:
The waving wench on the dock and the land-loosed lad,
The widow, the warden, the jail, and the son gone mad—

We two who were sentenced on earth to be braver far
Than any except what Our Lord and Our Lady are,
Shall singly shine henceforth, as a star and a star;

And not interfere any more with each other's light,
No matter how murky the mist, how dismal the night,
Or whether the clouds conceal or reveal us right.

Now, mind you, I do not want you even to pray for me.
Let our dismissal be done in a downright way for me,
And neither be sad about it, and neither be gay for me.

For nothing can grieve for nothing, is that not true?
And nothing plus nothing is nothing, not one nor two,
And you willed to know me as nothing, and I willed you.

And God will be pleased, if God can be pleased at all,
As we raise between us the sky and the high sea-wall,
So to slake our souls in the wastes where His pities fall.

She sailed to South America on a small boat. The boat weighed only five thousand tons. I was on the dock, pretending to be one of the baggage boys, looking among the visitors for him who would miss her most. But I could find no one bidding her farewell.

I watched the ship till it reached the crest of the horizon, and sank in the far southeast.

Only two corollaries on this subject remain in my notes, a sestet and a double quatrain, on an identical theme. It is a difficult theme to handle, and I often laugh at my efforts, for they are perfectly contradictory.

The first:

> I must regret my partings more,
>   Renounce, not just refuse,
> And make a face, and pace the floor,
>   And burst into boo-hoos,
> When someone ambles out the door,
>   I am so pleased to lose.

The last:

> What soared into the sun
>   Will return one day,
> Remolded and respun
>   In a rarer ray;
>
> Identical, yet different,
>   Indeed, Divine;
> And what was never, never meant
>   For me, will be mine!

THE IMAGINATION GUY

IT IS NOT OFTEN you can stare into a person's eyes without causing embarrassment, but you could with the Imagination Guy. And the reason was because he saw you only in a blur. You were less than a silhouette to him when you entered his room. You were perpetually prismed with the wrong colors, shrouded in a haze, covered with a cloud around the edges of which would come floating the sound of your voice:

"Good morning!"

"That you, kid?"

"Yes."

"Come in and sit down and tell me how you are."

"I'm fine."

"That's the ticket!"

Then he would inquire if there was a morning paper in the hall. And I would go and find that there was. Mrs. Hasenfus, his landlady, was usually making beds when I arrived, and she was glad to have someone take the Imagination Guy off her hands and entertain him until her chores were finished. He wore a bathrobe and slippers and sat in a comfortable chair. He usually remained undressed and unshaved until noon. His hair was grey, and he had a tooth missing here and there. He was in his middle fifties when I knew him.

I would return with the morning paper and seat myself in a chair opposite his.

Cataracts—that's what the doctor said the Imagination Guy had in his eyes. Cataracts! I was always peering into his eyes intently whenever they were wide open so as to find the little Niagara Falls I supposed were flowing in each retina. But he would invariably blink at the wrong moment and spoil the experiment.

"Mind reading me the headlines?" he would say when he heard me rumpling the newspaper, while he fumbled for a cigarette and lit it.

"I'll be glad to!" I would say. And I would unfold the paper and begin to read the largest words printed on the front page.

PLANS FOR ELEVATED GRADE-CROSSING COMPLETED. WORK ON CENTRAL SQUARE STRUCTURE TO BEGIN AT ONCE.

That was enough when you were reading to the Imagination Guy. You might then lay down the paper for a while and listen to him talk. That nimble brain of his would immediately begin to anticipate the story and tell it far better than it was written in the news.

"It's about time they got going on that thing," he would say, as he visualized the whole construction with closed eyes. "There's been an average of twelve people killed down there every year as far back as I can remember. Imagine having a railroad running right through the main street of your city! And we're supposed to be up-to-date! That's the worst of living in a town that was founded in sixteen hundred and twenty-nine. Never seems to want to grow up, if you know what I mean. Gets cluttered up with a lot of old fossils who want to impede our progress. I don't expect anyone has been able to keep track of the number injured down at that crossing. I nearly got knocked off myself once. It was when the gates were down and I didn't hear the gong ringing. Pretty hard for anyone to hear it ringing with all the racket and noise and the jangling of the street cars. I expect this new plan will cost a lot of money. Three or four hundred thousand dollars, I should imagine. But it's worth it. They're going to have a lot of trouble, though, enlarging the street. There's Tobey's tobacco store. That's got to go. And I expect it will cut into Emerson's lunch room. And I imagine it will block off a lot of light in some of the shops. You won't be able to see yourself in Hooley's bar. Then I'm afraid those pillars that hold up the tracks will cause a lot of trouble. With automobiles coming along at the rate they are, there'll be a lot of them bumping right into those pillars. However, I'd rather bump into something than have it bump into me. And it's a crêpe and an undertaker sure, kid, if you ever get bumped by a railroad train . . ."

I used to sit in absolute amazement at the way the Imagination Guy could develop in soliloquy the barest suggestions from the headlines in the daily news. He seemed to have all Lynn tucked in his head, its lay-out, its inhabitants, its history.

"You're a wonder!" I would say to him.

"Who?"

"You!"

"Why?"

"The way you remember everything. The way you imagine everything. The way you *see* everything with those cataracts in your eyes."

"Aw, forget it!" he would say in a depreciative snarl. "After all, I've got nothing else to do. . . . But how about turning to the sports page and reading me about yesterday's ball games."

The lingo of the sports page is the most fantastic in the world. And it is all condensed like cream in the headlines. Centuries from now, when the English language has perished, I wonder if some scholiast of the future will be able to decipher one iota of meaning if he has at hand only the leaders from an American sports page. Yet there were nine innings' worth of rapturous instruction and entertainment in every one of these phrases as I read them out loud to the Imagination Guy:

MARANVILLE'S BUNT SAVES HAVERHILL. . . . TIGERS CLAW HOSE FOR SIXTH STRAIGHT. . . . PIRATES SINK REDS IN NINTH FRAME. . . . CARRIGAN'S PEG NIPS GEORGIA PEACH OFF SECOND. . . . CUBS RESCUED BY TINKER TO EVERS TO CHANCE.

Friendship with the Imagination Guy implied obligations as well as privileges. For it seemed that every place you went you should be storing up things you had noticed and liked, so as to be able to tell them to him on your return. I might have remained his scout for years were it not for the following incident.

"Been swimming?" he said one day when I returned from a dip in the ocean.

"Yes."

"How was the water?"

"Cold."

"I mean how did it look?"

"Same as always."

"Was it blue or green?"

That stopped me.

"Don't you know the difference between blue water and green water?"

"No."

"Well, when it's calm and the wind is down and there's no storm brewing, the water is blue. It's just like a mirror, and takes it color partly from the sky. But when the wind is up and it's rough and a storm is threatening, it gets restless, frantic, green, ready to leap up in high waves!"

"I never noticed that."

"Well, you ought to. For pity's sake, don't let that beach get wasted on you, kid. We've got the most beautiful beach on the Atlantic Coast. King's Beach! There's nothing like it from Maine to Florida. Ever notice how Dow's Rock extends out on one side and Red Rock on the other, taking a large armful of ocean and hugging it right to our shore? The Bay of Naples has nothing on our little bay, I'll tell you. And haven't we got our own Egg Rock out in the distance, pretending it's Vesuvius? I love every inch of sand on that beach, and all the little pebbles. I love the small boats anchored off the point, bobbing up and down in the tide. I even love the sand pails and toy shovels of the children, and the colored umbrellas that shade the ladies when they bring their families down there for a day's outing."

I paused long enough to allow this rapture to dissipate. And then I glared at him with a rebellious look in my eye.

"Now see here!" I said, "I was the one who went swimming today, not you! And King's Beach isn't nearly as lovely as you say it is. Nothing is as lovely as you say it is. You make things lovely by the way you think about them and talk about them. No wonder they call you the Imagination Guy!"

He smiled a disappointed smile, showing all the vacancies in his teeth. He realized he had lost his hold on me. He dropped his head and sighed.

"I see you're on to me," he said.

"Doesn't everyone get on to you after a while?"

"Shhhh! Here comes the landlady!"

THE CLASSICS

IT IS STRANGE that I remember the days of my middle childhood—that is the years from seven till fourteen—better than I do the period of the next four years that followed. The Jesuits were responsible for that.

At the age of thirteen I was taken from the charge of the nuns, and sent to Boston to be educated by the Jesuits. It was a most fortunate choice on the part of my parents.

I was just at an age when a vivid fancy and an undisciplined fondness for day-dreaming were ready to roam for no serious purposes, and deserved to be checked. It was the precise time when the essential intellect, in itself and for itself, needed to be given something substantial to do: to stop amusing itself by way of reverie, and to be informed with the habit of reflection.

Up till fourteen, a boy's imagination is as aimless as a butterfly, and it is best to let him browse through books as he pleases, rather than harness him with commands to read only what is important in literature. Up till fourteen a boy is too sensitive to be in charge of anyone save a woman. Up till fourteen the psychological differences between a boy and a girl are so slight that they often thrive on the same stories and play the same games.

But at fourteen, a boy's world changes. Henceforth he mus

set his face toward the life ahead with a military outlook and a soldier's reserve. Co-education after fourteen is a farce. There is a world for woman and a world for man, and you will confound the two at your peril.

I got a head start on the critical age by one year.

The Jesuits, though soldiers, did not put uniforms on us or give us guns to carry. The Jesuits, though psychologists, did not outline for us through biological charts and graphs the emotional evolution through which we were passing. The Jesuits plunged us into the classics.

It was well enough to think, but did you know what you were thinking and why you were thinking it? And had you noticed, in your blank moments, the frightening dependence that must exist between thinking something and expressing it?

"Let us take thought out of the mould of language in which you are now using it," said the Jesuits, "and recast it in another mould, so as to show you exactly what its face value is. Let us choose as a medium of expression that used by men at the highest points of culture in the world's history, the civilizations of Greece and Rome. You are young American boys employing a hybrid, uninflected language, bristling with so many and such diverse rules that not even a professional grammarian knows them all, a language completely dissociated from its origins and all but unintelligible in its etymology save to the most meticulous savants. Is that a nice language for a boy to learn how to think in? No, not if there is a better at hand. And there is!"

"We will teach you," said the Jesuits, "the two most beautifully ordered and inflected languages in the history of the world. Let us see you try out your thoughts in those languages! You may have them as rich and pure and free from mongrel importations as little boys once received them in ancient Greece and Rome. Then you will know what is worth saying, and how best to say it, from having first learned what needed to be said at all. And it will fill your life with purpose.

And you will begin to be refined little gentlemen. And you will always know what to do."

We began with Latin grammar, and had hardly got on to the syntax and vocabulary of that, when it was followed by Greek grammar. We began to study the by-paths and delicate detours of human thought in such matters as intention, purpose, result, causality, wish, surmise, exhortation and command. We learned the "moods" that could affect a statement by reason of indicative, infinitive, subjunctive and optative colorings. We took sentences apart and studied their complexity, dependence, and the various ways in which an idea or phrase could be qualified. We watched a single word alter its ending as it went from nominative to genitive, to dative, to accusative case, always letting you know *what it was* by its root formation, and *what it was doing* by its variable syllable. In no time we were reading the letters of Cicero, listening to the stories of Herodotus, surveying in a virginal, poetic vision, the whole of life with Homer.

What with themes, tasks, exercises, memory assignments, translations, parsing—the Jesuits left you time for little else in life besides your lessons. One would almost say they allowed you as few distractions as an angel. You took language completely apart, and reformed it with the graces of personal choice. It was the birth in you of what is known as "style."

In a short time you found that you were thinking differently from other boys in your neighborhood, more fundamentally, with more care in your statements, more maturity and sureness in your judgments. You could detect fallacies in what others had to say, and were inwardly censoring what you had to express yourself. Other boys noticed this in you, and either avoided you as one above them, or else came to you for advice. There might be a tendency in this training to make one a snob, but a touch of snobbery in a boy, like a touch of vanity in a girl, is not necessarily dangerous, and often the foundation of future greatness.

Back, back, back you went with the Jesuits, through the history of Western Civilization, back through the Middle Ages, back to the times of the Roman Emperors, even back to the Greek gods and the twilight of mythology. Civilization became the most important word in your vocabulary. And little by little you began to be civilized, to differentiate what was of the spirit and what of the senses, what was trivial and what important, what was ephemeral in man and what never changed.

The Jesuits put no premium on your being clever, only on your being intelligent, and on your ability to give reasons for what you thought and said. They weaned you away from a world, then known as Lewis Carroll's, and now as Walt Disney's, and drove you to an admiration for the Roman valor and the Greek restraint. You were able literally to *trace* thought, classical and purposeful, in the outlines of the Doric, Ionic and Corinthian columns. Imaginary figures derived from abstractions began to people your mind: Minerva and her wisdom, Ceres and her fruitfulness, Juno and her righteousness. Thought came first with the Jesuits, and symbols second, reversing the order of the kindergarten. Illustration followed the values established by essential reason. The day of the picturebook had passed. The day of the dry text had begun. Mother Goose had flown off on a broomstick, never to return. Santa Claus had at last died in the frozen north.

"If you send your boy to school to a slave," so runs an old Greek proverb, "he will become a slave!"

If you send him to school to a Jesuit, will he become a Jesuit?

It so happens, sometimes.

FAREWELL WITHOUT TEARS

WHEN ONE is seated in a dentist's chair, with one's mouth full of dentist's fingers and dentist's instruments, it is difficult to hold a conversation. One becomes all yawn, and the only word it would seem possible to pronounce is the name of the town in the Tyrol where they put on the Passion Play.

"How old are you?" said the dentist, while he elongated my mouth to suit his convenience.

"Oberammergau!" I replied.

"What!" he exclaimed, withdrawing all his tools at once.

"Seventeen!" I answered clearly, as I rinsed my throat with water and spat into a little silver whirlpool on the arm of the chair.

"That third tooth from the front never came down, I see. It's embedded in the gum. I'd give it a few more years though. It may grow down yet!"

"Thanks."

I rose from my chair, paid him his bill, and bade him adieu.

"What's this I hear about you?" the dentist said, as I was getting my hat.

"It's true," I replied. "That's why I came to have my teeth examined."

"Well, good luck!"

"Thanks."

Then I went to the doctor's for a more protracted investigation.

"What's this I hear about you?" said the doctor.

"It's true."

"You're young."

"I'm seventeen!'

"Are you sure you know your own mind?"

"I think so," I said, expanding my chest. "But how about my physical condition?"

He examined me a long time, required me to remove my shirt and take many deep breaths, and then said: "You're fit!"

"Good-bye, doctor!"

"Good-bye!"

Then there was the clothier's to go to for a couple of black suits. And the shoe store for extra pairs of shoes. And the haberdasher's for shirts, stockings and linen. And the parish rectory for my Baptismal certificate. And the baggage store for a trunk. And, oh yes!, to the men's furnishings shop for an umbrella.

It was my first unborrowed umbrella.

I was about three weeks in getting everything I needed.

Finally, all washed, dressed and packed, I stood one day at the top of our front stairs, ready to knock on the door of my mother's room.

Good God, what was I doing? Was this the result of a classical education? Or is there a sense in which a boy does not know his own mind?

I knocked on my mother's door.

She was dressed in bright colors, endeavoring to please me. She kissed me one, twice, a dozen times, saying nothing.

My father, speaking for both of them, embraced me and said: "Good-bye, dear!"

My little brothers looked unhappy, and my little sister wept and would not be consoled with a million kisses.

I took a last look at all the rooms in our home. A last look at our neighbors' houses, and the traffic going to and fro in the street. A last look at our lawn and our lovely verandah. A last look at the number on our front door. A last look at the beaches below us, where I used to swim.

The by-gone beaches and limbs of brown,
When hoops were rolling around the town,
And London Bridges were falling down!

The car was ready, and my belongings packed in the rear.
The gears shifted, and we were off.

The next day I was in New York. It was September 7, 1914.
I received Holy Communion at the Church of St. Francis
Xavier. I ate breakfast in an automat lunch. I took a walk on
Riverside Drive and visited Grant's Tomb.

At noon I took the boat that sails up the Hudson.

I arrived in Poughkeepsie at five-thirty.

A short auto ride brought me to the Novitiate of St.
Andrew-on-Hudson, the training school for young Jesuits in
the Eastern States. It was just six o'clock, Angelus time, on
the Eve of Our Lady's Nativity.

We were fourteen novices entering on that day, and pretty
raw recruits we were, and looked, even to each other. We
were first brought to the chapel to say a prayer. Then we
went to the dormitories and were shown the hard beds on
which we were to sleep. Then to the cubby-holes where we
were to put our clothes. Then to the washrooms, where each
was given a small wash-bowl for himself, with one spigot in it,
spouting a stream of icy cold water. I had brought a safety
razor, and my first blade lasted me two years, and my first
cake of shaving soap, four.

We were taken to the refectory for supper.

After supper we were brought to the Master of Novices for
a first inspection. We entered his room individually. He was
a short, slight man, about five feet, two inches in height, and
weighed not more than a hundred pounds. His name, appro-
priately, was Father Pettit. He was *little* Father Pettit to us all
from then until he died. And it was not I who coined him the
adjective.

This is the story of what I chose to be at the age of seventeen, and exactly the story of what I would want to be again, were the choice once more to be mine.

But I forgot to tell what the Jesuit Master of Novices said to me when I visited him that first night in his room.

"I see you have a tooth missing!" he said. "We'll have to have that fixed!"

THE FIRST COMMAND

THERE is a great heritage bequeathed to aspirants in all Religious Orders by their spiritual forebears. It is the First Command.

There are copious rules developing around this initial order of obedience, but nothing can be attempted in the ascetical life until it has been established. You do not find it placarded in the cloister corridors as you do in a busy office or a hospital. It is the essential atmosphere into which you move, and you either accept it as sacred, or else profane it with every unnecessary sound of your voice.

The First Command can be issued in a single word, the most thunderous in the world when shouted. Birds begin to twitter when it settles in the air. It is the cricket's opportunity and the dove's delight. In it you can hear the leaves crinkling on the trees, the leaves turning in the books. It is the language of resignation, patience, forgiveness of injuries. Beethoven utilized it to compose the world's great symphonies. Christ hid in it for thirty years, preparing Himself for His mission. It is all that is audible of the planets circling the sun, of buds growing in the field.

In fulfillment of the First Command one notices the time passing, knows that it is time, knows that it is not eternity.

"There cannot be two hundred men in this house! It is impossible! Where is everyone? I hear nothing! What are they all doing?"

Recreations were merrier because of the observance I mention. A bell would ring and a burst of voices be heard, anxious to tell the happy thoughts that had been saved up during the day. A bell would ring again. Sociability ceased instantly and all reverted to the call of the First Command.

When you had any of what was offered you by the First Command you had all of it at once, and each had it all to himself. It was measureless and immeasureable, wider than the ocean and as large as God.

They were building an artesian well at St. Andrew and I used to count the strokes of the heavy drill plunging in the rock. I figured that it would strike a hundred and seventeen thousand times in a month.

I have seen two ascetories filled with novices kneeling for solid hours and hours of prayer in perfect tableau.

Some could not stand the monotony imposed by the First Command, and they packed their trunks and returned home to their mothers.

But on it went after their departure, the inexorable rule of the Religious, which when he forgets he figuratively tears down the walls of the cloister and shatters the great pillars of peace.

The First Command brought the uninitiated to the edges of the spiritual desert where alone the voice of God is to be heard. Yet there were moments of bewilderment when you had so much of it on your hands you knew not what to do. You drew little circles on paper with a pencil; you plucked blades of grass; you examined the bark on trees; you counted ants scampering into the little holes in their hills.

Poems

———◆———

THE CLOUD

Song should come promptly when the eye beholds
A Himalaya floating off in folds,
In wayward vales of silent plume-like lather:
Song should be swift the gist of that to gather,
Have fixed in snow-flame phrases and dispensed
This continent of quiet uncondensed,
Ere the explosion into forks of fire,
The crash and downpour of a frail empire
Whose trickling ruins the minnow shall be fond of
Soon, and paper boats sail on the pond of.

SUN AND MOON

The sun begets the shadow,
   The moon the silhouette;
The noon is for Narcissus,
   The night for Juliet.

The image in the water,
   The idol in the sky,
Are opposites that alter
   The angle of the eye.

343

The love behind the window,
  The truth within the wave,
Will keep the heart unhappy
  And make the head behave.

The bridge is set for vanity,
  The balcony for pride:—
Beneath a man his body
  And above a man his bride!

THE KITE

Over the purple crags,
  Over the snowy waste;
Not tailed with trailing rags,
  Not paper, board, and paste:

Over the raging ford,
  Over the twirling mill;
Not tethered to a cord,
  Not tugged by a human will:

He soared into the sun!
  He vanished in the blue!
A bird and a boy in one,
  Himself was the kite he flew!

THE WHISTLER

Seldom the soaring rocket-light will rise
Up from the flaming heart and reach the eyes.
Often the song of ecstasy, half-sung,
Will find no footing and fall back in the lung.
But one sweet bird up-warbling from the south

Will never miss the mouth.
The whistler's way is best, the school-boy's scheme:
The simple O that pipes away the steam
Lightly escaping from a lonely dream.

THE BUTTERCUP

I always come in multitudes; I am part of a festival
Of buttercups, each buttercup so rare and dear and small,
Alone, I guess I am practically no buttercup at all.

What praise I get a million ways must promptly divided be,
Who am but one little flaming note in a vast symphony
Of buttercups in your meadow, as far as your eye can see.

The rather common kitchen nomenclature that I wear,
Like a good humble buttercup, perforce, of course, I bear;
Though the items in my title were a much later affair

Than I, who in ancient Paradise Our Father did allow
To grow and become a buttercup as sweet as I am now,
Aeons before your crockery, centuries before your cow.

THE EWE

The little ewe will eye you,
   Leading her lamb to nurse.
The little ewe will spy you,
And try to terrify you,
   And cast at you a curse;
And then will want to woo you,
Come running half way to you,
   Then pause, and then reverse,
And never quite construe you
   For better or for worse.

THE DOVES

The doves,—they fly to the moonlit elms and cry: Tickitacoo!
    Tickitacoo!,
The whole night through.
They tell their loves in a song that has but a note or two:
Tickitacoo! Tickitacoo!
That's all they do.

And on and on till dawn, while the world is sleeping and all
    the other birds are too,
They wake and shake the silvery leaves with a strain that is
    never old, and never new.

There's snow upon their feathers, but their breasts are full of
    flame.
The seasons change, but still their melody stays the same:
Tickitacoo! Tickitacoo!
Ever soft and true.

TEARS

Through metal and through glass
The transcendentals pass.
Water must forgive
The sieve,
And sunshine dare not say
The window was in its way.

So, in the alternate enterprise
Of light and liquid in the living eyes,
That soak with sorrow every sweet surprise,
Perhaps when people weep we should not rue
That it is good and we are glad they do.

AFTER THE SHOWER

After the shower I went abroad:
All the wells in the world were full;
Lightning elapsed in the goldenrod,
Thunder subsided inside the bull.
Worms were soaking above the sod;
Lambs regamboled and birds resang.
God flung a violet boomerang,
Arched the ocean from coast to cape,
And, oh, it was great for a guy to gape
At Hope set up in a horse-shoe shape!

FOUR APOSTROPHES TO SILENCE

I

I am harried and hounded with Hush, Hush,
All through the voice-vacated night.
Whirlpools of respite around me rush;
Quiet consumes me quite.

Finger on lip, is the countersign.
A whisper were worse than a word;
While a delicate thunder I know is Divine,
Booms, and is never heard.

II

Nothing is ever hid:
Nothing you ever dreamed or did.

It gets into the gestures,
It trickles through the tones,
And in our ultimate vestures
Will rearrange the bones.

No voice is ever drowned.
Nothing becomes a stillness that once was a sound.

III

My only grievance against God,
Towards Whom no grievance could ever be,
Is that all even is never
And two and one are always

IV

Little Miss Troubled Heart is trying
To say what love cannot say:
Slumberless all the night and sighing,
Half asleep all the day.

Little Miss Troubled Heart is telling
With breast sobbing and eye welling,
Not even a millionth part
Of what is troubling Little Miss Troubled Heart.

What the spirit knows
Gives us repose.
But what the spirit wills is
What kills us.

THE INCOMPARABLE

A little less softly than a breeze
The Incomparable goes;
But this because of the necessities
Of substance, I suppose,
And the noisy abundance of her hair:
A distinctly relative affair,
Not noticed until I am compelled to compare
The Incomparable with a breeze that blows.

A little more muffled than a bird's
Her voice leaps into sound;

But this because of the natural weight of words,
Which even in the most thrush-like throat is found
Of all our gentle daughters.
The Incomparable's ways are wilder than the waters,
And her innocence most poised to please
When least assaulted by my similes.

THREE SOLDIERS

Three soldiers rose up from their tents,
And went to join their regiments.

And one said: "Captain, I report
Because I think that war is sport!"

And one said: "Captain, I am here
Because my duty makes it clear."

And one said: "Captain, I'm afraid
I was not for a soldier made."

So one in fervor, one in fun,
And one in fright took up a gun.

Three soldiers step for step went forth
And wheeled from south to west to north,

And while they marched, as drilled dragoons
Respectively in their platoons,

Beneath three helmets one could trace
A grinning, grave, and groaning face.

Three soldiers lay upon their backs
When bombs came down on bivouacs,

And wildly bursting in the air,
Destroyed all soldiers everywhere.

So one for pleasure, one for pride,
And one for love a soldier died.

THE EVERGREEN

When crimson beauty stales an autumn sky,
And leaves in lovely rot come floating down,
The birch, for shroud, will shade its swaddling gown,
The maple will be fickle to its dye;
Sumac and elm will both begin to sigh
For alien tints of lavender and brown,
Envy a golden evening cloud's renown,—
But I my true love-hue will not lay by.

Earth bred me in the mead, aye in the mud,
And in no sunset lacquer will I preen;
Fidelity is in my root, my blood,
And color-loyal all my tribe hath been.
Leaf vowed to leaf, whatwhile we were in bud,
To ever be forever evergreen.

RABBIT

Rabbit's eyes are pink,
And they are, I think,
Less to watch with than to wink
With: they are ornamental:
Sight in them is incidental.
All sensation goes
In through rabbit's ears and nose.
Rabbit runs around

With jump and rebound,
Sniffing every sound,
Listening to the light
Falling on the clover.
Rabbit *wants* to be afraid:
He delights in fright,
And is soft all over.
He is lovable and white,
And by God was made,
Out of man some tenderness to take:
Just for pity's sake.

SNAILS

Snails obey the Holy
Will of God slowly.

THE MOTH

The little muslin moth,
Whose food is flame and cloth,
Flitting in rapid flight
From linen-chest to light,
In its intense desire
To be dissolved in fire,
Many manoeuvres made
Around my red lamp-shade,
That so enchanted me—
To it I faithfully
Promise appropriate praise
In my verse, one of these days,
As soon as I can get,
And put on paper down,
Some nimble epithet
And little noiseless noun.

THE ROSE

Perfume and petal
  Are qualities
That test love's mettle
  With too much ease.

Bramble and briar
  Will soon discover
Who is the liar
  And who the lover.

REFLECTION

When we were young and you were fond
Of rolling pebbles in a pond,
Remember how we waded out
And looked and found without a doubt
Our pictures near a silver school
Of little fishes in a pool?

Though round the world the rivers go
And into fussy fountains flow,
Our pictures shall remain
When waters rest again.
The mirror in the well will not
Forget us when we are forgot.

BOUNDARIES

Over us and under
Is a world of wonder:
In between we blunder,
Blunder in between
The unseen and unseen,
And on someone's word
Hear of the unheard.

From our faiths and hopes
In prophets and in popes,
And in microscopes,
Mites and sprites we know
Are above, below,
And vice versa so.

Amoebas and archangels
Send us their evangels:
In between the ropes
Where we stand and stare
At the empty air;
Seeing only sights
That are lit by lights,
Hearing only sounds
That are kept in bounds
By celestial sheriffs
On their ghostly rounds
In between the seraphs
And the fleas on hounds.

THE POET

Ladies and gentlemen,
A poet is one
Of the few things one can be
And save one's soul.
And even then,
'Tis done
With such difficulty
And continual self-control,
Avoiding the inspiration
Of the devil,—
Lifting the illustration
To love's holy level,
The level of a star,—

That very few
Come through,
And nobody knows who
They are.

I BURNED MY BRIDGES

I burned my bridges when I had crossed.
I never brooded on what I lost,
Nor ruined with rapine my holocaust.

Youth is a rapture we must forget;
Wither and wrinkle without regret,
Hobble to Heaven and do not fret.

Yet in my soul there is something still
Deeper than memory, mind and will,
Something alive that I cannot kill.

Part of me, put not in my keeping,
Awakes unwakened when I am sleeping,
Under my laughter it goes on weeping

For by-gone beaches and limbs of brown,
When hoops were rolling around the town,
And London Bridges were falling down.

ENTIA MULTIPLICANDA

In the little kingdom
Of thingdom
That has no soul,
A pebble will tinkle and roll
In a bric-a-brac bowl;
By the brewing and brothing

Of silver and steel
A knick-knack is never not nothing
And a trinket is real.
By repulsion, attraction
Devoid of all immanent action,
The length, breadth and thickness of stuff
Is existence enough
In the little kingdom
Of thingdom.

In the little kingdom
Of thingdom
Where shells become pearls;
Where diamonds are princes and princesses, emeralds earls,
The well-fueled ruby will flash,
The coin on the counter will clash;
There's a lovely alarm for the ear,
Were there someone to hear;
There's a mineral meaning to find,
Were there only a mind,
In the little kingdom
Of thingdom.

In the little kingdom
Of thingdom
Where hands are all handles,
The lady was pleased to put shiny white sticks under lily-
      white candles,
With one of her fingers residing in ringdom,
A beautiful pledge evermore
That was bought in a honeymoon store,
One day, in the little kingdom
Of thingdom.

REVEILLE

(*for the Carmelites*)

Now see them stand at strict liturgical attention:
  The athletes who teach the body how to pray;
Who think no work but worship worth the mention,
  Determined that there is no other way

Save through the solitudes to reach salvation
  And the secret singularities of the soul,
Each measuring her strength in meditation
  Before the plunge through darkness to the Goal.

There will be time enough for lights and lilies
  When veils are shed and lids lie on the eyes.
Now, at a soundless hour when sleep the sillies,
  Pull the bell-rope again and wake the wise!

VIRGIN MOST PRUDENT

May after May I see by candlelight
  Above an icon that I kneel below,
Her head in shadow nodding left and right,
  Most sweetly and discreetly nodding No.

Year after year I must agree to let her
  Decide what to provide me for my good;
Pray as I may, I cannot ever get her
  To grant what would be wonderful if she would.

Spring comes, and little birds make warble.
  Snow thaws, but not Our Lady of the Snows.
Tapers I melt before relentless marble.
  Poems I write from what to live is prose.

AFTER THE LITTLE ELEVATION

O wheat-like, white, little, still-as-death,
Circumferenced Jesus of Nazareth;
My duty, Your beauty to recondite,
To fashion You frangible, frail and light.

You come translucent to hold and handle,
To peer clear through, Dear, and see a candle,
With a tractable trait to elate my heart
Who make You and take You and break You apart:—

Yet sever You never, St. Thomas said,
For wetness to water is not more wed
Than these twin fragments I now expand,
In my left, in my right, in my either hand.

The Saints have gazed at in other guise
This Body, ecstatics with other eyes;
But sinners with semblances rest content:
Its measure and mould as a Sacrament.

So daily at dawn, by the grace of Mary,
With well-worn words in a voice I vary,
I give God God, and at God's behest,
For whatever may ease her or please her best.

RESURRECTION

In crocus fashion, sunlight-wise,
    The Body of Our Lord
Slipped through the stone-bound sepulchre,
    Streamed through the soldier's sword.

Though stripped and whipped and spat upon,
　　Sundered with nail and spear,
Thus did our dust in Him prevail
　　At the robin-time of the year.

Albeit our interval under earth
　　Must needs much longer last,
Let there be always ready the roll
　　Of drums and the trumpet blast.

With bones ablaze and flesh aflash
　　And hair set flying free,
So shall I come to you, loved ones,
　　So shall you come to me.

ADVICE TO VERSE-MAKERS

　　It is not information
　　That causes inspiration.

　　There are no lambs and Marys
　　In any dictionaries;

　　And no beanstalks and Jacks
　　In any almanacs.

　　Beauty's a thing to earn
　　More than a thing to learn.

　　It comes from simply seeing
　　The sharp bright point of being,

　　Whose vein of gold is struck
　　By labor linked with luck.

And when a rapture fills
The auricles and ventricles

And gives the mouth through art
Connection with the heart,

One can assign the season,
But never knows the reason.

IN THE ANTIQUE SHOP

There was a lady made of gold,
And at an auction she was sold.

She was a little lady wrought
In metal moulded by a thought,

And had a faultless face, a form,
A gesture, an extended arm,

And in a mirror on a shelf
She pointed proudly at herself

As if to say to someone: "See,
What a man's mind has made of me!"

"Take her away!", the auctioneer
Bawled to a bidder in the rear,

A grand dame in a gaudy gown
Who paid a hundred dollars down,

And called her limousine and rolled
Off with the lady made of gold.

And oh, I wonder after that,
What in the world she pointed at!

FINALE

When the Angel has blown on his trumpet a rat-a-tat-tat,
And the final encounter of armies is finished and fought;
When the ultimate wire has been snapped on the ultimate rat,
And the ultimate saucer been licked by the ultimate cat;
When the last little flower has pined in the last little pot,
And the last little ditty has come to the last little dot,—
I will surely be happy—who wouldn't?—at that being that;
Though I wonder if really I will be as much as I ought.

RESIGNATION AT MIDNIGHT

Sleep has already come to other eyes,
    Dreams are not driftwood gathered in their thickets;
Nobody else is left without allies
    To count the clock-ticks and applaud the crickets.

But self is self, assignment without appeal,
    However restlessly one plays the part.
Out of another's slumber my soul would steal
    Home to its ache in this accustomed heart.

SOMETHING WITHIN ME

Something within me is delighted
When a little quatrain is completed;
Something within me does not care.
I have a half desire to hear it recited,
And by a voice I love repeated:
And I have half a loathing for the whole affair.

SONG FOR A LISTENER

1

This is a song of something said
For ears left hanging on the head
Weary of words that will not wed;

A song in which I trust is found
The pretty echo and rebound
Of sound off sense and sense off sound.

Our tuneless asses cannot climb
Parnassus, so perhaps it's time
For reason to return to rhyme.

2

The squirrel's scamper no one sees,
The measured arc, the branch, the breeze:
The perfect leap among the trees.

The stars, long snubbed, themselves resign,
Beginning about eight or nine,
To simply stick it out and shine.

The unmolested little mouse
Goes bric-a-brac throughout the house
Where artificial cats carouse.

3

One gathers wisdom coarse as this:
Two lips resisting cause a kiss,
And bondage is bereft of bliss,

And soldered selves each other slay
In incommunicable clay.
I thought it was the other way:

That out of selves new selves could come,
The hive, the hubbub and the hum,
The little dolly and the drum.

4

The heart is bruised below, above;
The ill-conditioned state thereof
Unfits it for the beat of love.

Much rubbish mixed with faint desire,
It seems more fuel now than fire,
And tries at all its tasks to tire.

In lacquered bosoms when it swings,
If cooled by hands aflame with rings,
Psychiatrists will tell it things.

5

There's no more music in the voice.
Music is now a nightmare noise,
And rowdy instruments employs.

The breath of life from being blown
Incessant through the saxophone
Has worn the body down to bone.

Starvation is the fad in food;
There is disgrace in amplitude;
Only the skeleton is wooed.

6

Our lanky lads and skinny lasses
Come crowding in to college classes
To find what flunks them and what passes.

They are compelled in curious courses
To trace through manuscripts and sources
The origins of river horses,—

Which, after long didactic fusses
Conjoined with therefores and with thuses,
Are labeled: hippopotamuses.

7

A tattered scarecrow tends the farm,
And nothing's kept from hurt or harm;
The cows can roam, the bees can swarm.

The gay harmonica is stuffed,
The artful lips no longer puffed,
The sweet sonata never snuffed.

And barefoot boys, who whistle well,
Have ceased to whistle, so they tell,
Since what befell us all befell.

8

Because the title was alluring,
Because one's friend was reassuring
And said that it was worth enduring,—

Miss Tupper's lecture one attended,
And Smotherhood one heard defended,
And one was grateful when it ended;

And with Miss Tupper on the brain
One walked home in the streaming rain
Till two and two made four again.

9

Because his lyre was newly strung,
Because the poet still was young,
One read some lines that Spoundel sung;

And found that what he thought untoward
He wallowed in, and thanked the Lord
He was not bored with being bored,—

And made elliptical allusions
To obfuscate his own confusions
And ostracize his own exclusions.

10

Because the curtain rose at four,
And S.R.O. was on the door,
One went to witness "Nevermore";

And saw O'Reilly on the stage
Attempting to become of age
And read the simplest primer page.

He hoped that we would not be pained
To hear the alphabet explained;
And hoped we would be entertained.

11

Allow me when the dawn comes down
Over the mountain to the town
To light my candle, get my gown,

And as I climb the crimson stairs,
Unleash the bloodhounds of my prayers
On these defeats and these despairs.

For well I know how worn and thin
The simple certitude within,
Though braggartly stuck out the chin.

12

I must in pity cease to prod
These getaways from good and God,
And spare the child and spoil the rod.

Which if I ever dared to use
To beat and brandish as I choose,
Would flash and flare into a fuse,

Unhide the hindrance in the heart
And hold it to the light apart!
'Tis well I amble in my art.

13

I know their game: each self-exhorted
And solipsistically sorted,
Fancies his own support supported.

The A's will feel they are secure
Because the B's and C's are sure
That what the D's and E's endure

Was verified by F's and G's
And so through X's on to Z's
And other unknown quantities.

14

I know their tricks: they sit and wait
Until some drunk goes by the gate,
Then after him perambulate.

And if it happens, as it may,
He drops his Beads along the way,
Why then the clue is clear as day!

For how can the Annunciation
Be part of Christian Revelation
In view of such intoxication?

15

Remember, gracious Virgin Mary,
Mother and Maiden, quite contrary,
Of this wild welter to be wary.

Preserve thy stately *Vous* between
Our *Je Salue*, and be our Queen
Aloofly more than thou hast been.

Be distant, keep atop the stairs,
Unharassed by our foul affairs,
And when thou willest, hear our prayers.

16

There is a Holy House of Bread
Where friends may feast and foes are fed,
And none is starved, none surfeited;

Where souls can relish the ideal
And bodies revel in the real:
Where mind and mouth can make a meal;

Where simpletons who suck their thumbs
Can share the carvings and the crumbs
With Constantines and Chrysostoms.

17

Within this Fortress I was brought,
A little thing without a thought,
And given all for giving nought.

I was anointed with a Sign,
And someone's promise, made for mine,
Attached my branch unto a Vine

Of Immortality and Love,
With Intimations from above
That Wordsworth was not thinking of.

18

Arriving at the age of two,
I found the faith I held as true
Enhanced my infant point of view.

I could believe a rubber ball,
Although somewhat phenomenal,
Would really bounce against a wall;

A jumping-jack when squeezed would squeak,
As though unwilling, so to speak,
To wait for reason's pure critique.

19

I took for granted at my side
A friendly lady kindly-eyed,
Another's daughter, sister, bride.

Two simple sounds, each sound the same,
Easy to mumble and exclaim,
Seemed to suffice her for a name.

And numbers, numbers: *one* and *three*
She kept on whispering to me
Until I learned a Mystery.

20

If I grew, if I may boast a bit,
Familiar with the Infinite,
And everywhere looked round for It;

But never thought to find It small,
And stumble on It in a stall,
So simple to approach and all;

So kindred, kissable and such,
In measurements that were not much,
With little hands and feet to touch.

21

When toys were trunked and school begun,
I was, among a many, one
Entrusted to a wimpled nun:

A virgin vestaled with three vows
Who had the Holy Ghost for spouse,
And tried devoutly to arouse

An aptitude for long divisions
Involving cerebral collisions
With theological precisions.

22

This gentle girl in cape and coif,
With softest silver in her laugh,
Prepared me for my epitaph:

"Here lies a lad whose sins were sins,
Not streptococcic orange skins;
Nor were his virtues vitamins.

He learned the rules and knew the game;
If Hell or Heaven hold the same,—
Himself, not spinach, was to blame."

23

This modest maid did not abhor
The monkey as the metaphor
For capers in the corridor;

But while she twitted, could but please,
Seeing but similarities
Between what had and had not fleas.

She held, as evolutionist,
That Eve and Adam led my list:—
My missing link was never missed.

24

This merry menial,—how came she
To lease her services to me
Without a farthing for a fee?

In what behavioristic school
Reaped she her rapture for her rule,
Found she her fashion as a fool

Willing to wilt along the aisles,
In marches mounting up to miles,
Where changing children flow in files?

25

This busy bird, as light as air,
Was never cumbrous in her care;
Her presence vanished everywhere!

A shadow?—none more softly strewn,
Nor—sunbeam?—from a nether noon
More mildly mirrored by the moon.

One knew not till her glow had gone
In dusk antipodal to dawn
That one had been so shone upon.

26

But dame and damsel disparate
And dealt in a divided state
I quit, and came to contemplate

A creature of a clearer kind,
A marvel moving in my mind
With both accomplishments combined;

A Lady whose aloof largesse
Ended in ways too choice to guess,
The Holy Ghost's unfruitfulness.

27

The barn was ready and the straw;
I saw what nudging angels saw,
And shepherds open-mouthed with awe.

I found what hitherto had been
The fragments of the feminine
Welded at last, without, within.

My happy Heaven had begun:
I knew the nursery and the nun,
The convent and the crib in one.

28

When once the heart has been up-hurled
And glimpsed this Glory in the world,
Whatever's ringleted or curled

Takes on a newer, nobler guise,
Usurps the function of surprise,
Asserts a symbol in the eyes,

Which one is soon intrigued to trace
In the most worn and wrinkled face,
In the most mean, improper place.

29

Because of Her who flowered so fair,
The poor old apple-wench will wear
A sprig of roses in her hair;

The strumpet strolling on the quay,
Who puts in pawn her purity,
Will sue for sailors' chivalry;

The lily, garbaged in a brawl,
Out of her refuse-heap will crawl
Back to her trellis on the wall.

30

Because this Beacon blanched our shore,
Our daughters dazzle us once more,
Our mothers mellow as of yore.

And though this sentiment I sing
Is fraught with an old-fashioned ring,
"In case you like that sort of thing"—

In case I don't, I hope it's true
A good old-fashioned brimstone brew
Someday in Hell will coax me to.

31

The crown and crest of creaturehood
Has not been seen so great, so good
As in our race, as in our brood.

The Cherubim and Seraphim
Have been o'er-vaulted and made dim
By something slender, something slim,

Assembled on our satellite
To move as any maiden might,
Familiar to our common sight.

32

Truth to attraction one must tether;
Reason and rapture rolled together
Will settle whether not or whether

The philosophic proof must pass
Inspection near the looking-glass
To learn the logic of a lass

And find if in mythology
What sense there is, if sense there be,
Was not a need for such as She.

33

A girl did God, I do believe,—
Created, courted by,—conceive;
And would that every word I weave

Her Sire, her Spouse, her Son might please
In this frail ditty darned in threes
With threads of triple harmonies.

One riddle, and my rhyme is through:
A bull will butt at red, but you,
Beelzebub, will butt at blue!

Verse

METAPHYSICS IN THE MARKETPLACE

I am fond of the beginning of a fact:
A potency in progress toward an act,
A sorrow getting set to be a sigh,
In a love-song the lurking lullaby;
Half a hymn and half a syncopated third,
The flutter of a fledgling on its way to be a bird,
The murmur of a whisper on its way to be a word.

Likewise, I like the respite and the pause,
The suspense in a sentence, the comma in a clause,
The little *will-be* where there was a *was*.

Lastly, my predilection for an ending,
When existence in pretense has stopped pretending:
The infant's second innings in the old,
Survival of the glitter in the gold;
I love a story when a story's told,—
And the muffle of a bell,
And the echo in a well,
And the open gate of Heaven and the slammed door of Hell.

AFTER THIS, OUR EXILE

It's just as dreary out in South Dakota,
It's just as tiresome down in Tennessee;
New habitats don't help us one iota—
Take it from me!

Nor does it matter if or whom one marries,
Despite what's written in romance and rhyme.
Helen, you know, was bored to death with Paris,
After a time.

Our set-up is a permanent nostalgia,
Our peace apportioned to another scene.
Life is a pain without or with neuralgia,
At sixty or sixteen.

If there were any other hope but Heaven,
If joy could flint from any other spark,
Think you, my loved ones, for a moment even,
I'd keep you in the dark?

LOVE IS A LOYALTY

They left no literature of their love,
    Rosie and Harry;
He had a pedlar's cart to shove,
    She had a wash to carry.

Valentines, verses, and *billets doux*
    They were unaware of.
Drudgery, more than a dream come true,
    They had their share of.

In separate roamings an unseen rope—
    In wet and dry weather—
Some fibrous fidelity, hempen hope
    Bound them together.

That they were childless, God willed to be,
    Though gossips were ruthless;
But you can ask Abraham Blum, M.D.
    If this be truthless.

Through tittle and tattle and tenement talkings,
  Through shadow and shame,
She cooked his cabbage, and washed his stockings,
  And bore his name.

Not much of a marriage to tell of this is,
  For better or worse;
But surely some sort of a Mr. and Mrs.,
  In a sort of a verse.

THE WAY OF THE CROSS

Along the dark aisles
  Of a chapel dim,
The little lame girl
  Drags her withered limb.

And all alone she searches
  The shadows on the walls,
To find the three pictures
  Where Jesus falls.

SISTER JEREMY

There was once a young nun with a truth-troubled face,
And a will like a whirlwind ungeared of its whirl,
Who survived the election and blinding of Grace
With the grace of a girl.

And they gave her a cross, and they gave her a ring,
And they lengthened her dress and unlengthened her hair;
And they said: "Now, my lady, you're ready to sing
Any song that you care!"

But the process that proved her was rather precise,
And her surplus of feathers they sheared from the dove
Who was bound on a flight through a forest of ice
With no warmth but her love.

And her story, electrotyped, printed and bound,
And dispensed in the shops of aesthetic regard,
Is the one you will find in most convents around,
If you look very hard.

THE DOVE

Learn from a little dove,
　　The Holy Spirit's symbol,
The qualities of love,
　　And what it must resemble.

Notice its note will vary
　　At different seasons,—
A wild bird, and a wary,
　　For different reasons.

When sunlight warms the roof,
　　And moonlight fills the nest,
Innocent, soft, aloof,
　　Unruffled and at rest.

But when the storm is raging:
　　Clawing, battling, crying;
A bird beyond all caging,
　　Furiously flying.

THE BEE

God, to some
Sticky stuff
Not yet alive
In a hive,
Said: "Come! Hum!
Glorify Me!
Be my bee

And buzz
As I bid!"
And sure enough,
It was!
And it did!

POOR TURKEY

The melancholy turkey-cock,
Of every bird the laughing stock,
Stands bewildered beside the barn,
Endeavoring to gobble a yard of yarn;
And folds his foliage like a fan,
And pecks at popcorn in a pan;
And wobbles and winks and wonders why
For all his feathers he cannot fly,
Hysterically hiccuping
A little song he cannot sing.

SHEEP RITUAL

Oh you should have seen the miracle
   I saw when I was in Wales,
Where myriads of sheep go munching up
   And lunching down the dales;
And graze along the meadow marsh,
   And nibble around the mill,
Cross the bridges over the brook,
   Bleat and eat and fill
Their bellies full of blossoms;
   Then lie awhile and sleep.
Then slowly up the slope again
   And slowly down the steep,
Their little mouths meandering on,
   Bite by bite they pull,

Inch by inch, the sweet grass
  While all the beautiful
Valleys of Wye from stream to sky
  Are turning into wool.

THE WHALE

Out in the bay arose a whale;
And in a flash from surf to sight,
From far-off wave to steamer-rail,
A whale a millionth of its size
Was matrixed in a beam of light,
And wriggled nimbly through my eyes—
Then plunging wildly in my brain
Became enormous once again.

Somewhere a whale is still in motion,
Lashing an ocean in a notion;
He dives through breaker, brine and billow,
Locked in a skull upon my pillow.
How such a wondrous whale can be
Remains a mammoth mystery;
But I must let him splash and spout
Till deep sleep dries his image out.

BRIEF LITANY

Softly out of nowhere
  Blows a summer breeze,
Wrinkling in the sunshine,
  Trembling in the trees;

Swings a little trinket
  Hanging in the air,
Keeps a penny pin-wheel
  Twirling at a fair;

Starts a wee melodeon
    Pumping in a flea,
Stops and drops a lobster
    A bubble in the sea;

Turns into a tremolo,
    Flows through a fife;
Lends a tiny hop-toad
    A lungful of life;

Falters on the hill-top,
    Tumbles down the glen,
Buried in a world
    Without wind. Amen.

THE FEATURE FEATURE

The owl is meant to emphasize
Especially the art of eyes.

The elephant's long rubber hose
Insists upon the art of nose.

The ostrich runs around and begs
Attention for the art of legs.

The art of neck belongs to the
Giraffe quite unmistakably.

The pretty peacock will prevail
In making known the art of tail.

The elk extends its chandeliers
To crown the lovely art of ears.

The art of mouth is obvious,
Due to the hippopotamus.

The art of chin is left to man,
Assisted by the pelican.

ADMIRING MAURA

The metaphysics of a dimple
Is rather more involved than simple.

But when she smiles, at seven weeks,
Two pretty nothings in her cheeks

Make Maura most admired where she
Is Maura most reluctantly.

For nature capers most with grace
Through unfulfillments in her face;

And one sees most to rave about
By looking at what God left out.

X.

Little Unknowns in the waters,
    Little Unknowns in the breeze,
O ultra-violet daughters
    Of Light: Let X equal these!

Beauties too infinitesmal
    To cope with the glare of an eye;
Daintinesses too decimal
    For a Muse to identify.

Dragons engulfed in a fungus
    A lyrical lens would amaze;
O never to rise up among us
    In a photograph or a phrase!

AUNT ABIGAIL

Oh, once I was a débutante
    And wore a social curl.
Now I am someone's aged aunt,
    No longer like a girl;

No longer like the rose in spring
   They said I once resembled.
I find it hard as anything
   To get myself assembled.

I don't know what o'clock it is
   Or if I'm late for tea.
I can't find where the pocket is
   In which I keep my key.

I think I'm late for supper too,
   My lettuce and cold lamb.
I'd yawn if it were proper to,
   To show how old I am.

I think my mind is wandering,
   I think my head is through
With puzzling and with pondering
   What am I next to do;

I wear a bonnet on it
   So I'll still know where it is,
And the little flower upon it
   Is to throw you all a kiss.

THE DEVIL'S MAN

God the Father made sleep, and God the Son the vigil;
But the Devil made insomnia.

God the Father made food, and God the Son fasting;
But the Devil made dyspepsia.

God the Father made speech, and God the Son silence;
But the Devil made sullenness.

God the Father made love, and God the Son chastity;
But the Devil made coldness.

God's man is the Father's and Son's, beloved of the Holy
Ghost. If he does not sleep, eat, talk or love as much as
he might, it is because he is waiting for a Kingdom that
is not of this world.

The Devil's man is a sullen dyspeptic, a sleepless misogynist. He
does not need to wait for Hell. He is already in it.

THE FAIRYLAND

All that enters through my eye
My intellect must simplify;

For nothing in my mind can be a
Guest unless it's an idea:

A spiritual accident
That has no weight and no extent.

For I am half an angel and
Must alter what I understand,

And rid it of the stubborn stuff
That makes it hard or makes it tough,

And turn its essence into air,
And hoard it underneath my hair.

But if some night my intellect
Should fail its function and neglect

To give some object, as it ought,
The proper lightness of a thought,—

Oh, how I'd toss around in bed
With moons and mountains in my head!

Oh, how I'd yell aloud in pain
With bulls and boulders in my brain!

TO AN INFANT

Marcia was lent us to illustrate
How little was God when His love was great,
When flesh disguised the Divinity
In millimeter and milligram
And showed the size of Infinity
To the ox and the ass and the lamb.

THE DONKEY

I saw a donkey at a fair
When sounds and songs were in the air;
But he no note interpreted
Of what the people sang or said.

Hitched by a halter to a rail,
He twitched his ears and twirled his tail;
In every lineament and line
He was completely asinine.

Though I had heard in local halls
Some eulogies on animals,
I thought it would be utter blindness
To show him any sort of kindness.

It seemed to me that God had meant
To make him unintelligent,
And wanted us to keep our places,
I in my clothes, he in his traces.

And so I turned my mind to things
Like banners, balls, balloons and rings,
For which I had to pay my share
And went on purpose to a fair.

But down the mid-ways while I went
On all the pageantry intent,
I stopped, and started to remember
A little stable in December,

Battered by wind and swathed in snow,
Nearly two thousand years ago,
When one poor creature like to this
Saw Mary give her Child a kiss.

So back I sauntered to the rail,
And stared at him from head to tail,
And gave his cheek a little pat,
And simply let it go at that.

STANZAS FOR THE UNASTONISHABLE

Their noses are assailed with smells,
Their ears are beat upon by bells,
They see the outward coverings
And watch the surfaces of things,
And relish to a slight degree
The savory and unsavory,
And knock their knuckles lightly on
A door or two, and then are gone.

Explore a clue or think it through,—
They find it too fatiguing to.
Their yearnings all in yawnings end
Who never to one fact extend
The simple courtesy of wonder,
That rends more reverently asunder
The lips, and makes the mouth let go
A less unpleasant "Ah!" and "Oh!"

If Beauty be but bubble-fair,
A breath of soap-surrounded air

That bounces briefly like a ball
And makes a moisture on a wall,
Then must we leave them to their senses
And save our own intelligences.
Though Christ Himself be whelmed in wheat,
They could not taste, so would not eat.

REFLECTION ON A FLEA

Let not my little Muse
Deceive you or confuse.
Not in the pose of art
Do I disclose my heart;
Nor do I use, to pray with,
The poems that I play with.
Rhyme is my little toy
To make-believe with and enjoy.

Not listening in shells
For the booming of beaches
No tide ever swells,
No ship ever reaches,
Do I pretend to find
Foundation for my mind.

I loathe the aesthetic attitude,
The literary languish,
The anguish after anguish,
The hunger for hunger, not for food,—
The joy that is not jolly,
The making tears a trade,
The professional melancholy,
The fear of being afraid.
I hide my whole head under
The sheets when I hear thunder.

Things and not theories
Frighten and make me freeze.
And, by the way,
Speaking of how to pray,
Dogmas come first, not liturgies.

The dilettante hand
That took art seriously,
That outlawed fairyland
And stripped the Christmas tree,
Now tries another trick
And has revived Our Lord
To go with the candle-stick
It has so long adored.
Of faith it finds a clue
In hyphenated points of view,
Whose novelty is never new,
And whose waste-land has got
A penny watering-pot
Filled up with drops of dew.

A doubt is still a doubt,
Even turned inside out.

Truer tonight to me
Is one small factual flea,
Whose stinging certainty
Impressed upon my nose
Is not a poem, or a pose.

COWARD NOËL

A stupid horse and cow, they say,
    Called for convenience, ox and ass,
Stood in a stable munching hay:
    A rather stupid sort of grass.

It seems a village girl was there:
    A rather stupid sort of maid,
Whose husband was a carpenter:
    A rather stupid sort of trade.

Her child was lying in a stall:
    A rather stupid place to sleep;
And stupid shepherds came to call
    With stupid lambs and stupid sheep.

The angels sang, *et cetera*,
    Some songs of this world and the next,
And so fulfilled from Isaiah
    A rather stupid sort of text.

THE PIANO TUNER

    Do, re, *moo!*
    Do, re, *meow!*
      Sounds so far
      Like a cat or a cow.

    Do, re, *miff!*
    Do, re, *muff!*
      Guess I haven't
      It tight enough.

    Do, re, *measles!*
    Do, re, *mumps!*
      Turn it too tight
      And back it jumps.

    Do, re (listen!)
    Do, re, MI!
      There's the little bird
      I heard in a tree!

THE MILKMAN

When the one o'clock cock begins to crow
    They drag him out of a dream,
And he stares at the stars in the Milky Way
    And the meteors made of cream.

When the sky is a meadow of molten oats
    Sickled with flaming steel,
He hitches his horse to a cart of cans
    With a squeak in its wheezy wheel,

And under the twinkle of sundry suns
    And miscellaneous moons,
His rattling bottles in sleepy lanes
    Tinkle their lonely tunes.

JEREMY

Lucy said to Jeremy, "Jeremy!"
    Jeremy said to Lucy, "What?"
"Don't you remember what day today is?
    Surely you've not forgot?
Didn't you notice the special pudding,
    And the little blue vase of flowers?
Whose anniversary is it, Jeremy?"
    Jeremy said to Lucy, "Ours."

Lucy said to Jeremy, "Jeremy!"
    Jeremy said to Lucy, "What?"
"I've been waiting till I've been weary
    Keeping your supper hot.
All day long I've been so excited!
    Didn't you like your tea?
How many years are we married, Jeremy?"
    Jeremy said to Lucy, "Three."

Lucy said to Jeremy, "Jeremy!"
  Jeremy said to Lucy, "What?"
"You seem dreadfully unromantic;
  Maybe we fuss a lot,
But aren't we still the same old lovers,
  Summer and winter through?
Tell me who was your sweetheart, Jeremy?"
  Jeremy said to Lucy, "You."

Lucy said to Jeremy, "Jeremy!"
  Jeremy said to Lucy, "What?"
"Remember the first year we were married,
  Out in the garden plot?
The moon was lovely, and you said I had
  Something as blue as skies,
What did I have so pretty, Jeremy?"
  Jeremy said to Lucy, "Eyes."

Lucy said to Jeremy, "Jeremy!"
  Jeremy said to Lucy, "What?"
"Remember the winter we went to dances?
  Remember the gown I bought?
We danced one night at the Grand Pavilion,
  And you wore an evening suit;
And how did you say your wife looked, Jeremy?"
  Jeremy said to Lucy, "Cute."

Lucy said to Jeremy, "Jeremy!"
  Jeremy said to Lucy, "What?"
"Remember the poems we read together,
  The maiden of Camelot
And the Knight who lived in a wondrous castle,
  Holding her hand in his?
Didn't they used to thrill us, Jeremy?"
  Jeremy said to Lucy, "Zzzzzz!"

NIGHTLY OUTRAGE

They draw the curtains
  And lock the door;

They keep it dark
  From ten till four

At Small and Small's
  Department Store,

While lackadaisical Elsie
  Scrubs the floor.

Her dress is dirty,
  Her knees are sore,

Pushing her pail
  From ten till four.

I think it's small
  Of Small and Small,

Even though Elsie
  Is lackadaisical,

To pay a woman
  To crawl and crawl

And clean their floor
  Like an animal.

I'd rather have
  No floor at all.

MRS. WHITTLE

I'm 'bout
Worn out . . .

I'm nearly
Eighty-three

You know,
And so

I guess I'm
Near my time . . .

I gits
Coughin' fits

Terrible,
I'll tell

You
I do . . .

But that ain't
My worst complaint . . .

I sleep light
At night . . .

My heart
'll start

Pumpin'
An' thumpin'

'N I wakes
With headaches . . .

My stomach
Has gone back

On me
Awfully;

I gits sick
'N anemic.

Guess my blood
Ain't good . . .

Sally's dead.
So's Ed . . .

These
Were my babies . . .

John,
He's gone . . .

He was my husband
And

I ain't got
No one but

Jeff,
'N he's deaf,

'N Mame,
An' she's lame . . .

They're weary
Tendin' me,

Fetchin' my cushion
'N pushin'

My wheel-chair
Everywhere . . .

They're fed
Up, they said . . .

They say I'm
All the time

In the way.
That's what they say . . .

So don't show 'em
This *poem*.

A PRAYER FOR PROTESTANTS

May God be kind to captive fish
Who dwell in little bowls and wish
To swim, and can't, and have no notion
Of what has happened to the ocean.

And may He bless in aviaries
Continually caged canaries,
Who wonder, when they try to fly,
What can have happened to the sky.

HAIR RIBBONS

When we were young, we looked on them as creatures
Inalterable in nature, as in form and features;
Diffidently to be approached, and shyly to be attended,
Extravagantly to be admired, and valiantly to be defended.

We needed no vile diagrams, being not such fools;
Innocence was not yet outlawed in primary schools.
With swift clean flashes of thought we were able to sense
What was their similarity, and what their difference.

And in order to make this clear distinction clearer,
And preserve those distances that keep the genders dearer,
They wore bright symbols of their strict inalterability:
Hair ribbons they wore, who were, yet who were not as we.

Manners have gone to the dogs since the hair ribbons departed;
Song is not sweet, nor verse versatile, nor folks open-hearted.
There is a blur in the eye, and the mind is annoyed
By a mania, and the ear by a monosyllable inaccurately em-
    ployed.

ST. JOSEPH'S CHRISTMAS

Not envied, not desired,
Only admired:—

A girl on this will thrive
As on no thing alive.

And such was God's rare plan
For Mary's man.

He watched his loved one flower
Hour after hour,

With footstep caused no fear
In angel-anxious ear,

Gave her his husband's praise
In nought but gaze:

The exquisite adulation
Of contemplation

That lets a fact reveal
Itself as real,

And, in Our Lady's case,
As *full of grace*.

He must have marveled most
When of the Holy Ghost

Her little Son who shivered,
At dawn was delivered.

He must have feared and feared
And hid behind his beard

When what was not his life
He welcomed from his wife

And his bride's Babe and Lord
Adored and adored.

At Christ's Nativity,
St. Joseph, I love thee.

WARNING TO CONTEMPLATIVES

The soul can overburdened be
With thinking of Infinity,
And over-eager for the place
Assigned it in the realm of Grace,
And so go straining for a goal
Beyond its valor as a soul.
And then—what water in the eyes
Will well, what aches, what agonies
Assail the bones and speed the heart
And rend the body most apart!
And then—the query for the cure,
The symptoms that are never sure,
The hours unbearable in bed,
The endless ice-pack on the head:
Undiagnosable disease,
The pain that is and is not peace,
When Christ has offered wounds for wealth,
And often not so good for health.

THE MISTRESS OF NOVICES

The Mistress of Novices is the nun's nun,
The courage and comfort of the just begun,
The discreet deterrent of the overdone.

The Mistress of Novices is the sister's sister,
The not all is gold because it seems to glister,
The not all is nonsense when a few resist her.

Her heart is an oasis for the saint's aridity,
A burning bonfire when the taint's tepidity,
The wisdom of the witless when the complaint's stupidity.

In a part unchosen, neither worst nor best,
As at Cana or Bethania she will greet her guest,
And be Mary or Martha at her Love's request.

The Mistress of Novices with fine finality
Is Charity's ultimate in impersonality,
Is everyone's secret and her own sodality.

O LOVE

O Love, and have You come to share
Our bones, our breath, our lungs, our air?

O Weightless, shall Your burden be
Our leaden Law of Gravity?

Within our fetters dare you, Fleet,
Go groping with our hands and feet?

And must our senses be assigned You!
Ears to deafen, eyes to blind You?

If I were God I swear I'd loathe
Myself in measurements to clothe.

Were I the Father's Word, no earth
Would straw and stable me at birth.

My tale would run—I must be honest—
Et Verbum caro factum non est.

AVE VERUM CORPUS NATUM

What little lambs and ewes
Went running to peruse. . . .

What baby calves and goats
And chickens out of shells
And heifers with their bells
And fillies lately born
Espied among their oats. . . .

What dull-eyed oxen saw
Commingling with their corn,
Strewn over with their straw. . . .

What donkeys with dismay
Found hiding in their hay. . . .

Abiding in our wheat,
In mystery complete,
At a far stranger manger
Is given us to eat.

FAREWELL

When you were nothing on the brink,
    I nothing on the verge,
The neighbors always thought, I think,
    That nothing would emerge
From what was less than nothing is
As symbol in geometries.

BUZZ, A BOOK REVIEW

"Therefore the transition from a coloured shape to the notion of an object which can be used for all sorts of purposes which have nothing to do with colour, seems a very natural one and we . . . require careful training if we are to refrain from acting upon it."

PROFESSOR PUFFLES.

Giddily in the garden
  The little bee blows,
With wax on his waistcoat
  And treacle on his toes,
  And a noise in his nose;
Pausing at a pansy
  And reposing on a rose.

Gee! but it must be jolly
  For a bee to be a bee,
And to jab a juicy javelin
  In a nice anemone
  That has objectivity,
As arranged by Aristotle
  In his strange philosophy.

Merrily in the meadow
  This fuzzy fellow fills
His engine full of honey
  On the sunny petal-sills
  Of delicious daffodils,
With an illative indifference
  To his inferential ills.

Really, it must be rapture
  To buzz about the brink
Of a violet that is valid
  Or an *a priori* pink,

Even though one's color kink
Is the fruit of careless training
In thinking how to think.

AND STILL . . .

And still . . . though maybe not one tenth the town
Believes what boon this Birthday brought us down,
We go on keeping Christmas just the same
With tinsel tricks, pretenses, and a name.

Whatever else one could or could not say,
(And who but God could deal us such a day?),
There must have come to notice, less or more,
That blinds are drawn in the department store.

And having soared in sales of Christmas cards
Inscribed with Christ-less rhymes by Christ-less bards,
Proprietor Mazuma sends the season's
Best greetings round to all for Christ-less reasons;

Bravely endures a one-day profit pause,
Appeased with turkey and cranberry sauce,
Then snoozes sweetly as a buttercup,
Or boozes indiscreetly, woken up.

And still . . . and still . . . the marvel Mother-Maiden
Is of her infant Lad and Lord unladen;
Emmanuel, grown little for our sakes,
Into our world His baby-entrance makes.

And still . . . above the Cave the stars are bright,
Some sheep and shepherds run with all their might;
And kings and camels from the Orient come,
While angels sing: Let there be Peace, for some!